# STILL THE BEST LOVED GAME?

# STILL THE BEST LOVED GAME?

## ENGLISH CRICKET IN CHANGING TIMES

**NEIL COLE**

THP
**TWO HENS PRESS**

First published in the United Kingdom in 2019 by
Two Hens Press
2 Hillcrest, Rogues Lane, Elsworth, Cambridge CB23 4HZ
twohenspress@gmail.com


A CIP catalogue record for this book is available from the British Library.

ISBN 978-1-9160969-0-5

Design and typesetting by Patrick Kearney

Printed by AF Ltd, Wroclaw, Poland

For Diana

# Acknowledgements

I am indebted to a number of people who have, in many ways, helped me to write this book.

First and foremost, I must give thanks to the late Geoffrey Moorhouse. It was he, through his classic book *The Best Loved Game*, who inspired me to write this book. If I have shamelessly borrowed the format, I can only state in my defence that imitation, even in its palest form, is the sincerest form of flattery

I should like, too, to thank Bill Higginson and Paul Roe, for warmly introducing me to disability cricket, and for generously answering my questions and providing information whenever it was requested. I also thank Hugo Barnard of the MCC's Cricket Office, for patiently answering requests for obscure statistics when he had far more important things to be doing, and Neil Robinson, the MCC's Library and Research Manager, Pat Ward of Essex County Cricket Club, and Karen Sadouki of the ECB for their quick and helpful responses to my questions and requests. I also thank the staff of the University of Cambridge Library for pointing me in the right direction when I was lost in search of resources.

Dr Nash Popovic overcame his disappointment that I was writing about cricket rather than politics – sorry Nash, next time – to provide much helpful guidance and advice.

Above all, though, I would like to thank my wonderful partner Diana Harper, without whose patience, generosity, support, encouragement and general cracking of the whip, this book would have remained simply an idea in my head, rather than reality.

Whether the reality is a good idea or not, I leave to you, the reader, to decide. However, some things are my responsibility. I have made every effort to ensure the accuracy of information in this book, and any mistakes are mine and mine alone.

Neil Cole
Cambridge, March 2019

# Contents

It is more than a game, this cricket.
It somehow holds a mirror up to English society.

Neville Cardus

# Introduction

In 1978, the writer Geoffrey Moorhouse spent the summer travelling around England watching cricket and writing about what he saw. His journey took in games at every level, from schoolboy cricket to Test Matches. The result was *The Best Loved Game*, a paean to England's national sport – or at least, what was regarded as such in 1978.

The past, as LP Hartley famously wrote, is a different country, and in the 40 years since Moorhouse wrote his book, both cricket and in the society in which it played have changed, sometimes out of all recognition. Indeed, it is hard to overestimate just how much has changed. In 1978, there was no internet, which is just as well as no-one had any computers on which to access it. There were no mobile phones or smart watches, and no satellite TV, just BBC 1, BBC 2 and ITV. Geoffrey Moorhouse would have used maps, not SatNav, to navigate his way to games, and he'd have recorded them using not a laptop or tablet – that was strictly something the doctor gave you – but pen and paper. The pace of life was much slower too. There was nothing like the range of activities that make demands on people's time today, and children generally made their own entertainment rather than having parental taxi services to ferry them through their packed social schedules every weekend. Sunday was a day of rest for the vast majority of folk, retail workers and Test cricketers included, unless you counted washing the car or mowing the lawn. Life was, in so many ways, so very different.

As society has changed, so too has cricket. A quick look at the terms in cricket's lexicon that did not even exist in 1978 gives a good indication of how things have moved on: Twenty20, day/night, List A, Sky, reverse sweep, reverse swing, the doosra, floodlights, white-ball cricket, MCCU teams, shirt names, ground naming rights, stump-cams, stump-mics, pay-per-view, online coverage, the IPL, Big Bash, Vitality Blast, neutral umpires, third umpires, red cards, hawkeye, DRS, hotspot, snickometers, the Duckworth-Lewis-Stern method, Kolpak players, the ECB, cricket websites, cricket apps… the list goes on. Durham was still a minor county, and two English Test stadiums, Durham's Emirates ground and the Rosebowl/Ageas Bowl in Hampshire did not exist. Bangladesh, Sri Lanka and Zimbabwe were still to gain Test status, never mind Afghanistan and Ireland. The all-powerful, all-conquering, invincible side back then was the West Indies. There was women's cricket, as there had been for decades, but it was hidden away like a maiden aunt only seen at Christmas. Most people had heard of Rachel Heyhoe-Flint but couldn't name a second woman player, and unless they had the good fortune to be the Queen, females (unlike schoolboys) weren't even allowed onto the hallowed turf at Lord's, let alone become MCC members.

Sometimes, it seems the only things that are still around 40 years on are *Wisden*, weaving its eternal, silky thread from cricket's origins to today and beyond, and Geoffrey Boycott. But then, no-one ever could get Boycott out. Cricket may still be played by eleven players against eleven others, using bats, balls and stumps, but there's hardly an aspect of it that has not changed, often radically, over the course of the last four decades. So, I wanted to revisit Geoffrey Moorhouse's journey and to see for myself how cricket is played today. My aim was not to show it as any better or worse than in 1978, which would have been a pointless exercise, but rather to look at the people who still watch and play this strange, wonderful, game and to examine its place in today's – and, perhaps more importantly, tomorrow's – society. It was a journey that took me to all corners of England, and to every level of the game, from its grassroots to the world's top-ranked Test nation. What I found confirmed some of my few thoughts, and confounded others. But then, if there is one aspect of cricket that is eternal and timeless, it is its ability to surprise.

This book is the record of that season. Each chapter, bar one, covers a single match, as I saw it at the time. As such, it is a collection of windows on the English season, with all the usual elements of triumph and failure, hope and despair, drama and comedy; the people who play it, and those who watch them. Together, it aims to provide a portrait of where English cricket has come from, where it is today and where it may be headed – and whether it really is still the best loved game.

# Chapter One

## Opening Day

Warwickshire v Durham MCCU
Edgbaston, Birmingham
Sunday 1 April

Whoever decided the first-class cricket season should open on April Fools' Day knew what they were doing. One of the longest, coldest winters in recent memory is refusing to relinquish its icy grip, like the last party guest who ignores the host's increasingly pointed hints for them to depart. It is a day for being indoors, by the fire, enjoying an Easter Egg – for it is also Easter Sunday – and steaming mugs of hot chocolate. Instead, with a smattering of other hardy souls (or, indeed, fools), I find myself rattling around the vast expanse of a near-empty Edgbaston, having fallen for an elaborate joke that it is the cricket season.

I nearly didn't come here at all, but to New Road, down the M5. Worcestershire were scheduled to meet Leeds/Bradford MCCU, the match I had selected to attend, but shortly before play was due to commence, I learned from my mobile phone (how Geoffrey Moorhouse would have found one of those useful in 1978) that the start had been delayed until at least lunch due to a wet outfield. I blame the prolonged cold spell for the misfiring of my brain cells that led me to think that watching a game at Worcester in April was ever a possibility, especially after one of the wettest springs in decades. Instead, a quick diversion has brought me here, where Warwickshire face the likely lads of Durham MCCU. They, at least, down from their northern hilltop colleges, may be more used to the freezing temperatures and biting wind.

The TV monitors in the walkway to the stands are showing football as I arrive, which seems out of keeping with the spirit of the day, though fully in tune with the conditions. There was actually meant to be cricket a week ago, two-day friendlies between counties and students. That really would have been something at which even the maddest of mad March hares would have baulked. In the end, the incessant rain, which has been falling for what seems a Biblical period, saw to it that the cricketers would not be called on to risk contracting pneumonia or trench foot.

Thanks to my diversion and consequently delayed arrival, I have just enough time to take up a position at the far end of the ground, in the Stanley Barnes stand. Edgbaston, as George Plumptre observed in *Homes of Cricket*, is, of all the English grounds, "the only one which gives the immediate feeling of being a stadium, an amphitheatre". Stadium is correct; it holds around 25,000 spectators when full. At a rough estimate, today's crowd is only about 24,950 short of that, though there will be some meeker folk taking refuge inside the pavilion. It is said that if you put two Americans into an otherwise empty stadium, they will invariably sit next to each other, while two English spectators will, with equal inevitability, find their own solitary space at each end of the ground. There is something in that today. We are small in numbers, we happy few, but no band of brothers. Instead, people are as dispersed as it's possible to be given the limitation imposed on us by most of the stands being closed. Despite the temperature struggling to reach 5C and the icy wind that makes it feel far colder, there is no crowding together for warmth here, no penguin-like huddle to help us endure the bitterness. Instead, it is each of us to his or her own. It is days like this that for centuries have shaped the English, and their remarkable capacity to suffer in silent solitude while absorbed in the pursuit of enjoying themselves. After all, we have, all of us, chosen to be here today when we could be at home in front of the fire, surrounded by friends and family, or, at the very least, chocolate. Those nations of more positive demeanour – and, invariably, sunnier climates – often chide the English for being negative. And yet, just turning up here today expecting to watch cricket – indeed, even inventing an activity that relies on warm sunshine and the absence of rain and then making it the country's national summer game – are acts of the purest optimism, albeit tinged with bloody-mindedness. If any curious foreigner wanted to understand the inherent contradictions in the English character, they would glean much from spending a day at the cricket.

And so, it is not just a smattering, but a scattering of spectators that greets the players onto the field. The students have won the toss and with the naivety of youth have put the pros into bat, which means they get to shiver while their older, wiser counterparts can enjoy hot mugs of tea in the comfort of the dressing room. The match is described as a warm-up, but there's little chance of anyone warming up today. The Warwickshire openers do the sensible thing and get out sufficiently early to grab their own teas before they have had time to go cold, and at 10–2 the students are congratulating themselves on their smartness in bowling first. When they break their huddle, it is to see the crease occupied by two former England men, Jonathan Trott and Ian Bell. It may be time for an extra sweater or two.

The last time I saw Trott and Bell bat together was in front of a packed house at a Test Match. One can't help wondering where, after all they have achieved, they find the motivation to scamper around in the icy cold against a group of undergraduates in front of an all-but deserted ground, but they will know that getting into good nick here could reap rich rewards later in the season. For the students, of course, it's a chance to test themselves against hardened pros. Time was, not so long ago, when it was a privilege enjoyed only by those at Oxford or Cambridge, but university cricket has broadened significantly in recent years. In 2005, the MCC began funding six university academies, then known as University Centres of Cricketing Excellence, around the country, covering a total of 13 institutions. First-class status came later, in 2012, and today the MCC estimates that around 20 per cent of all current English-qualified players attended an MCCU. Whether these games should have first-class status remains a perennial question. Personally, I rather like the fact that, in this era of 'professionalism' the game can still find room for such harmless anachronisms. Besides, the extension of the university system has enabled a lot of young players to develop their skills to a higher level than might otherwise have been the case, and perhaps helped more than a few of them become professionals. Unfortunately, though, it looks as if the MCC's funding may be coming to an end, so for now there is a little uncertainty over the future of the university sides.

Such issues will matter little to the protagonists today, however. Trott and Bell are defying the thermometer and wearing short-sleeved shirts, as is McGrath who is bowling. Indeed, few of the players appear to be feeling the cold, but then people seem increasingly not to these days. During the recent Beast from the East, the latest and most severe of several heavy snowfalls this year, a joke circulating on social media had someone from Durham's neighbouring city Newcastle complaining that if the big freeze continued, he'd be forced to put on a shirt before he went out for the night. That said, one of the students is sporting a pullover that may well be the longest seen on a cricket ground since the days of Percy Fender. It will keep his legs, never mind his upper half, warm.

McGrath tires as quickly as he has bowled and is replaced by Joe Cooke, whose shirt bears the number 57. Do Durham really have that many players in their squad? Or does Cooke, like countless students before him, have a predilection for a certain brand of baked beans and hold out hopes of the makers coughing up a term's worth in sponsorship? He gets encouragement from his team mates: "Here we go Cooky, on your way boy, on your way", though it's the ball that's on its way, to the boundary, "Never mind Cooky, back on it," He does get one to beat Bell, who is also dropped off Russell and narrowly escapes a run-out to a fine throw from Sohal. The biggest surprise, though, comes when the sun, a rare visitor in recent months, appears from behind the lowering grey clouds that have smothered the city all morning. The arrival of a bright, shiny object in the sky after such a long absence is likely to prompt claims of UFO sightings in the West Midlands area. I consult my weather app and it assures me, with a touch too much certainty for my liking, that there is a "100% chance of precipitation", but thankfully not until the scheduled close of play.

The students ring the bowling changes and the batsmen get their eyes in, and there are expectations that boundaries may start to flow, especially as the match is being played on the very edge of the square. But, with the occasional exception, the batsmen are content to make steady, rather than spectacular progress. As lunchtime approaches, the sun, having decided that the effort of trying to warm up the ground up is too much, retreats, not to be seen again, and the floodlights come on – "to enhance the natural light rather than replace it", we are informed. Whatever their purpose, the lights fail to spark much activity from Trott and Bell, who add just 14 in half an hour. Behind them, a steady stream of grey smoke rises from a small chimney attached to the pavilion, and it looks like one of those moments in every conclave when no-one's quite sure whether or not we have a new pope. The students, more to bolster their own morale than undermine that of the internationals, display some hubris – "Come on boys, let's get the third, let's make this our session" – and Sohal means business when he removes not one but two sweaters to bowl, but the momentum has swung. With lunch approaching, Bell finally relieves the torpor with a flurry of boundaries, and at the interval Warwickshire have reached 104–2, a score that hints at more fluent scoring than was really the case.

~~~~~~~~~~~~~~~~~~~~~~

As I sit and try, with little success, to warm myself up with coffee and soup, I think of where I might have been. The traditional curtain raiser to the cricket season is the clash between MCC and the champion county. Or at least, so people think. In fact, for a fixture widely regarded as 'traditional', the champion county match has been, for most of its history, nothing of the sort. According to Neil Robinson, the MCC's Library and Research Manager, "the perception that MCC v
~~~~~~~~~~~~~~~~~~~~~~

the Champion County is a long-standing traditional fixture was probably created by Geoffrey Moorhouse's book *The Best Loved Game* in 1978". Well, that's certainly where I got the notion from. In fact, the match's origins date to 1901 but back then it was played at the end of the season, immediately after the championship had been decided. After the 1935 match it ceased altogether for 20 years. It was revived, somewhat erratically, in the 1950s but it was not until 1970 that it was scheduled to open the following season. It hit more trouble in the 1990s, when the champion county either declined to take part or played England 'A' instead, and for five years around the turn of the century there was no match at all. It was revived again in 2004, but in 2010, with the season getting ever-earlier, it was taken to warmer climes as a test for day/night cricket. This year it moved from the Middle East to Kensington Oval, Barbados, where MCC defeated Essex by an innings a couple of days ago. Despite the contest's now clearly dubious claim to be the traditional opener, my plan for this book was to cover the domestic English season, and while the MCC match is classed as domestic, writing about the start of the English season from the warmth of the West Indies somehow felt against the spirit. Besides, my budget might stretch to games at Kennington Oval, but it certainly wouldn't get me to the Kensington one. So, instead of cou-cou and flying fish washed down with coconut water and rum in the sun, it's sandwiches, soup and shivers in Birmingham.

I take a walk, if only to get some blood circulating, and encounter a happy group of young men in suits and women in vividly coloured saris. They turn out to be a wedding party, bringing a welcome touch of brightness to a drab, grey day. I can only assume the happy couple are devoted lovers of the game, as well as each other, or had a very good rate for the reception room. Back on the field, the players re-emerge from the dressing rooms, hands deep in pockets, and it takes just a few minutes for Bell and Trott to reach their respective half-centuries. While they are accumulating runs, a steward starts doing the rounds of the spectators. Like a nurse checking on the welfare of people sheltering from the Blitz in a wartime tube station, she makes her way around the stands, making sure no-one's died of hypothermia during the lunch interval, or at least lost some digits to frostbite. When she reaches me, she assures me it's milder where I'm sitting than on the other side of the ground, but also suspects Bell and Trott, still clad in short-sleeved shirts, of having their thermals on underneath. A woman on a mission, she moves on to a trio making their first-ever visit to a match. One of them proudly tells her he has been studying *Wisden* ahead of the big day.

Out in the middle, Bell farms the strike and spends his time pulling and cutting, while Trott rests languidly on his bat and chats to the umpire. He looks an altogether more relaxed figure than the intense, sometimes troubled, batsman of old, and it's good to see. At the end of each over, they come together for the now obligatory fist pump.

Quite how or why this has become the custom among batsman, I have no idea, but there can hardly be a batter in the land, from Test player to schoolgirl cricketer, who does not, at the end of each other, walk towards their partner, clench their fist, and hit the other's outstretched glove. Do middle managers at business meetings, I wonder, get up after every agenda point to fist-punch their colleagues, even if their only contribution had been to pass the biscuits? "Come on, that's point 4, next month's sales forecast, sorted, only five more to go – let's take each point one by one and we can get through to any other business before the coffee's run out!".

By mid-afternoon Bell, untroubled and serene, has reached his century, but an over later, job done, he departs, caught behind off Cooke. Trott, meanwhile takes 90 minutes to add 12 to his lunchtime total. His new partner, Adam Hose, is in feistier mood and plants the ball in the pavilion, from where two fielders have some difficulty retrieving it. Tea arrives with Warwickshire, once 10–2, now 225–3. As the players head off, a young man asks me who's playing. When I tell him, he is puzzled. "Durham University? Are they professionals?" "Um, no, they're students", I reply. His frown deepens. "You mean, its professionals versus students? What is it, a warm-up match?". "Allegedly", I reply.

The crowd – if that's the right word, which it isn't – dwindles further after tea, to about 25, and my hands are almost too cold to write my notes. It's not the temperature that's the problem, but the accumulated numbness from sitting in it for six hours. Perhaps it gets to Trott too, as, after hours of Boycott-like accumulation, he gets a rush of blood and out of the blue plays a reverse sweep. It is like watching a guard who has been standing motionless for hours outside Buckingham Palace suddenly leave his post and do a cartwheel. Trott clearly feels it is time to up the tempo, and shortly afterwards brings up his century with a fine six. Hose reaches his own 50, which includes more boundaries than Trott's century, before getting caught in the deep going for another big hit. With the quicker bowlers needing to recover, the students persevere with spin, but it's too short and runs come quickly. With Warwickshire one short of 300, Sibley declares, giving his bowlers the chance to feast on student blood, or at least wickets. Possibly, in the gathering gloom, both.

Marshall and Plater walk out to get Durham MCCU's innings under way, but before the first over is out Marshall has already made the long walk back, to be replaced by McDonnell. Meanwhile, the Angel of the Eric Hollies Stand returns for another chat. As the students tentatively recover from their false start, she covers an impressive array of topics in a brief, albeit largely one-way, conversation. In just a few minutes she ranges from the day Warwickshire made 300–0 against the Army, and the Indian wedding in the reception suite, to the design of the roof over the stand and the sludge that falls through the gaps. In between, she finds time to discuss the manners of modern children, and the superiority of Sixties pop groups to their modern-day counterparts. Finally, she tells me she is leaving soon to visit a friend in hospital, who has injured herself while working at nearby Villa Park, home of Aston Villa FC. It seems she fell and tore a muscle away from a bone at the base of her spine, leaving her unable to sit down. It sounds very painful, but as one unsympathetic wag I mentioned it to a while later put it, "I always said watching Aston Villa was a pain in the arse". As the steward of mercy departs for her final calls of duty, I bid her farewell and reflect that, on this cold, gloomy day, she has probably done more than the cricket itself to raise spirits of the spectators who have stuck it out. Edgbaston might be a large Test ground familiar with vast crowds, but on days like this, with stewards like her, it manages to feel rather homely, even cosy.

In the meantime, a group of ground staff have gathered on the far side to watch one of their colleagues pummel a patch of ground with a mallet. The reason is not immediately apparent, and their faces do little so suggest any progress being made towards whatever their goal is. The scene brings to mind one of those old Bernard Cribbins songs, in which hapless workers in overalls scratch their heads and drink copious amounts of tea without actually achieving anything. Despite the distraction, Plater and McDonell make slow but steady progress and keep the professional wicket hunters at bay. They are doubtless relieved, though, when the bad light that's threatened all day finally forces an early halt to proceedings. Another first-class season is under way, Jonathan Trott has notched the first century of the year, and Durham MCCU will feel reasonably satisfied with an overnight score of 35–1.

Leaden grey skies greet the start of the cricket season on a bitterly cold Easter Sunday

**Warwickshire**

| | | | |
|---|---|---|---|
| W.M.H. Rhodes | c Sookias | b McGrath | 2 |
| D.P. Sibley * | c Sookias | b Russell | 2 |
| I.R. Bell | c Sookias | b Cooke | 100 |
| I.J.L. Trott | not out | | 111 |
| A.J. Hose | c Plater | b Graves | 68 |
| T.R. Ambrose ƚ | not out | | 10 |
| Extras | | 4lb 2nb | 6 |
| **Total** | | 78 overs | 299–4d |

Did not bat: K.H.D. Barker, O.P. Stone, C.J.C Wright, Sukhjit Singh, R.N. Sidebottom

**FoW:** 1–2, 2–10. 3–168, 4–280

| **Bowling** | **O** | **M** | **R** | **W** |
|---|---|---|---|---|
| A.H. McGrath | 15 | 2 | 45 | 1 |
| A.M.C. Russell | 12 | 2 | 34 | 1 |
| J.M. Cooke | 11 | 2 | 26 | 1 |
| F.W.A Ruffell | 10 | 0 | 39 | 0 |
| V.V.S. Sohal | 12 | 0 | 56 | 0 |
| B.W.M. Graves | 13 | 1 | 62 | 1 |
| C.M MacDonell | 5 | 0 | 33 | 0 |

**Durham MCCU**

| | | | |
|---|---|---|---|
| J.D. Marshall | c Ambrose | b Barker | 0 |
| M.J. Plater | not out | | 9 |
| C.M. MacDonell | not out | | 22 |
| Extras | | 1lb 2nb 1w | 4 |
| **Total** | | 13 overs | 35–1 |

Did not bat: B.W.M. Graves, W.A.R. Fraine *, J.N. Cooke, F.W.A Ruffell, A.H. McGrath, V.V.S. Sohal, J.H. Sookias ƚ, A.M.C. Russell

**FoW:** 1–0

| **Bowling** | **O** | **M** | **R** | **W** |
|---|---|---|---|---|
| K.H.D. Barker | 5 | 2 | 10 | 1 |
| C.J.C. Wright | 5 | 1 | 13 | 0 |
| R.N. Sidebottom | 2 | 0 | 7 | 0 |
| O.P Stone | 1 | 0 | 4 | 0 |

**Toss:** Durham MCCU elected to field.

**Umpires:** G. Lloyd, R. Warren

**Match drawn**

# Chapter Two

## The Youngest Fixture

### MCC v Wanstead and Snaresbrook CC
### Lord's, London
### Wednesday 18 April

MCC may no longer play the champion county at Lord's, but they are beginning what may well become a new tradition this year. Today, they take on the country's champion club, Wanstead and Snaresbrook CC, who claimed the title by winning the snappily named ECB Royal London National Club Championship at this very ground last September. Their reward is to be invited back to take on the most famous club of them all, the Marylebone Cricket Club. On a pleasantly warm spring morning, it is a day for best suits and finest dresses.

At the ground there is a friendly greeting from the stewards, and the one who pats me down for a security check is full of apologies for the infringement on my person. "Sorry", he says, in an embarrassed tone, "it's matchday regulations". The likelihood of an ISIS or Al Qaeda attack on MCC v Wanstead & Snaresbrook seems a little distant, if I'm being honest, and I'm not sure either would be wise to take on the MCC anyway, but such is the security-conscious age in which we live.

It's not the first match at headquarters this season. Middlesex played Northants last week in a county championship match that tempted fate by beginning on Friday 13th, but there are still signs that the new season is emerging only slowly from its winter hibernation. The Harris Garden is closed as lawns are re-laid; workmen are climbing up scaffolding with paintbrushes or staring down drain holes with little monitoring devices; stacks of chairs and tables are wrapped tightly in their winter plastic protection; and scores of water bottles stand on pallets, warming in the early sun. Unlike football, with its much-hyped Community Shield match and seemingly endless build-up, the cricket season awakes not with a bang but with gentle blinks and stifled yawns, like a reluctant riser groping vaguely for the snooze button. Much like me most mornings.

Perhaps it is why I love this part of the season; I can empathise with it. Besides, a lingering farewell to sleep is appropriate for this time of year. It is when we can all dream of a summer of long, hot, sun-baked days stretching into endless weeks and months; of triumphs and cups and titles, of glorious contests and heroic feats. No matter which club or county one follows, anything seems possible, even the impossible. After all, every team starts on 0 points. Well, unless you count Durham last year, of course, but that's another story. Such dreams may not survive harsh reality for long once the serious business begins, so all the more reason for the season's awakening to be savoured.

But today is all about Wanstead and Snaresbrook. They have earned their day in the sun, and have brought a fair number of followers across town to enjoy it, including a group of schoolchildren sitting in the Grandstand, eagerly anticipating their day's welcome escape from the classroom. Wanstead come into the match short of preparation, their two early-season friendlies having been cancelled, but at least their triumph here last autumn means they should not be too overawed by their surroundings. They've also brought their mascot, which is, for reasons not immediately obvious, a plastic inflatable heron. For now, though, it lies forlornly on its side on a bench, looking less like an inspirational talisman than a prop for Monty Python's dead parrot sketch.

MCC bat first, with the aptly named Jack Lord opening the bowling for Wanstead. Despite the early start – the first ball is delivered at 10.30 – it doesn't take long for the day's real business to begin. As Lord bowls his fifth ball, a voice behind me says "right, time for a beer". MCC also start swiftly, reaching 18 in even time before Ballard drives Shahzad into the hands of Das, to the delight of the visiting supporters. During the crossover, a young Wanstead player opens the pavilion gate to deliver something to one of his teammates. "'Ere,", cries a steward scurrying after him, "you'll get me sacked doing that yourself". Stoughton joins Thurstance at the crease and soon MCC are racing along,

65–1 and it's still only 11.15. The 100 comes up with just a solitary wicket down, and Wanstead's supporters are apprehensive. One, clad in a three-piece tweed suit, arrives with a pint of beer and is promptly asked to move to a different section of the pavilion. He walks about eight feet to the next bench and nearly spills his drink as Stoughton is bowled by Khan for 44. As the stocky figure of the beaten batsman walks up the pavilion steps, Mr Tweed grabs the heron. "Are you looking at my bird?", he shouts, to the hilarity of his companions. Thurstance, meanwhile, strikes a fine cover drive to take him to a half century.

Drinks are taken, but no-one's thought to take any out for the umpires, so the twelfth man returns to the pavilion in search of water. "Where do I get it from?" he asks plaintively. While the drinks are sought, I check my phone to catch up on what's happening elsewhere. As it happens, cricket is in the news. It's been announced that the BBC has been outbid by commercial station TalkSport for the rights to broadcast radio coverage of England's autumn tour of Sri Lanka and their trip to the West Indies in the new year. So, a year after celebrating the $70^{th}$ anniversary of *Test Match Special*, Aggers and Co. learn they will not be covering England's Test Matches this winter. In today's world of social media, fans are quick to vent their feelings, and most, it seems, are not impressed. "Literally the worst thing I have ever read on Twitter", says one, which hints at a somewhat sheltered life up to this point. It is, though, a blow to the BBC. Their media editor offers little comfort to distraught listeners: "For devotees of *Test Match Special* – an international club comprising hundreds of thousands of people, if not more – the sound of Jonathan Agnew and his colleagues isn't just part of summer. It *is* the summer. That is why today's news has caused shock and dismay. Fans need to be aware it could be a harbinger." "It is", he adds, "a warning to the BBC. Competition is only going to get tougher, as the likes of Amazon and Facebook finally move, as they have long threatened, into sport, just as BT have in recent years."[1] Unfortunately for the BBC – and for viewers without Sky subscriptions – money talks. Around the world, cricket boards are grabbing the dollars but not, perhaps, counting the long-term cost of smaller audiences. In this case, at least, commentaries will still be free to listeners, but it is another sign of significant shifts in the broadcasting of cricket.

Drinks over, the players at Lord's return to business. As so often happens, the interruption is followed by a wicket, Balmford caught off the bowling of Khan. Two more wickets swiftly follow and MCC, secure at 129–2, are wobbling at 158–5. The tall, watchful figure of Barrett and his new partner, Willetts, steady the ship with the old-fashioned virtues of solid defence and punishment of loose balls. They sail in relative comfort past 200, until Willetts is bowled by the splendidly named JSE Ellis-Grewal for 21. The new batsman, Hofbauer, sporting a snazzy yellow and maroon-quartered helmet, is greeted

[1] https://www.bbc.co.uk/news/entertainment-arts-43814257

halfway to the pitch by Barrett, who tells him "it's lovely" and downs a glass of water in one. To illustrate his point, he promptly crashes a six into the window of one of the Grandstand boxes. The next ball is despatched in similar vein and Shahzad, who's conceded 17 off the over, skulks away to his fielding position down the slope in the far corner. It's a perfect place to scheme revenge, and he scatters Hofbauer's wicket in his next over.

The new man, Lee, quickly runs through a whole gamut of options, the first three balls to him being met with an immaculate forward defensive, a mighty six and a near run-out. Two balls later there's another six for good measure. Lee is clearly a man who plays his cricket for its entertainment value. A few minutes later and the MCC innings closes on 298-7, Barrett unbeaten on a fine 82, Lee on a quickfire 14. It looks a challenging total, and someone from Wanstead will need a big score if they are to overhaul it.

In the interval, there's new of a further blow to TMS. One of their commentators, Ed Smith, the cerebral former Kent, Middlesex, and briefly England, batsman, is leaving the programme to be the new chief national selector. It's an interesting appointment. As well as being a former county captain (and, I predict, future MCC President – remember, you read it here first), Smith has a brain the size of the Oval and is an intelligent thinker and writer on the game. Despite spending much of his time at Cambridge playing cricket, he still came away with a double first in history. Not for nothing is he known as 'The Wordsmith' by his now former TMS colleague Geoffrey Boycott. Smith will be supported in his new role, the ECB state, by a network of "discipline-specific scouts" who will be supplying information on the players they see. Hopefully one of those players will be a successful opening partner for Alastair Cook, which England sorely needs, but that may be beyond even Smith's formidable powers.

I look up from my phone and take in the view. Even on a day like today, when it is mostly deserted, Lord's looks exquisite. If anything, its emptiness enhances its appearance. Row after row of white seats glisten brilliantly in the warm, mid-afternoon sun, while behind the Compton and Edrich stands, the flags of the Test Nations, joined now by those of Afghanistan and Ireland, flutter in the gentle breeze. If the players of Wanstead and Snaresbrook needed any reminder that this is no ordinary ground, a quick look out of their dressing room window will do the trick. Nevertheless, their openers, Arfan Akram, the captain, and Hassan Chowdhury, look composed as they walk out and take guard, though who knows what thoughts are racing through their minds. It's impossible, I would wager, for any player, even a Boycott or a Cook, to open the batting at Lord's and not feel the hairs rising. For players more used to walking onto pitches in Harold Wood than St John's Wood, the first task must surely be to overcome the natural instinct to freeze in awed stupefaction. If that is the private battle the batsmen are facing, it's shared by Osborne, the opening bowler, who can't get his length right and concedes

16 from his first two overs. Chowdhury looks intent on taking the game to the MCC, and Akram finds the boundary a few times early on before playing a horrible shot across the line to Barratt and getting caught.

As Wanstead progress steadily, if unspectacularly, a group of spectators in jackets and ties, who turn out to be committee men from the club, sit down alongside me. One in particular, Len, is chatty and tells me more about the club. It has, he says, some 350 members, a very healthy number, and an active youth section. "We see ourselves very much as a community club" he tells me, "and in a highly diverse area we like to think we're playing an important role in bringing the communities together". When I ask him about his side's chances today, he's less optimistic. "Not too confident to be honest… we've a weakened side, two of our lads from last year are off having trials with Essex". But, he and his colleagues have enjoyed a splendid lunch, courtesy of their hosts today, and whatever the outcome they are clearly enjoying every moment.

While we chat, Pack is brought on from the Nursery End to deliver his spin, his introduction greeted by a series of long, and probably unconnected, hoots from traffic on the Wellington Road. With the sun disappearing from the Pavilion End, I bid farewell to Len and his colleagues, wish them well, and head for the Compton Stand, which is still bathed in glorious sunlight. My walk takes me behind the new Warner Stand, opened last year to general acclaim, the Whacking Great (WG, geddit?) Sandwich Bar, closed for business today, and the banners and posters and statues of heroes from the ground's long history. Climbing the stairs to the broad, sunlit uplands of the Compton Stand, I emerge, blinking, into the still-hot rays of the sun. After what felt an interminable winter of snow and ice and permanently freezing temperatures, spring has finally, belatedly arrived, and to bodies unused to warmth it feels at least 10 degrees hotter than it probably is. Sharing it with me are 20 or so spectators who appear to be neutrals, enjoying not just the cricket but also the feeling of being outside without the necessity for multiple layers of thermal protection. Two men are deep in conversation about bus routes to and from the Oval; another, his shirtless back to the cricket, is engrossed in a book. Here, far from the pavilion, it is a place of baseball caps rather than Panamas, shirts off and feet lolling over the seat in front. There is a sense that folk are simply enjoying some welcome relaxation before the serious cricket gets under way, like cows, newly released from winter confinement, jumping up and kicking the air with the joy of freedom before getting down to some serious grazing.

Meanwhile, Chowdhury reminds us that, for Wanstead at least, this is serious cricket, and he heaves Lee through the covers to bring up the 100. It's only the 20th over, the pitch is benign, the MCC bowling looks rusty and the chase is on. The scoreboard tells us that Wanstead are well ahead of the Duckworth–Lewis score, though one suspects that won't matter today. Moments later, Chowdhury pushes the ball through the offside for a single and has 50 at Lord's. Though the season stretches out ahead and over the horizon, will it get any better than this for him? Milestones now tumble in quick succession. Chowdhury's partner, Das, has also been steadily, stealthily, accumulating runs and soon the 100 partnership is reached, then Das's own 50. Drinks are taken, and there's more on the *Test Match Special* story. A defiant BBC says it is "still the home of cricket on the radio" and reminds people that they have the rights to all England's home matches to 2024, and the next three Ashes series. They have been stung, and it shows.

Back on the pitch, the refreshments have been consumed, and gloves and helmets replaced. I used to hate drinks intervals when I was batting, not that I often batted long enough to see one, as the break in concentration was so often fatal. An interval has already accounted for one batsman today, and sure enough, this one does the same. Das, the taste of orange juice still fresh in his mouth, forgets himself and takes a huge swipe at Pack, misses the ball by a country mile and is stumped by Hofbauer. Chowdhury's spirited innings comes to an end soon after, and Wanstead are 162–3, with just a hint of clouds on the horizon, metaphorically and literally. They gather as Velani falls cheaply, and the question now is whether the Wanstead nerves will hold out. For the bus route devotees, there are more pressing matters. "Did you know", asks one of them, spying a pigeon searching for crumbs, "that the pigeons at the Oval are direct descendants of birds that used to be eaten, whereas the ones here are much more upmarket". So even when it comes to pigeons, Lord's claims superiority over its south London counterpart. There's no Henry Blofeld around to advise whether this information is true or not, but the bird in question certainly looks like he'd made an ample meal.

Far from such thoughts, Cummins and Ellis-Grewall apply some soothing balm to their side's innings, and Wanstead reached 200. They've prevented the stumble from becoming a collapse, but at the expense of the run rate, prompting a most un-Pavilion-like cry of "Come on boys!" from somewhere in the members' area. By the time six overs remain, they require another 54 runs. Thurstance replaces the tiring Barratt and the stylish Cummings hits him for 11 off the over. At the other end, Lee is bowling short, but there's not enough bounce and the ball sits up, waiting to be hit. When Ellis-Grewall skies the ball only for it to be dropped at third man, things seem to be going the way of the visitors, who now need 35 off 24. Four extras and a six get the Wanstead contingent cheering, the scent of a famous win now hanging in the air, but the cheers are stifled when a horrible mix-up sees Cummins run out for 47. He's done a sterling job, potentially rescuing a victory that was slipping away, but it's an agonising score to be dismissed for at Lord's, and to a run-out at that. He's philosophical as he returns – "that was always going to happen" – but it would take a stony heart to begrudge him adding a mere three runs in later years when he tells grandchildren on his knee of the day he played at Lord's. Ellis-Grewall, meanwhile, is on his knees in sorrow. There are shades of Trent Bridge, 1977, and Geoff Boycott, in his comeback Test, standing in forlorn isolation, face hidden behind gloved hand, as local hero and run-out victim Derek Randall jogs tearfully off, boos from the Nottingham crowd ringing in Boycott's ears. The scoreboard, though, is unsentimental, and tells a stark message – Wanstead are 280–5, needing 19 runs off 18 balls. Barrett is driven for four by Das; his next ball is scooped up but manages to find the short boundary, the third flies over the batsman's head and races away for four more. Barrett, trying to vary his length but looking increasingly like Malcolm Nash bowling helplessly to Gary Sobers, tries a leg-side delivery but Das whips it away to the Mound Stand for yet another boundary. Suddenly just three are needed, and they are obtained in spectacular fashion as Das wallops Barrett's fifth ball for six, prompting jubilation from the Wanstead contingent. Their batsmen have timed their chase to perfection with a performance worthy of England's champion club. "Always had it in the bag", says one of their supporters, tongue firmly in cheek and grin as wide as the Long Room. As the players clamber up the steps into the old pavilion, there are smiles and backslaps and kisses from the Wanstead supporters, and genial indulgence from the MCC stewards and members, genuinely happy that their guests have enjoyed a wonderful day out. Whatever Wanstead achieve in the season that lies ahead, it's very unlikely they will top this.

## MCC

| | | | |
|---|---|---|---|
| G.R. Thurstance | lbw | b Fayyaz Khan | 77 |
| E.C. Ballard | c R Das | b Shahzad | 8 |
| L.R.F. Stoughton * | | b Fayyaz Khan | 44 |
| G.W.C. Balmford | c Lord | b Fayyaz Khan | 9 |
| E.G. Flowers | | c&b Velani | 7 |
| C.A. Barrett | not out | | 82 |
| C.J. Willetts | | b Ellis-Grewal | 21 |
| G.D. Hofbauer † | | b Shahzad | 7 |
| W.W. Lee | not out | | 14 |
| Extras | | 14lb 2nb 13w | 29 |
| **Total** | | 50 overs | 298–7 |

**Did not bat:** M. Osborne, R.J. Pack

**FoW:** 1–18, 2–109, 3–129, 4–157, 5–158, 6–235, 7–281

| **Bowling** | **O** | **M** | **R** | **W** |
|---|---|---|---|---|
| J.R. Lord | 6 | 0 | 40 | 0 |
| Z. Shahzad | 9 | 0 | 55 | 2 |
| J.J. Das | 10 | 0 | 45 | 0 |
| M. Fayyaz Khan | 10 | 1 | 42 | 3 |
| J.S.E. Ellis-Grewal | 10 | 0 | 68 | 1 |
| K.S. Velani | 4 | 0 | 31 | 1 |
| R.J. Das | 1 | 0 | 3 | 0 |

## Wanstead and Snaresbrook

| | | | |
|---|---|---|---|
| A. Akram | c Barrett | b Willetts | 17 |
| H. Chowdhury | | b Willetts | 75 |
| R.J. Das | st Stoughton | b Pack | 54 |
| K.S. Velani | | b Barrett | 14 |
| T. Cummins | | run out | 47 |
| J.S.E. Ellis-Grewal | not out | | 45 |
| J.J. Das | not out | | 18 |
| Extras | | | |
| | | 5b 5lb 22w | 32 |
| **Total** | | 47.5 overs | 302–5 |

Did not bat: Z. Shahzad, J.R. Lord, S. Balage Don, M.F. Khan

**FoW:** 1–39, 2–142, 3–162, 4–187, 5–280

| **Bowling** | **O** | **M** | **R** | **W** |
|---|---|---|---|---|
| M. Osborne | 9 | 0 | 61 | 0 |
| C.A. Barrett | 8.5 | 1 | 49 | 2 |
| R.J. Pack | 10 | 0 | 51 | 1 |
| W.W. Lee | 10 | 0 | 53 | 0 |
| C.J. Willetts | 5 | 0 | 33 | 1 |
| G.R. Thurstance | 5 | 0 | 45 | 0 |

**Toss:** Wanstead & Snaresbrook elected to field.

**Umpires:** N.L. Bainton, P.W. George

**Wanstead and Snaresbrook CC win by 5 wickets**

# Chapter Three

## The Tourists in the Midlands

Leicestershire v Pakistan
Fischer County Ground, Grace Road, Leicester,
Saturday 19 May

Finding Leicester on a bright, sunny morning is one thing; finding Grace Road, in the absence of my SatNav, is a different matter altogether. After searching for signs to the ground without success, I finally locate one when I am about one street away from the entrance, by which time the floodlights make it unmissable. There's a further delay as the gate attendants umm and aah about whether my cans of soft drink can be allowed into the ground. Eventually, after a phone call to the security head office, they decide they are acceptable "as normal ground regulations don't apply today". Thank heavens it's not the fierce cauldron of a County Championship clash with all the inflamed tempers that provokes.

Finally allowed in, I settled into a seat. It's a warm, sunny day, one of many in what is turning out to be a lovely May, and certainly a marked improvement on my previous visit to the Midlands last month. The outfield is green and lush,

the ground itself, well, functional. I've never actually visited Grace Road, and there's always something wonderful about exploring a new cricket ground. Each one has its individual character and personality. I know football fans will rise up against me at this point, but I find far greater uniformity at soccer grounds, with their four stands and regular layouts, than at cricket grounds. Cricket offers pavilions in an endless variety of styles, from large, futuristic extravaganzas like Headingley's to little wooden edifices that look like branch-line stations repurposed after Beeching closed the railways. There are nooks and crannies, places to wander to and watch the players practice, and patches of grass where you can have a go yourself, at least if you're a kid or have some in tow. And everywhere there is history, from the names of the stands to the little plaques and pictures and memorials and statues and banners that adorn cricket grounds, like stations of the cross in a Catholic church.

All that said, Grace Road has few obvious signs of such devotion. There are various suites, including two named after Ray Illingworth and David Gower, but the stands and the pavilion are just called, well, stands and the pavilion. Most of them are open and exposed, though a few seats are covered by white parasols, like those one might find by a bar on a Caribbean beach. Any hope, though, of recreating a tropical atmosphere is undermined by the rows of Victorian terraced houses immediately behind them.

Perhaps the lack of an obvious sense of history here is not surprising, for the relationship between club and ground has not always been an easy one. Leicestershire first played here back in 1877, but upped sticks and moved in 1901 due to a lack of public transport leading to poor attendances. They did not return until after the Second World War, and many of the structures have a post-war feel about them. Several look like they date from the 1970s, apart from one large building that houses a café and gives the impression of having been relocated from a wartime RAF base. Hopefully the public transport has improved since 1901 (something far from guaranteed) and there'll be a decent crowd today. Leicester has a large population of south Asian heritage, so a game against Pakistan offers the promise of a sizeable audience. It's hard to judge numbers, as the crowd is widely spread, but there appear to be at least a couple of thousand here for the start.

It is only mid-May, yet the visitors arrive on the back of a Test victory, though only just. Earlier this week they defeated Ireland in Dublin, in the home side's inaugural Test Match. After two innings, Pakistan had a comfortable lead and seemed set to romp home, but after recovering from understandable nerves, Ireland fought back strongly and when Pakistan were reduced to 14–3, chasing 160 to win, an upset looked distinctly possible. In the end, the more experienced side got home by five wickets, but they'd been rattled, as their captain Sarfraz Ahmed admitted. They are probably expecting a less stern challenge today. There was a time when counties would field their strongest teams against touring sides, keen to claim the scalp of a Test nation. Those days, though, are long gone. Today, such matches are seen as a chance to rest leading players and try out young blood. So it is with Leicestershire. Six of their side are 25 or under, including two teenagers, Harry Swindells and Ben Mike. Neither has made his first-class debut yet, and another five players made just nine Championship appearances between them last season.

Pakistan bat first and make a confident start, 19 coming off the first five overs, mostly from the bat of Zaman. They run hard between the wickets too, intent on forcing the pace in this two-day game. There's life in the pitch though, and Klein sends down a bouncer that would have hit the ducking Azhar Ali if only he had been standing on the top of a ladder. Ten overs in and Richard Jones is the first change of bowler. At the other end, Taylor walks back to his mark between deliveries with the demeanour of Just William after suffering another serious injustice. Aadil Ali meanwhile, is performing a smorgasbord of stretching exercises, occasionally eliciting help from Taylor who lifts him up while he bends his back almost double. It's reminiscent of Alan Knott, who back in the 1970s would regularly carry out similar muscle-stretching exercises at every opportunity. He was thought of as eccentric for doing so, like vegetarians and people who grew organic food. It seems that, like them, he was merely ahead of his time.

In the stand behind me, a ventilator comes on, and a faint, incongruous, aroma of the sea permeates the seating area. An air of peace settles on the stand, with the low murmur of gentle chatter and the occasional call of "Come on lads" from a Leicestershire fielder keen to show his captain he's immersed in the game. Pakistan progress serenely to drinks at 47 without loss, though Zaman spurns his refreshment and stays at the crease where he goes through his repertoire of strokes. Refreshment taken, Klein returns to the attack, overpitches, and Zaman flicks him nonchalantly through square leg to bring up the 50. Soon after, another boundary is prevented by a smart piece of fielding, which prompts a sudden and unexpected blast of what sounds like a foghorn from the vicinity of the Meet Café, and is met with chuckles. Zaman bats handsomely, elegant drives and wristy flicks off his legs, and as he reaches his 50, the hosts start to settle in for a long day in the field. Zaman seems set for a large score, so it's a surprise when, with lunch approaching, he plays a rare loose stroke and is caught. The interval arrives soon after, the visitors heading for lunch at 121–1.

I wander over to the Meet Café, and, with a mixture of amusement and concern, notice that the room at the foot of the stairs leading to the café houses the medicine department. Outside, in the bright sun, there is a holiday feel in the air. Families are strolling around, wheeling pushchairs or keeping little ones from clambering onto the outfield. Others search for food or drink, and a sizeable queue quickly forms when the ice cream stall opens. Two members of the Pakistan squad walk around the outfield, laughing merrily, while a pair of sizeable rooks strut up and down the pitch with a proprietorial gait, like security guard birds from a Terry Pratchett novel. Lunch over, the rooks reluctantly make way for the returning batsmen. Aslam plays out the remaining four balls of Wells' interrupted over, before Azhar Ali brings up his 50. It's a surprise to hear that his half-century has taken only six balls more than Zaman's, and with the same number of fours. His batting has never looked as fluent as his departed colleague's, but lunch has helped him find his rhythm and he looks more settled. He starts attracting comments from a supporter in the pavilion, who loudly proclaims "Come on Ali, let's score some runs – let's have a four". Instead, Ali ducks underneath a bouncer. "OK, get some wides and then a four!". He duly obliges. "OY, OY, OY" comes the gleeful response. Meanwhile, Ben Mike's run-up is met with a rising crescendo from Ali's new friend, culminating in a loud exclamation as the ball is hurled towards the batsman, but there's no crowd-pleasing boundary this time, just a straight bat. The PA announcer cuts in to inform us of prayer facilities on the ground. Shortly after, Klein returns to the attack and shatters the wicket of Aslam, who either hasn't said his prayers or is keen to go and do so. His innings has never quite got out of third gear, and he departs for 8, Pakistan now 156–2 The tall figure of Salahuddin comes in, composes himself at the crease with the superior air of a prince mingling with his subjects, and elegantly flicks his first ball to deep fine leg for 2. My neighbour stands up and heads off to his prayers, leaving his bag in place to keep his seat. It's a pleasing thought that, in this day and age, people at cricket matches still leave their bags on their seats, trusting others not to run off with them. I can't think of too many other public places where items can be safely left without risk of either theft or controlled explosion.

In the meantime, the Voice is back. "Let's have a six – a six!" he shouts. "Come on, I paid a fiver!". He has to make do with a single, but it keeps him content for the moment. A short while later, Ali tries to oblige with a big heave, and is bowled by Klein, whose bowling is much improved since lunch. Another loud horn blast greets Sarfraz Ahmed. The crowd has swelled appreciably in the afternoon sunshine, but they are now treated to a lengthy delay as Salahuddin receives treatment for a blow to the elbow.

While that's going on, two of the Leicestershire players stroll to the crease and start inspecting his bat, in which they display considerable interest, examining it as if it were a suspected weapon found close to the body. It does look like a pretty chunky piece of willow, as is the way with modern bats, designed for bludgeoning, rather than caressing, the bowling. It's probably twice the thickness of my first full-size bat, back in 1978, but that would be seen as positively matchstick-like today, when power and size are to the fore. That same year, in *Cricket and All That*, Denis Compton complained of "massive bats… How much simpler is it to swat a fly with a rolled-up newspaper than with a telephone directory?[1]". His bats, he said, "weigh 2lb 2oz (1kg)" while "The more recent range of bats brought out by some manufacturers come in weights of between 2lb 8oz and 2lb 9oz." Contrast that with today, when 2lb 8oz would be considered light and many weigh well over 3lb (West Indies star Chris Gayle reportedly uses a whopping 4lb bat, while Compton's would today be no more than a medium-weight junior bat). Of course, it's this increase in bat size – restrictions have even had to be brought into curb their growth – and the additional shots it allows batsmen to play, that's helped fuel the explosion in scoring rates, certainly in Test Matches. It's little wonder that run rates today often bear as much resemblance to those of forty years ago as the 0–60 time of a Bugatti Veyron does to that of a Morris Marina.

Salahuddin's elbow mended, I realise my bench has become very uncomfortable – I have left my trusty cricket cushion at home – so I take myself off and find a seat nearby that has more legroom than a first-class seat on a 747. An entire row of seats would fit in between mine and those in front. All that's missing is a reclining option. I settle into my new surroundings, puzzled as to why this luxuriant section of seating is so sparsely populated. I soon find out. Sarfraz lets a ball go past him and from a few metres away a loudspeaker lets forth another mighty foghorn blast. Any notion of relaxing in comfort is banished. Sarfraz hits the next ball for six, there's another warning to shipping and the batsman then holes out to Hill, prompting a third blast and the day's first cries of "Leicestershire, Leicestershire". Pakistan are 199–4 and I'm on the move again.

The latest wicket encourages Aadil Ali, who's been spending much time wheeling his arms and making bowling motions. The thought occurs to me that, when Leicestershire bat, we could see the pleasing scoreline of Ali c Ali b Ali. Pakistan's 200 comes up to muted applause, as one scoreboard lags behind the other and still shows 199, and for the second time today they lose a pre-interval wicket when Saad Ali is caught and bowled by his namesake. Going along serenely at lunch, the tourists have now lost four wickets for 51. As they head for tea, a woman comes round taking orders for coffee and cake, which is rather fine. When play resumes, the Leicestershire players try just a little too hard to make further inroads. Khan faces a ball from Jones that bounces high above his head, and even though he jumps high with bat upraised, like someone trying to dislodge a kite from a branch, it still evades him and races to the boundary for extras. He doesn't survive much longer though, as Wells knocks over his middle stump in the next over. Salahuddin survives a long, loud LBW appeal, and the fielders are so engaged in appealing that they forget about the ball, and another four extras are only prevented by the hurried despatch of a rescue party. There's a brief scare when Faheem Ashraf, at the non-striker's end, is felled by a ball from the spinner, Javid, which is accidentally driven into him by Salahuddin, and he looks out for the count. "He won't be getting up for a while", says someone authoritatively. Almost immediately, Faheem sits up and within seconds is back on his feet, but it's shaken him and soon after he groggily lobs a simple catch to Wells. Minutes later, Hasan Ali is run out. Despite Salahuddin's very loud cry of 'No', Ali hares down the pitch only to realise that, like Wile E. Coyote pursuing the roadrunner, the ground beneath him has disappeared. He gulps, and resigns himself to his fate. Salahuddin, meanwhile, reaches his 50 with a fine drive. It's been a watchful, determined innings, rather than the dashing, princely one his arrival promised, but he'll be satisfied enough. With the clock nudging 5.45, Pakistan reach 300. Taking his cue, Salahuddin opens up and plays some crisp, elegant drives and pull shots, but the day closes when Abbas, playing against the county he has signed for this season, is out for 16. There's no time for a new batsman, and no tricky two or three overs for the home side to face. On a decent pitch, apart from the odd exaggerated bouncer, Leicestershire have done well to take eight wickets since lunch, while Pakistan have recovered from a mini slump to end the day with a respectable total. With tomorrow being the final day, though, a win for either side looks distinctly unlikely – as was the case right from the start, in truth.

**Pakistan**

| | | | |
|---|---|---|---|
| Azhar Ali | | b Klein | 73 |
| Fakhar Zaman | c Javid | b Wells | 71 |
| Sami Aslam | | b Klein | 8 |
| Usman Salahuddin | not out | | 69 |
| Sarfraz Ahmed * † | c Hill | b Javid | 17 |
| Saad Ali | | c&b Ali | 2 |
| Shadab Khan | | b Wells | 17 |
| Faheem Ashraf | c Wells | b Javid | 15 |
| Hasan Ali | run out | | 5 |
| Mohammad Abbas | c Hill | b Ali | 16 |
| Extras | | 4b 8lb 9nb 7w | 28 |
| **Total** | | 89.5 overs | 321–9d |

**FoW:** 1–121, 2–156, 3–176, 4–199, 5–207, 6–245, 7–267, 8–272, 9–321

| **Bowling** | **O** | **M** | **R** | **W** |
|---|---|---|---|---|
| D. Klein | 18 | 3 | 44 | 2 |
| T.A.I. Taylor | 17 | 2 | 49 | 0 |
| R.A. Jones | 13 | 1 | 73 | 0 |
| T.J. Wells | 14 | 3 | 45 | 2 |
| A. Javid | 15 | 3 | 42 | 2 |
| B.W.M. Mike | 7 | 1 | 28 | 0 |
| A.M. Ali | 5.5 | 0 | 28 | 2 |

**Leicestershire**

| | | | |
|---|---|---|---|
| H.E. Dearden | c Fakhar Zaman | b Saad Ali | 19 |
| S.T. Evans | lbw | b Shadab Khan | 22 |
| L.J Hill * | c Hasan Ali | b Shadab Khan | 33 |
| A. Javid | retired out | | 54 |
| A.M. Ali | st sub | b Fakhar Zaman | 41 |
| T. J. Wells | c Fakhar Zaman | b M. Abbas | 25 |
| H.J. Swindells † | not out | | 2 |
| T.A.I. Taylor | not out | | 17 |
| Extras | | 4b 2lb 7w | 13 |
| **Total** | | 75 overs | 226–6 |

Did not bat: B. W. M. Mike, D. Klein, R.A. Jones

**FoW:** 1–51, 2–52, 3–102, 4–165, 5–203, 6–207

| Bowling | O | M | R | W |
|---|---|---|---|---|
| Mohammad Abbas | 12 | 4 | 42 | 1 |
| Rahat Ali | 14 | 4 | 50 | 0 |
| Hasan Ali | 10 | 4 | 18 | 0 |
| Faheem Ashraf | 9 | 5 | 10 | 0 |
| Shadab Khan | 13 | 4 | 32 | 2 |
| Saad Ali | 5 | 0 | 20 | 1 |
| Fakhar Zaman | 12 | 0 | 48 | 1 |

**Toss:** Pakistan elected to bat.

**Umpires:** P. Hartley, C. Watts

**Match drawn**

# Chapter Four

## One-Day International

England v South Africa
New Road, Worcester
Saturday 9 June

New Road is one of those grounds one can be familiar with, without ever actually having been there. Every spring, it crops up in photographs in newspapers and on the BBC website. Sometimes is it is covered in snow, the city's ancient cathedral forming a graceful backdrop, but more often it is completely flooded, a lake where once there was a cricket ground. Such is its record of flooding that it even has noticeboards recording weather records and water levels for spectators to study during breaks in play, which are frequent and lengthy early in the season. This year, in fact, the county cricket club even went so far as to ensure their first two matches of the season were played away from home, so certain were they that the ground would be unusable. They were right, too. Today, though, spring is far behind us, summer well under way and it hasn't rained for weeks. Indeed, not a drop since the sweet showers of April. Instead, we have had weeks of glorious sunshine, and

Worcester looks at its finest. It is the sort to day to make you feel that, even with the Battle of Brexit raging furiously, all, or nearly all, is well with the world.

Yet despite this, as I walk across Chapter Meadow on my way to the ground, I have to sidestep large puddles. Where have they come from? And if they are still here after 40 days without rain, what was it like two months ago, after one of the wettest springs on record? No wonder the players decamped to drier ground elsewhere. Surely New Road must have dried out by now? Guided by the early morning music blaring from the stands, I arrive to find, thankfully, a perfect-looking pitch and a good crowd for the first of three one-day internationals between England, the reigning women's world champions, and South Africa. It's 321 days since England's last match on home soil, that remarkable triumph at a packed Lord's, and their supporters are impatient to see them in action again.

It's fair to say that women's cricket has come a very long way in recent times. Rather like the Beatles, it's become an overnight success after years – more than two centuries' worth in this case – of hard work and frustration. The earliest recorded women's game was in 1745, when Bramley took on Hambledon in what the *Reading Mercury* described at the time as "the greatest cricket match that was played in this part of England"[2]. Hambledon won by eight runs. The first women's club was founded in 1887 and three years later a touring

[2] www.telegraph.co.uk/only-in-britain/first-recorded-womens-cricket-match/

team, the Original English Lady Cricketers, was formed, but was forced to disband when the (male) manager made off with the profits. The Women's Cricket Association was founded in 1926, and eight years later the first women's Test Match was held, England beating Australia by five wickets in Brisbane. By 1973, women had their own world cup, beating the men by two years, but not until 1976 did they finally win the right to play at Lord's – prior to that, if you were a woman wanting to enter the Long Room you had to be the Queen, which rather restricted opportunities.

Even after that, progress was slow, and the women's game remained on the fringes, or even beyond, though inching slowly closer to the mainstream. The Women's County Championship was established in 1997, and counties started integrating women's teams more fully into their fold. The BBC began introducing women commentators, then coverage of some women's matches. But it was only last year that the game finally broke through the glass ceiling, or boundary in this case, and entered the mainstream. With society moving ever-more towards greater inclusivity, the World Cup, held in England, caught the public's imagination – or at least, a much larger swathe of it than previously. Properly promoted by the ICC, the tournament saw every match broadcast live around the world, to no fewer than 139 countries. Helped by the home side's success, the final at Lord's was played in front of a packed house, every seat filled except, shamefully, for rows of empty benches in the members' pavilion. It was a great occasion too. A wonderful atmosphere, a dramatic match, and thousands of new fans hooked. Some of them will be here today, and it's wonderful to see so many young women and girls enjoying the cricket and watching role models they can truly call their own. No longer do female fans have to make to do with men's names on their shirts – they can sport Knight and Shrubsole, Taylor and Brunt on their backs with pride. That said, there's a pleasing number of men here too, testimony to the growing realisation that women's cricket offers up exciting sport for everyone. Today's match is being broadcast live on Sky; over the course of the season, TV and radio will broadcast many more women's matches live. Men's cricket may still cast a long shadow, and there are still, sadly, too many who decry the female game, but for those who look ahead with eagerness, rather than back in fear, women cricketers have finally stepped out of that shadow into light of their own. It begs the question as to whether we should even be calling this women's cricket any more, or referring to the England women's team? Surely now it is simply cricket, and England?

I find a seat near the top of the D'Oliveira stand, and make myself comfortable. It is 50 years this year since the D'Oliveira Affair spectacularly erupted. Basil D'Oliveira, a so-called Cape Coloured (mixed-race) cricketer from Cape Town, where he was unable to play international cricket for the all-white South African team, had come to England and made his way into the Test side. Controversially omitted from the England side to tour South Africa in 1968–69, he was brought into the squad when Tom Cartwright withdrew due to injury, prompting accusations from the South African government that his selection was political. The ensuring row led to the tour being cancelled and to South Africa's cricketing exile, which lasted until 1991. Many of the South Africans playing today will not even have been born when apartheid ended, but they will certainly know the history and the name D'Oliveira.

It's a cloudy, humid morning. There are patches of blue sky, but conditions seem perfect for bowling. It's a surprise, then, when England, having won the toss, choose to bat. Jones, tall and erect, starts strongly, racing to 19 of the first 20 runs before being bowled by Ismail, whose diminutive stature belies her lively bowling. The crowd are buoyed by the arrival at the crease of Sarah Taylor, one of England's World Cup stars and a hero for many of the young women who've come to Worcester today. Ismail, though, is determined to spoil the party and has Taylor leg before for just 2. When England's captain, Heather Knight, follows her back to the pavilion three balls later, South Africa's cheers can be heard back home on the high veldt. Khaka replaces Ismail and promptly bowls Beaumont for six with a ball that cuts back beautifully, and the world champions are in disarray on 39–4. South Africa are bowling to those timeless virtues of a good line and length, and so far, England cannot deal with it. They can't blame conditions either – the fault lies squarely with loose batting across the line or failing to commit to the stroke. The champions are looking distinctly rusty.

Wyatt, the new batter, enters somewhat hesitantly, and will need to improve on a career average of 18 if England are to get back into this contest. There was a time when anyone would have been chased out of town for using the word batter, and the older hands on *Test Match Special* still dislike it, but the rise of women's cricket has also brought about a challenge to some of the gender-specific language in cricket's lexicon. Deep Third Man seems likely to stay, if only because Deep Third Person sounds faintly sinister, but batter has caught on, in the men's game as well as the women's. And why not? Traditionalists object, and it is not, I agree, an elegant word. But, after all, we say bowler rather than bowlman, so why should batsman be sacrosanct, especially when the person with the bat is not a man? Far below me, Wyatt has more pressing concerns, and her concentration is tested by a skein of geese that comes into land on the outfield, looking like a squadron that's returned from a bombing mission. Sciver, another World Cup star, mistimes a hoist and spoons the ball to van Niekerk, swishing her bat angrily through the air as she departs, and the crowd are left stunned. This wasn't the homecoming party they'd planned. Katherine Brunt arrives at the crease, with more than a hundred ODIs' worth of experience behind her, but she averages below 15 with the bar, so it's with hope rather than expectation that the crowd greets her.

Behind me, a small child goes to sit on her seat, but it tips up and she performs a Chaplinesque slide onto the floor, provoking considerable amusement from the rest of her family. “Not funny”, she grizzles. “Well, it did look quite funny”, replies her mother. “NOT FUNNY”, insists the child, her brother now laughing heartily and both parents trying, not very successfully, to avoid joining him. “It is!”, says the mother. A few minutes later, the child wanders along the row to some other members of the party and starts grizzling again, presumably in an attempt to elicit the sympathy for her mishap so lacking the first time round. As she does so, yet another wicket falls, and I suspect there are plenty of other spectators who share her mood.

England, wickets falling with alarming frequency, become becalmed and manage just ten runs in as many overs, though at least without further loss. Van Niekerk rings the bowling changes, but Brunt finally gets England’s first boundary in what feels a very long time (it is, I later discover, 13 overs) and the PA announcer-cum-DJ at last has a chance to play a burst of music. The cheers that accompany it express relief rather than confidence, but it’s short lived. In the very next over, Tryon’s tricky, sliding, deceptive action fools Gunn, who has taken 41 balls to reach just four. England are 80–7, well into the tail, and I’m anticipating an unexpected early evening at home.

The crowd, though, who are almost entirely supporting England, are backing their team and there are huge cheers as Anya Shrubsole strides to the wicket. It was Shrubsole who took six wickets – and ran out a seventh – as India collapsed from 191–3 to 219 all out to concede the World Cup Final, a performance that propelled her to the front cover of *Wisden Cricketers' Almanack* this spring, the first women to receive the accolade. It's made her a star, and an idol for many here today, but even she can't stop the rot and is run out for 7. Two wickets left, and England still not into three figures. When they eventually crawl to the landmark, there is much applause and cheering – and unlike the ironic cheers one would hear if the men's team were in a similar position, this applause is genuine. Indeed, throughout what's been a thoroughly miserable morning for England, there has been a noticeable absence of any frustration or impatience from the crowd, just enjoyment and encouragement. Perhaps it's because this England side has achieved so much and can be forgiven an occasional lapse, but I suspect it's more to do with a different mentality emanating from the different composition of the crowd.

Whatever the reason, it makes for a very pleasant atmosphere, despite England's predicament, and the players will take heart from the support. Brunt certainly does, launching a series of cuts and drives at odds with everything else we've seen all day, and her half century receives a tremendous ovation. More boundaries follow, the increasingly vociferous crowd shows its delight, and suddenly South Africa are unable to stem the flow of runs. Brunt, belying her average, is having one of those innings when everything she tries comes off. Full of strength, even brutality at times, her batting is defiance personified. When the England innings reaches the 50th over – something few would have bet on half an hour ago – Brunt plays an extraordinary shot, lying practically flat on the ground and scooping the ball over her head for four more. Supported by some stubborn resistance from her teammates, she has reached 72no, a one-day best despite her 100+ caps, and has dragged England to respectability. 189 may not be enough to win the match, but it gives the bowlers something to aim at, and the crowd hope.

Polite applause greets South Africa's batters, the grinning Lizelle Lee alongside the tall figure of Laura Wolvaardt. Wolvaardt is only 19, but already playing her 33rd ODI, which shows how much cricket is played these days. As for England, cometh the hour, cometh the woman, and Katherine Brunt, who's barely had time to catch her breath since her batting heroics, is handed the new ball. When she bowls Wolvaardt for 2 in her second over, the adoration for her is palpable. It's just the start England had to make, but it gets even better soon after, when Luus is stumped by as fine a piece of wicketkeeping as you'll see all season. Standing up to Shrubsole's bowling, Taylor, with lightning reactions, collects the ball outside leg stump and whips the ball across to remove the bails. It's the sort of moment on which matches can turn, and reminds us all of just how good Sarah Taylor is behind the stumps. South Africa are 5–2, Brunt's performance is taking on a Bothamesque stature and the crowd are loving every moment.

Near me, two young women are discussing women's cricket at their club. They are regular players, but frustrated at the fact the same two or three people are left to mark out the pitch before each game and put everything away afterwards.

I sympathise, though I suspect pretty much every other cricketer at every club in the land would recognise the problem. One of them, though, raises a pertinent question: "Where", she asks her companions, "are all the women umpires?" She has never seen any, and I must admit, neither have I. One, Claire Polosak, did umpire the England men's team in a match in Australia earlier this year, but female umpires are undoubtedly rare. All five of today's officials are men, and it is curious, and disappointing, that the huge growth in the women's game has not seen a commensurate increase in the number of female umpires. Like the young women in front of me, I can only hope the ECB is aware of the issue and has a plan to resolve it.

Back on the pitch, England's bowlers toil but they lack penetration. Brunt is recalled in the hope of finding a breakthrough, but even she cannot magic one up. The two batters are well set; Lee playing with a solid defence and strong, lofted shots over the covers, van Niekerk slashing a series of cuts on the offside, and the target drops below 100. "It's surprisingly tiring, watching a cricket game", says a woman near me. "There's a lot of concentration needed", her partner agrees. "It's not like football, it's seven or eight hours". "It is, it's hard to keep awake for a full day". She pauses before adding "well, it is if you've had alcohol!".

Lee is having no difficulty concentrating, despite van Nierkerk's departure, and hits a huge six towards the TV broadcasting stand, prompting the day's first exasperated cry of "Come on England". On 68, she is finally drawn into a mistake, mistiming a lofted pull shot and being caught on the boundary by, inevitably, Brunt, who cannot keep away from the action. England rejoice, the crowd, with South Africa needing barely more than 50, have slim hopes reignited, and Lee walks off to well-deserved applause. Or rather, she's about to walk off – she is literally one step short of the boundary rope, her replacement Marizanne Kapp already taking guard – when the fourth umpire instructs her to stop. The eagle-eyed off-field officials have spotted from TV replays that Brunt has grounded the ball, though from the angle at which she took the catch, it seems unlikely that she'd have been aware of it. Lee is reprieved, and England's deflation is visible. Lee resumes where she briefly left off, while England, shoulders slumped, look weary, even ragged. Their bowling has lost what little edge it had, even the sublime Taylor misses a stumping chance, and South Africa make light work of the remaining 55 runs. Fittingly, Lee seals the win with a huge six into the pavilion, to seal her side's first ODI win against England in this country in 15 years, and get some revenge for a tense World Cup defeat last year. The South Africans are naturally jubilant; while England must contemplate a third defeat in four matches, after two losses in India in the spring. As the old saying goes, getting to the top is hard; staying there is harder still.

**England**

| | | | |
|---|---|---|---|
| A.E. Jones | b Ismael | | 19 |
| T.T. Beaumont | b Khaka | | 6 |
| S.J. Taylor ƚ | lbw | b Ismail | 2 |
| H.C. Knight * | lbw | b Kapp | 4 |
| N.R. Sciver | c van Niekerk | b Khaka | 16 |
| D.N. Wyatt | c Luus | b Khaka | 7 |
| K.H. Brunt | not out | | 72 |
| J.L. Gunn | c Lackay | b Tryon | 7 |
| A. Shrubsole | run out | | 7 |
| L.A. Marsh | b Ismail | | 15 |
| S. Ecclestone | not out | | 12 |
| Extras | | 3b 10lb 12w | 25 |
| **Total** | | 50 overs | 189–9 |

**FoW:** 1–20, 2–24, 3–29, 4–39, 5–61, 6–64, 7–80, 8–97, 9–148

| **Bowling** | **O** | **M** | **R** | **W** |
|---|---|---|---|---|
| S. Ismail | 10 | 2 | 25 | 3 |
| M. Kapp | 10 | 1 | 51 | 1 |
| A. Khaka | 10 | 2 | 42 | 3 |
| R. Ntozakhe | 10 | 1 | 21 | 0 |
| C.L. Tryon | 5 | 0 | 21 | 1 |
| D. van Niekerk | 5 | 0 | 16 | 0 |

**South Africa**

| | | | |
|---|---|---|---|
| L. Lee ƚ | not out | | 92 |
| L. Wolvaardt | b Brunt | | 2 |
| S. Luus | st Taylor | b Shrubsole | 0 |
| D. van Kiekerk * | b Shrubsole | | 58 |
| M. du Preez | not out | | 36 |
| Extras | | 1lb 4w | 5 |
| **Total** | | 45.3 overs | 193–3 |

**FoW:** 1–3, 2–5, 3–118
Did not bat: M. Kapp, C.L. Tryon, A. Khaka, R. Ntozakhe, S. Ismail, S. Lackay

| **Bowling** | **O** | **M** | **R** | **W** |
|---|---|---|---|---|
| K.H. Brunt | 10 | 2 | 31 | 1 |
| A. Shrubsole | 10 | 0 | 36 | 2 |
| J.L. Gunn | 6 | 0 | 39 | 0 |
| S. Ecclestone | 10 | 0 | 32 | 0 |
| N.R. Sciver | 2 | 0 | 11 | 0 |
| L.A. Marsh | 7.3 | 0 | 43 | 0 |

**Toss:** England elected to bat. **Umpires:** M. Burns, R. Robinson
**South Africa win by 7 wickets**

# Chapter Five

## The University Final

### Durham MCCU v Loughborough MCCU
### Lord's, London
### Wednesday 20 June

Many years ago I phoned one of the country's largest bookmakers to place a bet on Cambridge for that afternoon's University Boat Race, only to be taken aback when the person who took my call asked me "Who is it between?". Her question would have made more sense, perhaps, had it been about cricket. Cambridge and Oxford still corner the market in televised student rowing contests, but they certainly no longer have it all their own way at the crease. They will meet later this week, on this very ground, for their annual clash, though whether or not it's still *the* University Match is a moot point. The Lord's contest is a one-day affair these days, and though Cambridge award blues for it, Oxford reserve the honour only for the four-day game that now alternates between The Parks and Fenner's. Meanwhile, there are new kids on the block.

Today's university match is the final of the MCCU tournament. Originally set up as the University Centres of

Cricketing Excellence Scheme in 2000, changing its name four years later when the MCC took over its management and funding, the initiative saw the setting up of six regional centres, each of which would draw on talent from a range of local institutions (ironically, today's finalists are the only teams whose players are drawn exclusively from one university). Oxford University, together with Oxford Brookes, formed one; Cambridge, with Anglia Ruskin, another, with similar centres at Durham, Cardiff, Leeds/Bradford and Loughborough. The years since have witnessed nothing less than the passing of the old guard and the rise of the new. A quick flick through the pages of this year's *Playfair Cricket Annual* reveal that 47 current county cricketers have come through the MCCU system. Only one, Sussex's Abidine Sakande, went to Oxford University; none were at Cambridge. Yet just a generation ago, in 1993, when Mike Atherton became the 71st captain of England he was the 34th to have attended one of the two ancient universities. He may well be the last for a very long time. How can two universities that supplied so many captains of England now produce just one cricketer, let alone international, between them?

The fact is that the two ancient institutions, which once provided the likes of Peter May, Colin Cowdrey, Tony Lewis and Mike Brearley, simply no longer care about cricket – academic success is all, and anything that interferes with it is discouraged. There have even been Oxford MCCU games against counties that have not featured a single player from the older of the city's two universities. The last Cambridge-educated county cricketer was Zafar Ansari, who retired prematurely last year while on the cusp of the England team. As he put it, "There is the expectation at Cambridge that everything you do is dedicated towards your academic work, which is on a pedestal… with some of my tutors, if I said I have to go and play this game, there was a sort of scepticism about it, asking me 'why in a world-class academic institution I was playing a game that doesn't really matter.'"[3] Thankfully, other universities take a more rounded view. Durham alone have provided more than 40 Test and county players in the last quarter of a century, two England captains, Hussain and Strauss, among them. Eight current county pros studied there – mostly at the aptly, if coincidentally, named Collingwood College – and even more took their degrees at Loughborough. Loughborough have dominated this tournament too, winning the first three editions and the last three, and another three in between (Oxbridge manage three between them). Their flag flies proudly over their changing room this morning (their opponent's flagpole sadly bare in contrast). Durham, meanwhile, despite their success in unearthing talented cricketers, have just a solitary title to their name, back in 2010. They come to Lord's today as definite underdogs, having finished well behind an unbeaten Loughborough in the group stage.

I arrive late, which will surprise no-one who knows me. My excuse is a very late night, having arrived home in

---

[3] https://www.oxfordstudent.com/2017/04/30/ansari-retires-end-innings-oxbridge-country-cricketers/

the wee small hours after a Rolling Stones concert at Twickenham. The Rolling Stones may be nearly as old as the standing ones at Stonehenge – remarkably, they have been performing for more than a quarter of the entire lifespan of Lord's itself – but Mick Jagger, at least, is considerably more mobile, and the band still put on a lengthy, energetic show. At the end of it, with 60,000 revellers attempting to leave the ground all at the same time, the PA announcer informed us, in the unmistakably smug tones of someone who has a taxi booked, that Twickenham station was closed due to problems on the line, and we'd all have to walk to Richmond. No-one would get any satisfaction from the tube last night. Of course, Jagger is cricket mad himself, an MCC member no less, though I can't spy him at the ground this morning. Apparently, he runs – sprinting, not trotting – seven miles a night when performing, so his absence this morning can be excused.

As I arrive, I am greeted by the unexpected sight of a queue at the Grace Gates, all of whom seem to be from India. For a moment, I wonder if English student cricket has a huge and hitherto unsuspected following on the sub-continent, but it turns out to be a party of tourists booked onto one of the excellent ground tours the MCC provides daily. As I find my seat in the Mound Stand, I realise that the crowd is very much of the size I had expected. It's a slightly mixed bag that have gathered. There are small groups who look like friends of players, a few alumni, and various parents, even an entire family or two. Up in the

Tavern there is the sound of early jollity, which I suspect will get louder as the day goes on. Loughborough have won the toss and put Durham in to bat. It's one of those curious English days when, despite almost total cloud cover, sunglasses are still needed to avoid the glare, though no-one's quite sure where it's coming from. It's a little bit humid too, the pitch looks greenish, and Loughborough's captain, Tillcock, clearly feels there are early wickets to be had. Fraine and Plater are the batsmen aiming to defy them, Fraine promoted to opener since my previous encounter with Durham's students on a freezing Easter Sunday at Edgbaston. Pereira opens the bowling with considerable enthusiasm and tennis-like grunts. His energy finds rewards, as Fraine is dismissed for 7 and Plater, bat held high even by modern standards, sends up a catch to Sehmi behind the stumps. Pereira wheels away, arms outstretched, like a schoolboy pretending to be a fighter plane in a playground. When Cooke goes the same way for a golden duck, Pereira upgrades to supersonic, and there are yells, whoops and hugs all round. Durham are 28–3, and one feels for Cooke, who may be in the first few moments of a lifetime's regret. A golden duck at Lord's is not the memory he'd have wanted to take away, but at least he can say he has played here, which in itself is more than most of us will ever manage. Meanwhile his replacement, Ben Graves, is introduced over the loudspeaker in a voice that suggests the overworked announcer feels liberties are being taken with his good will.

There are a few encouraging cries of 'Come on Durham', and Macdonell – a Derbyshire cricketer until leaving the county a few months ago to pursue other career options – is doing his best to respond. He puts on a mini-stand with Graves, but when the latter, hunched over his bat, legs wide apart, punches indecisively and sends the ball to the welcoming hands of Khan at mid-off, the northern university is 63–4 and Pereira has bagged all of them. He bowls straight through his allotted ten overs, wreaking havoc with Durham's batting order to finish with 4–30. Sohal departs soon after, and after yesterday's late night, I start to anticipate a welcome early finish. Nothing against Durham, of course – we are, after all, old acquaintances by now – but it would not go amiss. The prospect seems likelier still when Rishton, spurred on by cries of "lovely bowling there Rishy", entices Emanuel to edge another ball to the faultless Sehmi. It's as well Durham haven't brought a flag, as it would be hanging very limply right now. Alex McGrath comes in, Rishton appeals for an LBW and when it's turned down appeals all the louder. It matters not, as McGrath is bowled by Tillcock in the next over, having added just one.

Amidst all this carnage, MacDonell is doggedly holding up one end, with a Boycott-like protection of his wicket. With the enticing smell of bacon rolls wafting across from a kitchen somewhere, he and Sookias now start to build a stand, with snatched singles here, the occasional boundary there, and much punching of gloves in between. The 100 comes up, and at least a degree of respectability is being achieved. Eventually, on 118, the stubborn MacDonell is removed, deceived by a wily ball from Azad. Sookias can bat though, despite his lowly place in the order, and plays some fine strokes. Subramanyan, quick and nimble and with nothing to lose, throws his bat and to some effect, racing to 19 off his first 18 balls and having the temerity to strike a six into the Tavern Stand. Loughborough, not used to having runs scored off their bowling so far, seem taken by surprise and are short of ideas to stop it. The scoring slows, but keeps ticking over, and Loughborough start to lose their swagger; Durham progress steadily to 150, then 175, and the partnership passes 50 before Sookias eventually falls for a fighting 39. The last man, Russell, comes in, and he too displays some resistance; what it lacks in elegance, it makes up for in nuisance value. Against all likelihood, Durham have advanced from 77–7 to 213 before Russell, trying to hoik Khan, is bowled, leaving Subramanyan unbeaten on 45. While the target should be well within the champions' reach, you sense that Durham's tail has managed to punch a few small but vital holes in Loughborough's confidence.

After the break, it is Durham who emerge from the pavilion with a spring in their step. Is there just a hint of nerves in the walk of Loughborough's opening batsmen, Evans and Azad? If there is, it's justified, as their reply makes a disastrous start, Evans beaten by pace and deviation from Russell's very first ball. The favourites are 0–1, Durham are jubilant, and Lord's has a second golden duck of the day. There's urgency about Durham's fielding, the lively Russell is beating the bat with alarming frequency for the champions, and a lone call of "Luff-burrow" sounds more in concerned hope than expectation. When McGrath, bowling at the Nursery End, gets one to go down the slope, Azad edges it, it's 20–2 and he walks sadly back to the pavilion, accompanied by the strains of "walking in a cricket wonderland" from the gleeful Durham supporters. It's been a fine opening spell from Russell and McGrath, miserly with runs – just 24 conceded off 11 overs – and constantly beating the edge of flailing bats. But when they're replaced by Cooke and Subramanyan, the bowling becomes slower and less accurate, and the scoring picks up. Thurston and Soames require only four overs to more than double their team's total as they ease past 50, and momentum starts to turn again. It's as if the larking around of the first couple of terms have stopped and it's time to knuckle down to work and get through the final-term exams.

The commanding Thurston is the dominant figure in the partnership, muscular strokes finding the boundary with more regularity than Durham will care for. Soames is more reserved, but his steadying innings is no less valuable in its own way, and after those early wobbles Loughborough are starting to cruise. Thurston reaches 50 with a huge six and Durham bring on Ben Graves from the Pavilion End, the announcement eliciting a solitary 'YAY!" from a supporter. But, when Loughborough pass 100 in the 26th over, it looks like plain sailing. And then, inexplicably, Thurston gets his shot selection hopelessly wrong and instead of driving a delivery from Sohal for another boundary, merely lobs it up, presenting it on a platter to Plater, and departing for 62. It's the tamest of endings to what has been a domineering innings, and Loughborough are visibly jolted. At 107–3 they are exactly half way to their target, but are soon four down, captain Tillock bowled cheaply by Graves. The bowler seems to have friends and family here for the occasion, and he receives much applause and shouts of encouragement as he takes his fielding place on the boundary in front of the Tavern. Someone cries out "Come on Jerry, come on". Are they referring to Ben Graves? If so, is perhaps particularly fond of ice cream? "You are cool", a young woman informs him, and he grins bashfully, looking suitably pleased with life. Buoyed by encouragement, he gets Rishton stumped in his next over. Now there is full-blown leaping, whooping and high-fiving, and a group hug from Durham. There's even what might pass for a roar from the crowd, who are loving the latest twist. The game has shifted back to the older university, but they still have the dogged Soames on 37 to deal with. In the meantime, Graves arrives back at his boundary post. "Ben, that was wonderful", says his admirer, and it's hard to tell whether the colour in the young man's cheeks is from exertion or blushes. Loughborough are five down for 130, the run rate has crept past seven an over, and, symbolically, their flag now hangs limply from the flagpole. "Jerry, Jerry, give us a wave" shouts someone and when Graves' figures of 2–28 from ten overs are announced at the end of his spell, his chief fan runs down to the advertising hoarding and shakes his hand. She turns back to her companions, her face wreathed in the ecstatic rapture of someone who's just been winked at by Louis Tomlinson and may well faint with excitement.

In the meantime, Soames continues blocking and pinching singles, and reaches a stubborn half-century, but more wickets fall. When Khan, aiming for the boundary, is caught in front of the media centre, the entire Durham team race down to swamp the fielder. Loughborough are now 161–7, and their position worsens further when Sohal tempts Soames into a rare indiscretion and he's caught by Cooke. He's proved a fine anchor to the innings since his premature arrival at the crease, and clearly hoped to steer his side home, but he now cuts a dejected figure as he slumps off, his side on the brink of defeat. They need 52 runs and have 38 balls in which to get them, but only two wickets left. That's soon one, Rollings leg before for a duck. He's not happy, and briefly stands his ground before departing with all the enthusiasm of a man heading for the scaffold. "One wicket!", comes a helpful reminder from a Durham supporter.

As Durham close in on victory, one can almost feel the energy coursing through the team, and Loughborough can only prolong the inevitable. Pereira leans forward at the crease with bat held high, looking like a solitary swordsman about to defend a castle entrance against an entire army, but unlike Aragorn there is no victory over overwhelming odds. That said, it takes an extraordinary catch to end the match, when Sehmi launches a ball high into the air and a Durham fielder runs fast and dives far to pluck the ball out of the air. Loughborough are beaten, Durham are jubilant, and there's even a short-lived one-man pitch invasion. The long, happy drive up the A1 to the far northeast will seem a lot shorter than the weary trek back to the East Midlands.

Even when largely empty, as it was for the MCCU final, Lord's remains a sight to gladden the heart

**Durham MCCU**

| | | | |
|---|---|---|---|
| WAR Fraine * | lbw | b Pereira | 7 |
| MJ Plater | c Sehmi | b Pereira | 14 |
| CM Macdonell | | b Azad | 31 |
| JM Cooke | c Sehmi | b Pereira | 0 |
| BWM Graves | c Khan | b Pereira | 16 |
| VVS Sohal | c Sehmi | b Rishton | 4 |
| JF Emanuel | c Sehmi | b Rishton | 0 |
| AH McGrath | b Tillcock | | 1 |
| JH Sookias † | st Sehmi | b Khan | 39 |
| JS Subramanyan | not out | | 45 |
| AMC Russell | | b Khan | 11 |
| Extras | | 2b 7lb 12nb 24w | 45 |
| **Total** | | 49.4 overs | 10 – 213 |

**FoW:** 1–25, 2–28, 3–28, 4–63, 5–75, 6–76, 7–77, 8–118, 9–179, 10–213

| **Bowling** | **O** | **M** | **R** | **W** |
|---|---|---|---|---|
| Pereira | 10 | 1 | 30 | 4 |
| Rollings | 10 | 0 | 43 | 0 |
| Rishton | 10 | 0 | 46 | 2 |
| Tillcock | 10 | 2 | 27 | 1 |
| Khan | 7.4 | 0 | 35 | 1 |
| Azad | 2 | 0 | 23 | 1 |

**Loughborough MCCU**

| | | | |
|---|---|---|---|
| ST Evans | c Sookias | b Russell | 0 |
| MH Azad | c Cooke | b McGrath | 12 |
| CO Thurston | c Plater | b Sohal | 62 |
| O Soames | c Cooke | b McGrath | 53 |
| AD Tillcock * | b Graves | | 6 |
| JAJ Rishton | st Sookias | b Graves | 4 |
| NA Hammond | | run out | 1 |
| AH Khan | c McGrath | b Subramanyan | 14 |
| RT Sehmi † | c sub | b McGrath | 8 |
| WJL Rollings | lbw | b Subramanyan | 0 |
| WJ Pereira | not out | | 0 |
| Extras | | 2lb 7w | 9 |
| **Total** | | 46 overs | 10 – 170 |

**FoW:** 1–0, 2–20, 3–107, 4–124, 5–130, 6–133, 7–161, 8–162, 9–166, 10–170

| **Bowling** | **O** | **M** | **R** | **W** |
|---|---|---|---|---|
| Russell | 8 | 1 | 21 | 1 |
| McGrath | 8 | 1 | 20 | 3 |
| Cooke | 5 | 0 | 32 | 0 |
| Subramanyan | 5 | 0 | 30 | 2 |
| Sohal | 10 | 0 | 36 | 1 |
| Graves | 10 | 2 | 29 | 2 |

**Toss:** Loughborough elected to field. **Umpires:** T. Lungley, I.N. Ramage
**Durham MCCU win by 43 runs**

Durham's students bat, while Lord's ground staff look on

Durham supporters soak up the sun on a glorious day at their impressive ground

The far side of the ground, with the beautiful backdrop of Lumley Castle

# Chapter Six

## Day/Night Match

Durham v Warwickshire
Emirates Riverside, Chester-le-Street
Monday 25 June

Having watched Durham's students in action last week, it is the turn of the county cricket club. As I near the Chester-le-Street junction on the A1 I find myself, appropriately enough, behind a car with the letters MCC in its registration plate, but instead of turning off, as I expect, it carries on northwards. A few minutes later I arrive at Durham's impressive Riverside stadium. The car park payment machines take only cash, so when I get to the ticket kiosk, all my change now gone, it is with some apprehension that I ask the gatemen if he takes cards for payments. "I'll take anything", he replies reassuringly, "cards, cash, euros, loose women…". It's not his lucky day, I tell him, as sadly I have no euros on me, and I hand him a card instead. As I walk through the gates, I'm pleasantly surprised to find there is no security check, no bag search, not even a ban on alcohol, not that I am carrying any. Having been frisked and had every pocket of my bags searched before being allowed to watch a match between students last week, it makes a welcome change to come to a professional game and not be regarded as a possible terrorist, or at least someone likely to cause alcohol-related anti-social behaviour.

With today's match played across daytime and evening, the final session under floodlights, at least I was able to avoid setting off at an ungodly hour this morning to get here on time. Floodlit first-class matches, as opposed to limited-overs games, are still something of a novelty, though cricket has been played under lights for a long time. The first match is believed to have been, curiously, between Middlesex and Arsenal FC back in 1952, but it was only in 1979 that it started being played regularly, as part of Kerry Packer's World Series Cricket in Australia. It took a while to catch on in England, but eventually floodlights started appearing at some of the larger grounds. Even so, it was only in 2011 that the first floodlit Championship match took place, and not until late 2015 did Test cricket finally get a day/night match, Australia narrowly beating New Zealand. While the two captains were full of praise for the concept in public, the rest of the players weren't unanimous in their support; most felt improvements were needed to make it work, not least refining the new pink ball. It might be easier for TV cameras to spot a pink ball under floodlights than a red one but, they argued, the reverse was true for the fielders. The concept stayed, though, and England played their first day/night Test just 10 months ago, trouncing the West Indies by an innings and 208 runs (a scoreline which, back in the 1970s, would have seemed a far more extraordinary story than the fact it was under floodlights, but that's another story).

Of course, playing cricket under floodlights is a different experience for the players as well as the spectators, and these County Championship matches are primarily aimed at giving players the opportunity to get used to playing first-class games in this fashion. Last year, the matches all took place just ahead of the Edgbaston Test, but this summer, with no day/night Test being played, the matches are more spread out, to enable the ECB, they tell us, to evaluate different conditions at different times of the year. Well, after 2017's dismal summer, this one continues to shower sun, rather than rain, upon us, so we'll see how the pink Dukes ball fares in warm sunshine. It's 27C degrees today and set fair for several days. It's a far cry from 2016, when Sri Lanka had the misfortune to be sent here for a May Test Match, just after one at Headingley played in dismal, grey conditions and temperatures more suited to winter sports. The unfortunate visitors, unsurprisingly, lost both matches, despite a spirited fightback at Durham after trailing England by 397 runs, and must have left the north wondering how the English, with such a wretched climate, ever invented cricket. They weren't alone, as media pundits, players and fans alike questioned the wisdom of subjecting touring teams to Tests in the north before summer had even arrived.

Of course, it's not just day/night cricket that wasn't known here 40 years ago. Back then, any match involving

Durham would have been a Minor Counties game. Only in 1992 did they join the County Championship, the first county to do so since Glamorgan more than 70 years earlier. So rarely do new teams join the Championship that despite being around for more than a quarter of a century, they still seem new boys to me, like Ronnie Wood of the Rolling Stones. And, like his career with the band, Durham's 26 years have been quite a ride. By 2004, they looked out of their depth, bottom of the Championship's second division, near the bottom of the one-day league's second division, and last-but-one in their Twenty20 Cup division. But, when you're at the bottom, the only way is up. In 2005 they improved sufficiently to win promotion to the first division of the Championship. The following year they escaped relegation by the skin of their teeth, but, galvanised, in 2008 won the County Championship itself (a fine feat, given that Northamptonshire, Somerset and even Gloucestershire, Wally Hammond, WG and all, have yet to win the title (or at least the official one in Gloucestershire's case) in their far longer existences. Durham retained the crown in 2009, and won it again four years later, and have added one-day trophies to the cabinet too, but in 2016 it all went spectacularly wrong. Having over-extended themselves, Durham found themselves in deep financial trouble, owing money to creditors and having to reassure players their contracts would be honoured. Despite the distractions, the players performed remarkably in the circumstances, and the team finished fourth, 30 points adrift of champions

Middlesex. Off the field, however, storm clouds were brewing, and when the season ended the county agreed a bailout deal with the ECB. In return for a payment of £3.8 million to clear debts and put the county on a sounder footing, they would give up rights to stage Test Matches at the Riverside, which had been built specifically for such games, accept a revised salary cap and have prize money withheld. Most controversially of all, they would also be relegated to division two, with a 48-point penalty at the start of the 2017 season. It was a harsh punishment, and deeply unpopular with many, not least among the blameless players who had helped make Durham one of the most successful counties on the playing field.

The club's incoming chairman, Sir Ian Botham, who played for them in their inaugural championship season, was typically bullish ahead of life in the lower division. "Look, it's just two wins", he said. "The team are more than good enough to get those two early wins. In Division Two, we'll probably be the best side by a distance, and with the character and determination of the guys here it is not a case of if but when we get back to the top level."[4] His typically positive attitude had to be admired, but wasn't quite matched by results. Durham won just three matches all year and finished next to bottom, only perennial wooden spoon contenders Leicestershire below them. They're faring only slightly better this season, two wins out of five, three places and 18 points off bottom. They're even

---

[4] www.theguardian.com/sport/2017/feb/27/ian-botham-durham-chairman-restore

below Leicestershire this time. Ominously, things are going rather better for their visitors. Warwickshire are top of the table and looking like genuine promotion material, though they did slip to defeat against their nearest rivals, Kent, last week.

Another decent crowd has turned up to watch, and to enjoy the sunshine, though nearly all, it has to be said, are men of a certain age. I'm interested in seeing how the crowd changes, if at all, when the shops and offices close and the workers come streaming out in search of evening entertainment. There's certainly plenty of room for them, for this is a sizeable ground. Although it's new by cricketing standards – the first match was played here in 1995 – there's a reassuringly old-fashioned feel to it. The buildings are all modern, to be sure, but designed with tradition, as well as comfort, in mind. It was built deliberately to be large enough to host Test Matches – a condition of Durham's original elevation – so can seat far more than the few hundred gathered today. It also has a wonderfully picturesque setting, overlooked by the splendid 14th Century Lumley Castle, once the residence of the Bishop of Durham, later a rather luxurious hall of residence for Durham University students. In the past, the castle defended the local area from hordes of marauding Scots, not to mention marauding undergraduates, but today it has the more genteel role of hotel, where guests can enjoy a fine, if somewhat distant, view of the cricket.

Warwickshire have won the toss and decided to bat. Rhodes looks in fine shape early on and plays a particularly fine cover drive, only to be caught behind next ball.

He swats angrily at a fly and trudges off. Meanwhile, the bowler, Salisbury, appears to have forgotten his shirt and is wearing someone else's with the name taped over. Despite his early success, the chatter among the spectators is not of Warwickshire but of their recent conquerors Kent; or more precisely, their veteran all-rounder Darren Stevens. "He just keeps getting better as he gets older", says one, not inaccurately. "Amazing feller", says another. Durham, of course, know a thing or two about useful veterans, led as they are by the redoubtable Paul Collingwood. Meanwhile, Sibley and another of the game's senior pros, Ian Bell, accumulate runs steadily. Drinks are taken soon after the 50 comes up, and prove Bell's undoing as he's dismissed immediately upon resumption, to his evident displeasure. Drinks-related dismissals seem to be a recurring theme this season, and I start to wonder whether they should get their own entry on scorecards. It seems only fair.

His replacement is another veteran, Jonathan Trott. Rushworth, Salisbury's opening bowling partner, completes his spell and comes down to the boundary in order to keep the twelfth man occupied. "Gav? Gav? Water please." "Lager?", asks Gav. "No, water – a bottle from the fridge". Gav duly trots out with the water, but an over later his services are in demand again. "Gav? Towel please." "What?", asks Gav, who is either spectacularly hard of hearing for a sportsman or feels the role of twelfth man needs livening up. "A towel", shouts Rishworth, exasperation rising in his voice. Deciding Gav is a bail short of a full wicket, he then mimes the act of rubbing his face in the hope it might trigger some sort of recognition of what's needed. While all that's going on, Sibley and Trott make steady progress and at lunch – or is tea, no-one seems quite sure? – Warwickshire are 80–2.

As usual, I wander over to the club shop, which has disappointingly few books on sale. On the way back, I pass the signs for the loos, which say not 'men' and 'women', or 'gents' and 'ladies', but, in good north-eastern terminology, 'lads' and 'lasses'. As I get back to my seat, someone nearby says "Afternoon" to an old friend, adding quizzically, "or is it evening?". It's not yet half-past four, the longest day of the year was just four days ago, and the sun is scorching, so despite the puzzlement caused by the unfamiliar playing hours, I'll stick with afternoon. The PA announcer tells us the teams are returning, and leaves the mic on while he laughs long and loud at a joke not shared with the rest of us. It's certainly lost on Sibley, who faces a mere four balls before he's rapped on the pads and sent on his way. Lunch must have been treacle tart rather than salad, as Trott is equally immobile and also hit firmly on the legs. There's a loud appeal from the Durham players, as well as one of their supporters, who shouts "Give 'im out", from his ideal vantage point at square leg. "Give 'im out", he repeats, softly but menacingly, sounding like a Bond villain issuing instructions for a hapless victim to be fed to hungry piranhas. Bravely, the umpires ignore the request and Trott survives.

In the still heat of the late afternoon, a soporific mood falls upon the ground. No-one is actually asleep, but a few are engrossed in books or hunched over tablets. Most, though, are watching the game with keen interest but are simply, I suspect, too hot to make anything in the way of noise. That's left to the Durham players, who urge on the hard-working bowlers with cries of "Come on Rushy", or the equally original "Rimmy", depending on who's bowling. Whatever happened to witty, imaginative nicknames? I'm not sure there have been any good ones since Monde 'All hands' Zondeki retired a few years back. Chris Gayle sometimes answers to Gayle Force, though there's a pinch too much of the tabloid headline about that one. I still fondly recall Phil Tuffnell's soubriquet of 'the cat', awarded not because of his feline fielding qualities, but his ability to be found fast asleep in the dressing room at any hour of the day.

Trott, meanwhile, is proving as keen a gardener as Alan Titchmarsh, constantly prodding and poking the pitch between overs. Between each ball, however, he is statuesque, leaning on his bat, hand on hip and looking as thoroughly at ease as he did against Durham's students earlier in the season. Perhaps his recent announced that 2018 will be his final season has brought him some calm detachment. Trott has been a fine player for Warwickshire, and for England too, until undone by mental health problems that he courageously went public with. He's always been an intense character, and that can bring challenges, especially in such a precarious, public and mentally draining occupation as Test batsman, with relentless pressure and tiny margins between success and failure error. He was good at it though, a reliable number 3 – something England would give their collective right arm for today. He averaged 44 from more than 50 tests, and his one-day figures were better still. But for all his runs, perhaps his greatest legacy to the game will be, like his contemporary Marcus Trescothick, that he felt able to reveal his mental struggles to a wider world. In the tough, macho, environment of professional sport, admitting to doubts, fears and anxieties has all-too-often been seen as weakness, attracting 'jokes' at best, or more likely insults and mickey-taking, rather than the support that was actually needed. Things are, thankfully, albeit slowly, changing, in sport as in wider society, but there's still a long way to go to dismiss the stigma that remains over mental health. For all their runs and centuries for their counties and for England, Trott and Trescothick's finest legacy to the game may well turn out to be the greater openness and understanding in the game of mental health issues, and the strength others will take to open up about their own struggles.

Today, though, Trott is looking positively relaxed, enjoying himself in a successful team. He and Adam Hose have taken the score to 130 when the younger man mistimes a hook and the Durham keeper, Davies, take a superb running catch halfway to the boundary, and into the sun at that. Durham's bowlers, despite the heat, are keeping the bowling tight and with the visitors four down, the home supporters are encouraged. Not enough, though, to come flocking to the ground. The clock has reached the time of day when workplaces empty, and a few new arrivals do enter the ground, but they can be counted in tens rather than hundreds. And for all those who arrive, it seems nearly as many leave to go home for dinner. Trott reaches his 50, and it's an innings full of old-fashioned virtues – guarded, watchful, careful, leaving anything outside off-stump and punishing anything loose, with runs coming mostly (just) from singles and twos rather than fours and sixes. When he does strike a boundary, it's like listening to one of those people who doesn't speak much but when they do it is worth hearing. With Trott joined by Ambrose, who plays a series of fine strokes, chances dry up for the Durham bowlers. At 6:53, when we'd normally be heading home, the PA system announces the tea interval – "sponsored by English Tea Shop" – with the visitors a slightly more comfortable 173–4. Ahead of the final session, the floodlights come on and, on a bright, sunny June day in the far north, make not the slightest difference. The sun is still high and will not set for the best part of another three hours. There will be no rapid hastening of night, play dramatically illuminated by lights blazing fiercely against a pitch-black sky. The absence of one of the big selling points of floodlit matches perhaps helps explain why there is no evening surge in the size of the crowd. To all intents and purposes, the final session of the day is going to be little different from the first two, and therein lies a problem. At this time of year, day/night

Championship games simply aren't sufficiently different or appealing to attract a new audience. The scheduling of this year's matches suggests the ECB know this, and the games are used purely as a means of giving players practice playing under lights with a pink ball, with no serious attempt to appeal to a wider public. On an evening like this, even that seems spurious.

Instead, the two batsmen continue, untroubled, in the sunshine. Collingwood brings himself on to bowl, Graham Clark's solitary over is greeted with a cheery cry of "Come on Clarky, get 'em my son!", but the score climbs steadily. A few minutes after 8.00, Ambrose reaches his half century; Just before 8.30, Trott reaches three figures, and the only young couple I've seen all day depart. The heat, too, says, "enough is enough" and gives way to the cool of late evening, though a couple of hundred spectators stick it out for the last ten overs. They are rewarded by Ambrose's departure, caught in the deep trying to force a few more runs. The shadows from the floodlights finally replace those from the sun, and at 9.17pm play ends for the day, Trott unbeaten on 119, Warwickshire a little short of 300 and looking at a big score tomorrow. For the stewards, it seems the end has not come a moment too soon. Before the players have even left the square, the floodlights are switched off, and any of the few dozen remaining spectators hoping to visit the lavatories before journeying home are out of luck, as they are locked already. The lingering impression is that night-time cricket is tolerated, rather than embraced, a contractual obligation rather than exciting innovation. It's not catching on…

**Warwickshire first innings**

| | | | |
|---|---|---|---|
| Rhodes | c Latham | b Salisbury | 2 |
| Sibley | lbw | b Rushworth | 27 |
| Bell | c Steel | b Salisbury | 23 |
| Trott | not out | | 170 |
| Hose | c Davies | b Salisbury | 17 |
| Ambrose † | c Harte | b Rushworth | 67 |
| Barker | c Davies | b Salisbury | 27 |
| Patel * | b Rushworth | | 15 |
| Wright | c Davies | b Harte | 21 |
| Hannon-Dalby | c Latham | b Rushworth | 13 |
| Sidebottom | lbw | b Rimmington | 6 |
| Extras | | 14b 3lb 6nb 1w | 24 |
| **Total** | | 134 overs | 10 – 424 |

**FoW:** 1–17, 2–52, 3–81, 4–130, 5–265, 6–332, 7–351, 8–381, 9–405, 10–424

| **Bowling** | **O** | **M** | **R** | **W** |
|---|---|---|---|---|
| Rushworth | 38 | 9 | 101 | 4 |
| Salisbury | 35 | 9 | 111 | 4 |
| Rimmington | 25 | 5 | 81 | 1 |
| Harte | 15 | 2 | 54 | 1 |
| Pringle | 16 | 1 | 43 | 0 |
| Collingwood | 4 | 0 | 2 | 0 |
| Clark | 1 | 0 | 2 | 0 |

**Durham first innings**

| | | | |
|---|---|---|---|
| Latham | c Ambrose | b Hannon-Dalby | 50 |
| Steel | c Ambrose | b Sidebottom | 51 |
| Smith | c Ambrose | b Hannon-Dalby | 2 |
| Clark | c Bell | b Patel | 32 |
| Collingwood * | lbw | b Hannon-Dalby | 9 |
| Harte | c Ambrose | b Wright | 45 |
| Davies † | c Bell | b Patel | 0 |
| Pringle | c Ambrose | b Hannon-Dalby | 34 |
| Rimmington | c Bell | b Wright | 32 |
| Salisbury | not out | | 8 |
| Rushworth | c Rhodes | b Patel | 5 |
| Extras | | 8b 8lb 8nb 5w | 29 |
| **Total** | | 104 overs | 10 –297 |

**FoW:** 1–96, 2–98, 3–139, 4–150, 5–173, 6–175, 7–223, 8–277, 9–284, 10–297

| **Bowling** | **O** | **M** | **R** | **W** |
|---|---|---|---|---|
| Barker | 22 | 5 | 58 | 0 |
| Wright | 22 | 8 | 46 | 2 |
| Hannon-Dalby | 22 | 5 | 61 | 4 |
| Sidebottom | 16 | 2 | 70 | 1 |
| Patel | 22 | 9 | 46 | 3 |

**Warwickshire second innings**

| | | | | |
|---|---|---|---|---|
| Rhodes | | b Rimmington | | 9 |
| Sibley | c Davies | b Salisbury | | 18 |
| Bell | c Collingwood | b Salisbury | | 4 |
| Trott | c Clark | b Salisbury | | 53 |
| Hose | lbw | b Rushworth | | 15 |
| Ambrose † | c Latham | b Pringle | | 39 |
| Barker | not out | | | 32 |
| Patel * | c Latham | b Pringle | | 0 |
| Wright | | c&b Pringle | | 0 |
| Hannon-Dalby | c Steel | b Rushworth | | 0 |
| Sidebottom | not out | | | 2 |
| Extras | | 12b 1lb | | 13 |
| **Total** | | 52 overs | 9 – | 185 dec. |

**FoW:** 1–26, 2–32, 3–38, 4–102, 5–119, 6–179, 7–179, 8–179, 9–182

| **Bowling** | **O** | **M** | **R** | **W** |
|---|---|---|---|---|
| Rushworth | 14 | 3 | 44 | 2 |
| Salisbury | 16 | 3 | 57 | 3 |
| Rimmington | 10 | 1 | 40 | 1 |
| Pringle | 12 | 3 | 31 | 3 |

**Durham second innings**

| | | | | |
|---|---|---|---|---|
| Latham | lbw | b Patel | | 29 |
| Steel | c Bell | b Wright | | 2 |
| Smith | c Ambrose | b Hannon-Dalby | | 35 |
| Clark | c Ambrose | b Patel | | 17 |
| Collingwood | c Ambrose | b Patel | | 4 |
| Harte | c Sibley | b Sidebottom | | 18 |
| Davies | c Ambrose | b Patel | | 20 |
| Pringle | c Bell | b Sidebottom | | 3 |
| Rimmington | | b Patel | | 61 |
| Salisbury | c Ambrose | b Patel | | 19 |
| Rushworth | not out | | | 2 |
| Extras | | 10b 4 lb 2nb | | 16 |
| **Total** | | 66 overs | 10 – | 226 |

**FoW:** 1–14, 2–79, 3–83, 4–87, 5–120, 6–138, 7–144, 8–148, 9–179, 10–226

| **Bowling** | **O** | **M** | **R** | **W** |
|---|---|---|---|---|
| Barker | 11 | 1 | 42 | 0 |
| Wright | 10 | 1 | 26 | 1 |
| Sidebottom | 12 | 4 | 31 | 2 |
| Hannon-Dalby | 8 | 0 | 30 | 1 |
| Patel | 25 | 8 | 83 | 6 |

**Toss:** Warwickshire elected to bat. **Umpires:** G. Lloyd, C. Watts
**Warwickshire win by 86 runs**

# Chapter Seven

## The Cup Final

Kent Spitfires v Hampshire
Lord's, London
Saturday 30 June

Another day at Lord's, another cloudless blue sky. It is something to which we are becoming strangely accustomed this year. There has been a genuine heatwave this week, temperatures well into the 30s, and the followers of Kent and Hampshire have made their way in numbers along the A2 and M3 to enjoy a day in the sun. Consequently, long queues snake along Wellington Road, even as the players take the field, and a big crowd seems likely. It's short of a full house though, the top floor of the Tavern remaining closed. Time was when a Lord's Cup Final would have been a guaranteed sell-out, but the magic has waned in recent years. Attendances have fallen, not helped by an ECB attitude towards one-day cricket that at times seems dismissive. Twenty20 is the thing these days, and the 50-over game, once vilified as a form of cricket reserved for Messrs Bashem and Sloggit, and the ruin of the first-class game, is now viewed by some as too slow, too long, too old-fashioned. The hunter has become the hunted. The romance has gone too. The old domestic cups – the 50-over Benson & Hedges, and the Gillette/NatWest, ten overs longer – featured the likes of the Netherlands and Minor Counties and the Universities. The longer tournament was a proper, FA Cup-style knock-out tournament complete with occasional giant killings and provided the climax to the season. And, of course, matches were shown live on the BBC, and not just the final. It was one such match – a Gillette Cup semi-final between Lancashire and Gloucestershire – that first got me hooked on cricket as a small boy. It was 1971, and Old Trafford was packed, scores of teenagers crouching and kneeling wherever there was space, right up to the boundary rope, and sometimes over it. The match was spilling over, too, way past its expected finish time. Thankfully, my parents let me stay up late, for which I have a lifetime's gratitude. With the clock showing 8.45pm and gloom fast descending – no floodlights then – David Hughes swaggered to the crease. Twenty-five runs were needed off five overs; today, that sounds like a target batsmen would knock off with their eyes closed, but back then, with different expectations of what was possible and batsmen needing night-vision goggles to see the red ball, it was a different proposition. Hughes queried the light, only for the umpire, Arthur Jepson, anxious to avoid having to come back in the morning, to tell him "You can see the moon, can't you? How far do you want to see?". Hughes accepted the decision philosophically and promptly smashed 24 runs off one over, sending the crowd into delight and Lancashire into the final. He'd have loved playing Twenty20.

It wasn't just the fans who lapped up the excitement of the cup – the players did too. This was their big day out as well, and for the honest journeymen among them, a possibly once-in-a-career chance to play before a packed house at Headquarters. To be sure, they'd play here enough in county games, but a noisy, beery, chanting, cheering capacity crowd and the presence of TV cameras would be something special. If they were lucky, they'd even stay the night at a nearby hotel, rather than having to drag themselves along the motorway early in the morning. Some teams even kitted out their teams in shiny new cup final suits. In the days before Kerry Packer improved the financial lot of cricketers, that was worth getting excited about. There were other incentives too. Many a player was propelled onto a winter tour after a match-winning performance in a cup final, or landed a very welcome sponsorship deal. Sometimes, such a performance would even define an entire career, like Asif Din's century in the 1993 NatWest final.

Those glory days, though, are long gone. Over the last decade there has been continual, at times bewildering, change: to formats, names, sponsors, match lengths, scheduling… The One-Day Cup is actually, bewilderingly, the 17th incarnation of what was once the 40-over Sunday League. Not even Doctor Who has regenerated so many times. When competitions are subject to this sort of constant tinkering, they lose identity, and lose meaning for fans, and sometimes even for players. Just four years ago, when Durham triumphed here, the ground was half-empty. Today's final is not even the culmination of a knockout cup at all, but of a league system that has featured far too many games, and too many meaningless ones. With continual change, it's no surprise that interest has declined, and the ECB seems disinclined to stem the flow. It's been announced that, from 2020, the final will not even be played at Lord's, but at Trent Bridge. It's all very well spreading big matches around the country, but – and with no disrespect to Trent Bridge, a fine ground and one of my favourites – this is a downgrade, and many will see it as another nail in the coffin of what was once the climax of the county calendar.

All that said, the Kent and Hampshire fans who are here are full of enthusiasm and in good voice. That may be because both counties have been starved of success in recent years. Hampshire's last silverware was in 2012, in one of this tournament's many predecessors, the Clydesdale Bank 40, when for List A cricket they were the Hampshire Royals. Before that, they were the Hawks (that tinkering again), but in 2013 reverted to simply Hampshire. It was recognition, perhaps, that such artificial nicknames, rather than attracting new, young fans, are essentially meaningless and can actually distance clubs from their supporters. Kent, meanwhile, persevere with the appendage Spitfires, which has less to do with the plane that fought so many battles over Kentish soil, and more to do with a beer brewed by their sponsors. Their wait for trophies, at least in the men's game, goes back even further than Hampshire's, to a second division title in 2009 and a solitary Twenty20 triumph two years earlier. Their record in Lord's cup finals is approaching a thing of wonder. Since lifting the B&H Cup in 1978, the final year of their golden period, they have reached seven Lord's finals only to lose them all. Their long-suffering supporters – and here I must declare to being one – will be hoping today is eighth-time lucky, but on past form we will do so more with hope than expectation.

The ground is abuzz, as loud and vibrant in the bright morning sun as the red and yellow blooms that adorn myriad flower beds and borders. The Lord's hum is all around us – that curious, contented, harmonious murmur of eager chatter and anticipation, distilled into one organic, benevolent sound, like the mellow drone of a million contented bees. No ground anywhere *sounds* like Lord's on big match day. Other grounds may be noisier, livelier, certainly more raucous, but none have the dreamy benevolence of Lord's. It's the fans of the Hop county who have first reason to cheer, when captain Sam Billings calls correctly, but despite the blue skies he puts Hampshire into bat. Kent fancy their chances in a chase, but Hampshire will equally feel they can post a big score. It's not only the skies that are blue today. Kent are in navy trousers and mid-blue shirts, while Hampshire's batsmen, clad in dark blue kit with bright yellow helmets and pads, look like a futuristic SWAT team wielding bats as weapons. They start confidently, 18 runs flowing from the first four overs, though not without a point or two being made by Podmore and Henry for Kent. It's not long before the first cries of 'Come on you Kent' drift across from the Mound Stand. On a hot day, they will soon become beerier. Their boys are certainly eager, making excellent stops to save boundaries. Between overs, there is none of the usual gentle lobbing of the ball from fielder to fielder to bowler; instead, it is positively hurled between fielders while they run, like the Harlem Globetrotters mesmerising slower-witted opponents with their dazzling ball skills. The Hampshire openers, Alsop and Rousseau, are made of stern stuff though, and despite Kent's excellent fielding find the boundary with increasing fluency. The 50 is up on the 10th over, with ominous ease from Kent's perspective.

They turn to Darren Stevens, the veteran all-rounder who, though 42, seems to get better with every passing season. His introduction to the attack is met with loud applause from the Grandstand, Kentish territory for the day. Historians among the Kent supporters will take heart from the fact that in 1774, the year these counties first met, Hampshire were undone by a bowler called Stevens. There are few signs of a repeat though. The modern-day Stevens is treated with respect, but the two batsmen are well-set and looking too comfortable. Striking the ball hard and clean, helped by a hard surface untroubled by rain in weeks that sees the ball race to the boundary, they cut and drive with regularity. On the hour, Hants are 90 without loss, and

Alsop races to 50 from just 56 balls. Henry comes back, but despite a string of fine performances for Kent this season, he's being treated like a club bowler today. His first ball is swatted ruthlessly into the Tavern for six by Rousseau for his own half century. Another four follows, and it's all too easy. Kent finally turn to the slow left-arm bowling of Imran Qayyum, and land their first success since winning the toss, which already seems a very long time ago, as Alsop comes down the pitch in search of another boundary and is stumped by Billings. It begs the question why Qayyum wasn't brought on earlier, but Kent's belated joy is tempered at the sight of the Hampshire captain, James Vince, coming down the pavilion steps. Vince's England career might have stalled again, but he's already chalked up more than 500 runs in this season's One-Day Cup, and averages 63. It's a reminder of the task facing Kent if they are to end that long run of Lord's defeats.

Vince is an enigma. He bats beautifully, and few batsmen can get their innings going as quickly as he can. He can play delightful, nonchalant shots from the moment he takes guard, and does so today. Yet for all his elegant stroke play, there is a fatal weakness about his batting. Even when he appears at his most comfortable and in complete control – which is most of the time – Vince seems to find ways to deliver the ball into the grateful hands of waiting fielders. It's raising questions about his ability at Test level, but in the county game he is in fine form and will be looking for a major score today. It is not to be though.

On 23, having looked as comfortable as ever, he tries to nudge Qayyum away but succeeds only in holing out to Joe Denly, who snaffles the catch at long on. It heralds the arrival of Sam Northeast, and of an unsavoury change in atmosphere. As recently as last season, Northeast was the captain of Kent, but when he appeared reluctant to sign a new contract he was replaced by Billings, and soon after, left the county. It has left an unpleasant taste in the mouths of Kent supporters, and they let him know about it with a resounding chorus of boos. It is the sound of the football terrace, and it has no place in cricket – not at Lord's, not at Canterbury, not anywhere. And, like most such gestures, it's likely to be self-defeating, spurring the player on to greater efforts.

Rousseau needs no incentives. He is batting wonderfully, a craftsman in total mastery of his art, and the Kent bowlers have no idea how to stop him. The 200 is passed, and Rousseau tucks the ball away to reach his 100. He pumps his bat against his chest and to the dressing room, though not, disappointingly, to those applauding him in all corners of the ground. The trend of acknowledging team mates but not paying spectators has crept into the game over the years, and, like booing, it's not a welcome addition. It's a shame, because the applause is, deservedly, warm and generous from both sets of supporters, and his innings has laid the foundation for what could be a mammoth score. It's also setting up what could be an inner contest between compatriots, as Kent's leading batsman, Heine Kuhne, is also South African. But before Kuhne gets to show what he can do, Kent must find a way of keeping Hampshire in sight. Billings rings the changes among his bowlers, Rousseau responds with an enormous six that flies into someone's lunchbox in the Warner Stand, and Northeast, duly responding to his former supporters, accumulates runs steadily.

Billings turns to the part-time leg-breaks of Joe Denly, and the gamble pays off. Rousseau, sensing a feast, is caught unawares and when he attempts to drive Denly to the ropes he is caught by a jubilant Blake for 125. It's been a magnificent, at times brilliant, innings and a near-faultless one. The crowd rises to greet him (and all are acknowledged this time) and Kent heave a sigh of relief, but there is an inescapable feeling among their supporters that the damage has been done. Denly, though, has others idea; Dawson departs lamely to him for 8 – a wicket maiden at that – and after Northeast reaches his 50, to a mixture of polite applause and more unwelcome boos, McManus heaves a ball from Denly so high it looks like it might reach the helicopter circling the ground. Sean Dickson has time to make a cup of tea while waiting to catch it, and when it eventually returns, he makes no mistake. Hampshire, who were threatening to top 400 and leave Kent for dead, are also coming back down from such stratospheric heights, at least a little. Denly further repaying his captain's faith, accounts for McManus and Weatherley cheaply, and when Hampshire's innings comes to an end, they've made 330–7. It is well short of what looked possible at one stage, but it is still, we are told, the largest score ever made in a Lord's final.` That's quite a feat, given that sides in Gillette Cup/NatWest Trophy finals had an additional ten overs with which to score, but that just goes to show how scoring rates have climbed over the years. How pedestrian a one-day match from a generation ago would look today! And yet, strangely it is Kent who may be the more buoyant side in the interval. Hampshire may have set a record, but it's a smaller total than Kent feared they'd be chasing half an hour or so ago, and psychology can do strange things to teams. Denly's unlikely flurry of wickets may just have turned the momentum Kent's way.

After an enthralling few hours, it is time for the gathered thousands to stretch their legs and take in the surroundings. The gardens have filled up, bar staff are busy keeping up with demand for lager and Pimm's and prosecco, and a Dixie-style jazz band provides background music. Behind the Nursery End, something called croquet cricket and other activities are attracting attention. Meanwhile, children from the two competing counties are taking part in mini-matches on the outfield, part of the ECB's All-Stars Cricket initiative to get five-to-eight year-olds playing the game. They do so with plenty of enthusiasm, and get plenty of encouragement from the fans who've remained in their seats.

When the field is cleared, Daniel Bell-Drummond and Heino Kuhn walk out, the heavy weight of years of accumulated expectation on their shoulders. We've seen one South African take the game by storm already today; will the in-form Kuhn follow suit? Many think so. It might be unfair on his colleagues to say he has single-handedly put Kent into this final, but his four centuries in five innings, including one in a close semi-final win over Worcestershire, have certainly been worth their weight in gold. If he's to make another one, he'll need to get the better of yet another compatriot, Dale Steyn. Steyn may, perhaps, not be quite the bowler he was, but on a stage like this he'll be hungry to recapture past glories. He and Chris Wood start with intent, getting lift and movement, probing the batsmen's defences. Kent, though, start with aggression and intent of their own – have they any choice? The much-admired Bell-Drummond plays some gorgeous drives off his legs and Kuhn punishes Wood for bowling a no-ball by positively clobbering the resulting free hit for six. Steyn is bowling well, but when he too starts conceding boundaries, there are warning bells sounding in the Hampshire dressing room. Kent's 50 comes up in the 9th over, putting them, remarkably, ahead of their opponents at the same stage. But then, without warning, Kuhn gets a rush of blood to the head and hares off down the pitch for a single that was never there. It's only one wicket, but given Kuhn's form in this competition it feels to Kent supporters as if they've lost at least three. Worse follows, when Denly, the unlikely bowling hero, gets frustrated and, instead of hitting Berg out of the ground, manages only to lob the ball gently to Vince. Kent are 83–2, Hampshire once more brimming with confidence, while the Spitfires are starting to stall. As the afternoon wears on, the beer and Kent's need for runs keep the fans busy with chants of "Come on Kent, ra-ra-ra", and "Spit-fires, Spit-fires", but as the innings reaches the midpoint Kent are on 127, now 30 adrift of where Hampshire were and still more than 200 from their target. The Kent fans may be singing, but it's Hampshire's who are cheering.

Dickson plays himself in, then gets himself out, and when Bell-Drummond chops a ball onto his stumps, his solid but slightly laboured innings ends on 86, and Kent are staring yet another Lord's defeat in the face. More wickets quickly fall and soon they need 11 runs an over. Billings offers resistance and improvises with skill, but his teammates are forced into too many loose shots that, along with some brilliant fielding, prove their undoing. Perhaps harshly, it is the wicket of Billings that seals Hampshire's victory. He has reached 75, and played well for them, keeping the fight going, when he scoops a ball from Berg to the hands of Steyn. He drops his bat to the ground and rests his hands on his knees as around him the Hampshire players jump and dance and run and hug. Their supporters have left the songs to Kent all day, but now they break out in a chorus of 'Hampshire we love you, Hampshire we do'. The announcer tells us it's the biggest crowd for a one-day final since 2009 – life in the old competition yet, perhaps – but it's no consolation to a Kent side whose 40 years of hurt at Lord's will stretch into a fifth decade.

**Hampshire**

| | | | | |
|---|---|---|---|---|
| T.P. Alsop | st Billings | b Imran Qayyum | | 72 |
| R.R. Rossouw | c Blake | b Denly | | 125 |
| J.M. Vince * | c Denly | b Imran Qayyum | | 23 |
| S.A. Northeast | not out | | | 75 |
| L.A Dawson | c Blake | b Denly | | 8 |
| L.D. McManus † | c Dickson | b Denly | | 6 |
| J.J. Weatherley | lbw | b Denly | | 0 |
| G.K. Berg | | b Haggett | | 9 |
| D.W. Steyn | not out | | | 1 |
| Extras | | 2lb 4nb 5w | | 11 |
| **Total** | | 50 overs | 7 – | 330 |

**FoW:** 1–136, 2–193, 3–270, 4–287, 5–297, 6–297, 7–323

Did not bat: C.P. Wood, M.S. Crane

| **Bowling** | **O** | **M** | **R** | **W** |
|---|---|---|---|---|
| Podmore | 9 | 0 | 54 | 0 |
| Henry | 9 | 0 | 64 | 0 |
| Haggett | 3 | 0 | 34 | 1 |
| Stevens | 10 | 0 | 59 | 0 |
| Denley | 10 | 1 | 57 | 4 |
| Imran Qayyum | 8 | 0 | 80 | 2 |

**Kent**

| | | | | |
|---|---|---|---|---|
| D.J. Bell-Drummond | b Wood | | | 86 |
| H.G. Kuhn | run out | | | 32 |
| J.L. Denly | c Vince | b Berg | | 12 |
| S.R. Dickson | c Rossouw | b Crane | | 30 |
| S.W. Billings * † | c Steyn | b Berg | | 75 |
| A.J. Blake | run out | | | 9 |
| D.I. Stevens | c Weatherley | b Dawson | | 12 |
| M.J. Henry | c Alsop | b Steyn | | 0 |
| C.J. Haggett | | run out | | 1 |
| H.W. Podmore | | run out | | 1 |
| Imran Qayyum | not out | | | 3 |
| Extras | | 1b 4lb 2nb 1w | | 8 |
| **Total** | | 47.1 overs | 10 – | 269 |

**FoW:** 1–55, 2–83, 3–158, 4–179, 5–190, 6–217, 7–218, 8–241, 9–257, 10–269

| **Bowling** | **O** | **M** | **R** | **W** |
|---|---|---|---|---|
| Wood | 9 | 0 | 43 | 1 |
| Steyn | 9 | 1 | 56 | 1 |
| Berg | 9.1 | 1 | 43 | 2 |
| Dawson | 10 | 1 | 48 | 1 |
| Crane | 7 | 0 | 53 | 1 |
| Vince | 3 | 0 | 21 | 0 |

**Toss:** Kent elected to field. **Umpires:** D.J. Millns, N.G.B. Cook
**Hampshire win by 61 runs**

# Chapter Eight

## Canterbury Cricket Week

Kent v Leicestershire
Spitfire Ground, St Lawrence, Canterbury,
Sunday 22 July

Geoffrey Moorhouse once wrote, "If I had to show a foreigner his first cricket match, I should ideally like it to be here, during Canterbury Week." He was right to say so. Canterbury may, geographically, be the closest English city to the Continent, but its Cricket Week, with its marquees and beer and remembrance services and traditions, is as English as the White Cliffs of Dover just down the road. Pilgrims still journey to Canterbury, to gaze in awe upon Becket's magnificent cathedral, but for one week each year it is not Chaucer's "holy blissful martyr" they seek, but a different saint altogether, St Lawrence. They find him, or at least, the sacred site that takes his name, not at the end of the Pilgrim's Way but along the Old Dover Road, atop one of the steep hills that overlook the medieval city. They are drawn to festivities that have taken place here every summer for closing in on two centuries, and which are as rooted in the

Kentish soil as the orchards that gave the Garden of England its name.

Canterbury Cricket Week is the oldest such week in the world, 176 years old to be precise. Somehow it has survived the constant meddling and muddling with schedules and formats. It is one of English cricket's great survivors, even if it sometimes feels like one of those ageing actors who turn up unexpectedly in a TV programme long after you thought they had died. It is a throwback to a time when the championship was all, and traditions were embraced, not discarded. Other such weeks have vanished from the calendar. Google 'cricket weeks in England' and only Canterbury will appear. True, Scarborough Cricket Festival lives on, but that is an end-of-season jamboree, a final hurrah before the chill days of autumn send us shivering indoors. And besides, Canterbury is not about festival cricket; this is a week of serious competition with points to be won, and vital ones this year with promotion at stake. But while there is no frivolity here, there is certainly entertainment to be had. With the marquees and the beer tents circling the arena, the ground has the air of a country show. If a cake competition or best-in-breed contest were to spring up behind the seats, they would blend in effortlessly.

If I am waxing lyrical, it is because Canterbury and its Cricket Week are very special to me, and not just for cricketing reasons. It was here, or rather in the adjacent Kent and Canterbury Hospital that overlooks the southwestern corner of the ground, that as a very small child my personal innings nearly ended, barely before I'd troubled the scorer. Thankfully, the Almighty umpire gave me not out and having played myself in I've managed to reach my half-century. It was also here, a few years later – in 1978, as luck would have it, the very week that Moorhouse wrote the words above – that I saw my first-ever professional cricket match. Kent were playing Leicestershire, who, in another coincidence, are today's opposition too. Back then, the Foxes featured a promising young batsman with a shock of golden curls, who two months earlier had become the talk of English cricket after pulling his first ball in a Test Match for as sweet a boundary as you'll see. David Gower was born in Kent and schooled in this very city, but somehow slipped the county's notice and signed instead for Leicestershire. I managed to get his autograph that day, but not to see what all the fuss was about, as he made 4 and 0. Thankfully, the most elegant batsman of his era – perhaps since Kent's own Frank Woolley, to whom he was often compared – more than made up for that on many later days, when I saw him make batting look as graceful as a Michelangelo sculpture.

In those days, when three-day Championship games meant you could squeeze two matches into a single week and still have time for a Sunday League knockabout, my second match was just days later. It was 9th August, Warwickshire the visitors this time, and Geoffrey Moorhouse was here, on this very ground, watching the same match as an enraptured schoolboy. Perhaps I even saw him, notepad on his knee, pen poised, as he observed proceedings. Forty summers later the memories are too distant to recall whether I did spy him – and besides, Kent have more than their fair share of devoted supporters who religiously maintain the sacred scripts that are their scorebooks, and who could all, in the process, pass for scribes. Even so, it's a pleasing thought to know I may have sat near him, watching the same events unfold.

Later, as a teenager, I would make my second home here during the summer months. Borrowing Wizzard's attitude towards Christmas, I wished it could be Cricket Week every week. The city streets would be decked with brightly coloured bunting, while heavy shire horses would laboriously haul brewer's drays, laden with cricket-goers, up the steep hill from the ancient city walls. Each evening, the Old Stagers would perform their annual amateur dramatics, just as they had done every Cricket Week, except during wartime, since the first in 1842. The St Lawrence Ground (as it was called then, and with apologies to sponsors Shepherd Neame, still is as far as I'm concerned) was the perfect venue; white marquees gleaming in the sun; cars parked on the bank, windscreens covered with rugs to avoid reflected sunlight dazzling the batsmen; and the famous lime tree standing stubborn and defiant, alternating between deepish midwicket and deep backward point. Jazz bands played Dixie music in the intervals, women of a certain age paraded in their finest hats on Ladies' Day, and such was the timeless quality of the place that if a squadron of Spitfires returned to their old hunting grounds overhead and chased off some Messerschmitts, no-one would think it in the least bit unusual.

The horses and, sadly, the tree have long since gone (as, thankfully, has the embarrassingly outdated Ladies' Day – not all traditions are worth preserving), but I am unprepared for the shock of how much else has changed since my last visit. The seats from where I saw my first game all those years ago were replaced way back in the 1980s by the Cowdrey Stand, but in more recent years the club, in urgent need of additional income, has transformed one entire side of the ground. As I entered this morning, the first thing to greet me was not the lovely, red wrought-iron gates of old, but a rather unlovely supermarket. (The gates, I later found to my relief, have not been removed, merely relocated further back along the old driveway). Adjoining the supermarket is the Lime Tree Café and a social lounge for members of the University of Kent, whose colleges look across the city to the ground from their precarious hilltop location to the north. Running along the Old Dover Road side of the ground, there now stands a large development of retirement homes with balconies looking out onto the playing area. As a result, the Blythe Memorial – erected in memory of one of Kent's finest sons, the spinner Colin Blythe who went to Passchendaele and, like so many, never came back – has had to be moved. Where once it stood proudly inside the main entrance, seen by all, today I find it half hidden in a distant, shady corner of the ground, far removed from the main stands and pavilion. It has been restored and renovated, which is to the good, and the smaller Nackington Road entrance is close by, but even so, I fear it will largely go unnoticed here. The 100th anniversary of the Armistice is under four months away, lest we forget…

Perhaps the greatest change, though, at least symbolically, is the tree. The Canterbury lime tree made St Lawrence unique among the first-class grounds of England, and famous wherever cricket is played. It was already here when the ground was opened in 1847, five years after the club and its Cricket Week were founded. Most people, on finding a tree in their way, would have either laid out the playing area so the tree was outside the boundary, or simply chopped it down. Thankfully, the founders of the St Lawrence Ground were made of quirkier stuff. To their great and everlasting credit, they simply laid out the ground around the tree, and so it stayed, within the playing area and requiring its own rules for when struck by the ball. It also became a challenge for batsmen who would try to clear it with a mighty blow. Only four are recorded as succeeding, the great Learie Constantine among them.

The tree became as much a part of the ground as the old Victorian pavilion or the slope that makes Lord's look like a billiards table. Was a photograph ever taken here that did not feature the tree in the foreground? But by the late 1990s, the ageing lime was in trouble. It had a fungal disease and was given just ten years to live. Its end came on a stormy night in 2005. By the time the winds subsided, the trunk was broken in two and just a stump remained. The club, though, with a respect for both romance and history, not to mention good old English eccentricity, had been planning for the tree's demise and had grown a sapling, which was duly replanted to take its predecessor's place. It was a very English decision, though not everyone understood. The Australian coach, Dave Gilbert, was nonplussed. "It's typical of English cricket. A tree gets in the way for 200 years and when it falls down, instead of cheering, they plant a new one." Happily for Gilbert, though sadly for those with more romance in their soul, commercialism and money eventually won, as they always seem to in the end. When the retirement apartments were built in 2017, the boundary had to be moved, as otherwise it would be too close to the flats for safety. As a result, the tree now stands just outside the boundary, and the unique, quirky charm of the ground has been consigned to ever-fading memory.

~~~~~~~~~~~~~~~~~~~~~

There's a large crowd to welcome Kent today, buoyed not just by the occasion but by the county's promotion charge. When I saw them here in 1978, they were joint County Champions and would claim the title outright the following month – their seventh and, to date, final Championship. That triumph saw the club's golden era draw to a close, and Kent's fortunes, on and off the pitch, have steadily declined ever since. They have spent all but one of
~~~~~~~~~~~~~~~~~~~~~

the last ten years in the second division (or at least, the men have – the women, in the same period, have landed five of their record seven county championship titles). It's been a difficult time financially too. The club was even forced to sell the famous Albert Chevalier Taylor painting of a match here in 1906, the year of Kent's first championship, when the insurance bill rose beyond their means. Acquired by the MCC, it hangs in the Lord's pavilion these days, though Kent still display a copy. On the field, though, things are looking up, and promotion for the men's team is a distinct possibility. The disappointment of the Lord's final forgotten, or at least forgiven, there's warm applause for the opening batsmen as they stride to the wicket. It's doesn't last long, though.

In warm, overcast conditions, with Ben Raine swinging the ball sharply, Bell-Drummond survives – just – a vociferous LBW appeal before being caught for 9, and his replacement, Kuhn, is bowled first ball. Their departures are a serious disappointment. Kuhn has been in magnificent form; scoring centuries for fun, and where better to add to his total than in Cricket Week? I had also hoped to see a good innings from Bell-Drummond, a home-grown talent and another possible candidate in England's ongoing, seemingly endless, quest for a reliable opener. Bell-Drummond is also, sadly, one of an increasingly rare and endangered species in English cricket – the black cricketer. Interviewed in the *Guardian* at the start of the season, he said there are just seven black and mixed-race cricketers active across the 18 first-class counties[5]. That's about 2% of the total number of players, roughly half the proportion of black and mixed-race people in England and Wales as a whole, but far lower than the 33% of footballers at the start of the last Premier League season who identified as British and BAME (black, Asian and minority ethnic)[6]. Yet in 1992, England had three black/mixed-race players in a squad of just 14 for the World Cup. So why, in an age of supposedly greater inclusiveness have we gone so far backwards? And why has the game's popularity seemingly collapsed in one community while it continues to thrive in another – those of south Asian heritage (whose contribution to club cricket in England today is both enormous and vital)?

Fingers are pointed at numerous causes, from the decline of cricket in state schools, especially those in inner cities, to the ever-growing dominance of football (tellingly, the *Guardian* article relates how Bell-Drummond walked unrecognised along the streets of his native southeast London, while another local boy, Liverpool footballer Joe Gomez, was swamped by fans when he visited). Other sports, like basketball, have also grown enormously in popularity, and with the decline of the West Indies cricket team in the last 20 years, young black people no longer look to cricket for aspirational sporting figures. Attitudes at grounds haven't always helped, either. In the 1970s and

---

[5] www.theguardian.com/sport/2018/jun/12/daniel-bell-drummond-england-class-divide-low-income-areas-cricket

[6] https://talksport.com/football/269320/proportion-british-bame-players-has-doubled-premier-league-began-talksport-special-report/

'80s, when the West Indies blasted all opposition aside with the ferocity of a Caribbean hurricane, you would always know when they were in town. Test Matches would be carnivals, with whistles, cans, drums, flags and a noisy, happy atmosphere. Today, most of that has been regulated away, leaving fans unable to recreate the atmosphere of Bridgetown or Sabina Park (though incessant beery chants of Ingerland, Ingerland are deemed fine). Go to any cricket match in England today, and it's noticeable how few spectators, let alone players, are black. And, while cricket may have been central to those who grew up in the West Indies before coming to the UK, their children and grandchildren are English-born, may never have set foot in the Caribbean, and did not grow up playing cricket on the beach as soon as they could walk. They have their own cultural references, and cricket generally isn't one of them. In an attempt to take cricket into primary schools in the part of London where he grew up, Bell-Drummond has launched a new programme, the Platform Cricket Initiative. Hopefully it will succeed, if not in unearthing future professionals, then at least in reigniting interest in cricket among inner-city youth. It's sorely needed, because right now, those youngsters are being deprived of the chance to get active in the game, and English cricket is missing out on a wealth of talent.

But at this moment, in Canterbury, the crowd have other concerns. "Oh shit!", exclaims a voice behind me as another potential catch is spilled by a Leicestershire fielder.

"Oh Jesus!", says the same voice moment later, though this time the problem appears to be a cork flying out of a bottle with greater than anticipated velocity. Leicestershire, meanwhile, are an appealing team – they appeal loud, and often. When they're not doing that, they offer hard, Paddington-style stares to discomfort the batsmen. Do, they, I wonder, keep marmalade sandwiches under their white sunhats? Raine gives one such stare to Denly, with 'watch it' written all over his face. Denly doesn't heed his advice and edges Chappell to Eckersley behind the stumps. Shortly after, Dickson follows suit and kicks an imaginary cat as he, too, heads back indoors. Kent, looking for a good score against their promotion rivals, are teetering at 48–4.

As the tall, blond, nippy Zak Chappell rips the middle out of Kent's innings, a subdued air falls over the crowd. They take their cricket seriously here – second only to Yorkshire in passion, it's often said – but there's little to be passionate about so far today. When Kent finally stagger to a laboured 50, there's a smattering of applause that sounds derisory to the uninitiated, but is in truth a reflection of the quiet, stoic desperation of loyal followers who have suffered for too long. Many here today will remember Kent's glory days, of Alan Knott and Derek Underwood, Colin Cowdrey and Brian Luckhurst, Asif Iqbal and Bob Woolmer, Alan Ealham and John Shepherd. Relegation to 'small club' status hurts. They've had agonising near-misses too, like 2012, when they lost their last match of the season to Glamorgan and were edged into third place by Yorkshire.

More contentiously, there was 2016, when they finished runners-up, enough under normal circumstances to earn promotion. That year, though, the divisions were being restructured and only the champions went up. And, of course, there are all those cup final defeats. Another plucky failure is just too much to contemplate. Leicestershire's players, meanwhile, sensing the pressure Kent are under, strut around, shouting encouragement to each other in superior tones, the slips prowling like a pack of wolves more than foxes. When Billings falls for 10. Kent have lost half their men with only 58 runs on the board. A disastrous morning is rounded off when one Zak, Chappell, dismisses another, Crawley – a minor cricketing first, perhaps? – for a paltry 5, leaving Kent looking rudderless on choppy seas. One never truly knows what a good score is until both sides have batted, but Leicestershire head off for lunch with the air of a side that has a pretty fair idea.

One thing at Canterbury that, to my delight, has not changed is the policy of allowing spectators onto the outfield during intervals. It's a wonderful tradition, and I hope it never stops. Some inspect the pitch, but for 99% it's a chance to strike up impromptu games. Scores of fans, some young, others young at heart, grab bats and balls and rush onto the ground, and this little corner of Kent is temporarily transformed into England's answer to Mumbai's Maidan. To my left, triumphs from Kent's glory days are restaged; to my right, old Ashes battles are re-fought. The game in front of me, though, bears more resemblance to a Marx Brothers routine. If Kent's batting today has been poor, it's as nothing compared to that of the three 50-somethings who make up for a spectacular lack of talent with an abundance of enthusiasm. For a few glorious minutes they are schoolboys again, reliving old summer holidays as they try to smite Dennis Lillee or Shane Warne into the middle of the adjacent game. Alongside them, two dozen Ben Stokes smash England to more Twenty20 victories, while a score of Joe Roots bat for Test glory. It is wonderful to behold, and surely there are few better ways to inspire the next generation. If the Kent fans are passionate, it's because they are steeped in cricket and its traditions, their love for the game planted and nurtured in the very soil on which their heroes tread. The club understands the bond this creates. Other counties would do well to take note.

I take a walk to the pitch, zigzagging like a scout crossing No Man's Land in order to avoid the missiles flying in all directions around me. After a near three-month absence of rain, the pitch looks greener than expected, as indeed does the outfield ("This must be the only ground in the country that still has grass", remarks one fellow). The pitch does not excuse Kent's woeful performance, though. It requires care from the batsmen, certainly, but it is not spiteful. Curiosity satisfied, I take a stroll around the ground. There are no cars on the bank any more, seating now filling the space, and there are fewer tents than of old – just seven, half the number that would once have been here. The Royal East Kent Regiment – the Buffs, old friends of Cricket Week – are here, as are the Old Stagers, the oldest amateur theatricals group in the world. Founded specifically to stage plays during Cricket Week, they have performed every year since the first, apart from during the two world wars. The mayor has a marquee, as does the Kent County Cricket Supporters club, but there's no Association of Men of Kent and Kentish Men this year, to my dismay. In the marquees that are here, the convivial clinking of glasses and popping of corks is the sound of old friends enjoying a thousand reminiscences.

Or perhaps they are drowning their sorrows? The scoreboard tells a woeful tale, and not just of the Kent innings. As the players return to the field, the scoreboard lights shine brightly, as dark grey clouds gather overhead. The Leicestershire players form the obligatory team huddle while Stevens and Podmore stride defiantly, rather than confidently, to the crease. Parkinson patrols the boundary looking like a teacher waiting to pounce on an unsuspecting schoolboy late back to lessons after an illicit cigarette behind the bike shed. "Are you ready boy?", he calls; Raine bowls the first ball and Stevens thumps it for four. It's a determined start, but short-lived. Podmore, misjudging the flight completely, is leg before in the next over and Kent are 77–7. Stewart survives only two balls before going the same way, prompting an exasperated "Oh for goodness sake!" from an elderly woman behind me. Another spectator gleefully announces that while he lives in Kent, he comes from Leicestershire and can't lose, a declaration that receives a lukewarm reception from those around him. "Come on Dexy boy!" cries Parkinson to the bowler, before spotting someone he knows in the crowd. "Dream, isn't it?", he says, grinning from ear to ear, "batting at 9 and not having to bowl!".

The ever-reliable Stevens is doing his best to put up some resistance, and a wild pull that evades the fielder to take him into the 30s prompts a hopeful chant of "Stevo, Stevo". With his stocky build, bald head and mature countenance, there's a hint of Inspector Montalbano about Stevens. (Even his initials, D.I, play along with the idea.) His innings today has certainly been Montalbanoesque, a mix of the forensic, the instinctive and the passionate, with the occasional fiery boundary borne of controlled aggression. At 42, he's been playing probably the best cricket of his life over the last two or three years. He scored over 700 runs last year, with an average that matched his age, and took 60-plus wickets to land the Kent Bowler of the Year award. Not bad for a player once dismissed as 'the Vicar of Dibbly-Dobbly'. He might not quite be matching that *annus mirabilis* this year, but he's still one of the first names on the team sheet before each match. Funnily enough, though a Kent veteran, he began his career with Leicestershire, where he was born. Back then, in the last century, he was as an opening batsman. In just his fourth match for the Foxes he made a century against Sussex, a feat that so impressed a watching Colin Cowdrey that he felt compelled to present Stevens with a painting, which hangs on his wall at home to this day. Perhaps it was that gesture that sowed the seeds of Stevens' subsequent move to Kent.

Cowdrey, sadly, was no longer around to welcome him, but there's no doubt he'd have worn that gentle smile of his, knowing his early faith was justified, even if Stevens had dropped down the order a few places by then. But, for all his fighting qualities and menacing pulls, Darren Stevens cannot bat at both ends; unfortunately, neither can Kent. Podmore's dismissal is followed in swift succession by those of Stewart, Claydon and Thomas, who manage five runs and two ducks between them, leaving the veteran stranded on 38no and Eckersley with a wicketkeeping five-for. Kent have managed to pass 100, but only just, and after just two sessions of the first day they are in deep trouble. It's going to take some bowling effort to drag them back into this match.

The players back in the pavilion, I make a quick dash to the shop, where the front cover of one of the monthly cricket magazines has none other than David Gower on the front cover. I mention to the shop assistant my sighting of Gower here in my first cricket week 40 years ago. Immediately, a chap in a wheelchair close by chips in, reeling off a series of facts about the game. He only looks in his 40s – surely he was too young to have been here? – but remembers the game with extraordinary clarity. "Chris Balderstone made 90 for them and Davison got a century. Bob Woolmer made a big knock for us, 130 or more, and Asif got a ton too, but the rest didn't do much", he tells me. "They collapsed in their second innings though, only made 120, and we beat them comfortably ". I nod as sagely as I can in agreement, without the faintest idea whether or not he's right. "Blimey", says the shop assistant, "the curator's stepping down soon, you might want his job". Having started the conversation, I feel I ought to contribute something else, so mention being enthralled as Derek Underwood took 7–45 on a drying pitch. Statto gives me a quizzical look. "Hmm, yes, I remember him taking a few", he replies, with surprising vagueness for one so precise on all the other key points. I bid him a cheery farewell with the smug satisfaction that comes from having caught someone out at their own game.

Back in my seat, pull out my phone and go online. Could he really remember all that detail from an obscure county game 40 years ago, when he was about 2? I find a record of the match (how did we ever get by without the internet?). Sure enough, Woolmer made 137 and Asif Iqbal 104, while the last six Kent batsmen made just 25 between them. Balderstone did make 90 and Davison 105 in Leicestershire's reply, but needing 240 to win, they were bowled out second time round for 120. I take my hat off to the memory man, but there's more. Underwood did indeed take 7 wickets. Against Warwickshire, in the second match that week. And for 38, not 45. After 40 years, I am left with the realisation that the one statistic I could clearly remember from my first ever game was wrong. So wrong, indeed, that it wasn't even from the same match. No wonder I can't recall whether or not I saw Geoffrey Moorhouse. I console myself with a cheese roll and vow never again to fall into the trap of getting into a conversation on past matches with someone clutching a scorebook. There's only ever going to be one winner.

I manage to do all this research because we're awaiting a new batsman. The Leicestershire innings had commenced, and the first wicket had fallen, before I had returned to my seat. Under patchy skies, Leicestershire's progress is cautious, painstaking even, just 17 runs from their first 11 overs. Ackermann leans forward at an alarming angle, looking more like the Leaning Tower of Pisa than an illustration from the MCC Coaching Manual, but it doesn't help him as he too falls cheaply. His replacement is Mark Cosgrove, though older spectators might be forgiven for thinking that the ghost of Colin Milburn has appeared. In an era in which coaches place such a premium on fitness, and most cricketers, as a consequence, sport toned, athletic bodies, the portly Cosgrove is a throwback to a previous age. His physique has often been the cause of comment, and even led to him being dropped by South Australia once. But he can hit a ball well enough to have scored 14,000 first-class runs and to have played one-day matches for Australia. Besides, there should be room in cricket for those who sing to their own tune – it has always been a game that could accommodate non-conformists – and there is far too much dull uniformity around today, in cricket as in life. Cosgrove and Horton ease Leicestershire's wobble, and the game enters one of those periods in which nothing very much happens. A sizeable force of gulls takes advantage of the lull and starts languidly harvesting the outfield. Slowly, lazily, they cover half the ground before their peace is finally disturbed, when Horton is out for a patient 21. As the Kent players celebrate, the gulls rise up *en masse* like a scene from a Hitchcock film. Aggrieved, they circle the outfield but when they re-settle a few minutes later Kent immediately strike again and the whole episode gets replayed. Leicestershire are suddenly a lot less cocky, and head for tea at 63–4.

After tea, however, it is a different game. Runs don't exactly flow, but the little bit of life that was in the pitch has disappeared during the interval, as if it suddenly remembered an urgent appointment elsewhere. With no threat in the bowling, the batsmen are untroubled for the first time all day. Dexter and Eckersley play sensibly, gather runs steadily, and the game starts to drift inexorably away from Kent. At a little after half-past five, with the crowd starting to thin, Leicestershire take the lead. As the sun finally comes out and the shadows lengthen, Dexter is bowled by Ivan Thomas, who's bowled tidily all afternoon, for a neatly compiled 41, but there's little else for the remaining Kent followers to celebrate. There are moments, as when Claydon sends down a rogue delivery that pops and fizzes and forces Raine to spin 180 degrees before dropping to his knees facing the pavilion. Hands resting on the handle of his bat, he looks like Lancelot pledging allegiance to Arthur. For the most part, though, Leicestershire are content to play out the session. As the close of play draws near, an elderly spectator in shorts and Kent sunhat shuffles down to the boundary and obtains an autograph from Grant Stewart. He turns around, face beaming as he returns to his friends and his glass of red wine. He may have passed 70, but inside he is seven again, an eager schoolboy watching his heroes. Long may he continue to do so.

Elsewhere, farewells, at least until the 'morrow, are spoken, gulls squabble over discarded titbits, and Denly, who can do no wrong with the ball these days, gives Kent the last, hollow, laugh of the day as he bowls the final over and removes Raine. Leicestershire end the day 45 ahead, four wickets standing. If not totally in charge, they are certainly in the driving seat and will look to press on tomorrow and turn that lead into three figures. Kent, meanwhile, are still in the contest – just – but they'll need early wickets. It's been an intriguing day, and the spectators drift out satisfied with the entertainment. Sadly, though, none of them will be going to see the Old Stagers. It turns out that when ECB scheduling requirements forced Cricket Week from its traditional early August slot, the Old Stagers didn't move with it, and their production of *Quartermaine's Terms* isn't on for another two weeks. Shame, I should like to have seen it. Next year, perhaps.

**Kent first innings**

| | | | |
|---|---|---|---|
| D.J. Bell-Drummond | c Eckersley | b Raine | 9 |
| S.R. Dickson | c Eckersley | b Griffiths | 24 |
| H.G. Kuhn | | b Raine | 0 |
| J.L. Denly | c Eckersley | b Chappell | 5 |
| S.W. Billings * ł | | b Chappell | 10 |
| Z. Crawley | c Eckersley | b Chappell | 5 |
| D.I. Stevens | not out | | 38 |
| H.W. Podmore | lbw | b Dexter | 2 |
| G. Stewart | lbw | b Dexter | 0 |
| M.E. Claydon | c Eckersley | b Abbas | 5 |
| I.A.A. Thomas | lbw | b Raine | 0 |
| Extras | | 2b 4lb | 6 |
| **Total** | | 37.5 overs | 10 – 104 |

**FoW:** 1–25, 2–25, 3–44 4–48, 5–58, 6–65, 7–77, 8–77, 9–103, 10–104

| **Bowling** | **O** | **M** | **R** | **W** |
|---|---|---|---|---|
| Mohammad Abbas | 9 | 4 | 17 | 1 |
| B.A. Raine | 13.5 | 2 | 39 | 3 |
| Z.J. Chappell | 7 | 2 | 14 | 3 |
| G.T Griffiths | 5 | 1 | 17 | 1 |
| N.J. Dexter | 3 | 1 | 11 | 2 |

**Leicestershire first innings**

| | | | |
|---|---|---|---|
| H.E. Dearden | c Billings | b Podmore | 0 |
| P.J. Horton * | c Billings | b Thomas | 21 |
| C.N. Ackermann | c Crawley | b Stevens | 5 |
| M.J Cosgrove | lbw | b Stewart | 22 |
| N.J. Dexter | | b Thomas | 41 |
| E.J.H. Eckersley ł | | b Bell-Drummond | 74 |
| B.A. Raine | c Dickson | b Denly | 9 |
| Z.J. Chappell | c Dickson | b Stewart | 21 |
| C.F. Parkinson | c Billings | b Claydon | 4 |
| G.T. Griffiths | not out | | 9 |
| Mohammad Abbas | | b Claydon | 2 |
| Extras | | 9b 9lb 2nb 1w | 21 |
| **Total** | | 80.4 overs | 10 – 229 |

**FoW:** 1–0, 2–17, 3–47 4–51, 5–121, 6–149, 7–179, 8–198, 9–224, 10–229

| **Bowling** | **O** | **M** | **R** | **W** |
|---|---|---|---|---|
| H.W. Podmore | 19 | 6 | 39 | 1 |
| D.I. Stevens | 19 | 7 | 30 | 1 |
| I.A.A. Thomas | 14 | 2 | 39 | 2 |
| G. Stewart | 2 | 1 | 53 | 2 |
| J.L. Denly | 4 | 0 | 21 | 1 |
| M.E. Claydon | 11.4 | 0 | 27 | 2 |
| D.J. Bell-Drummond | 1 | 0 | 2 | 1 |

**Kent second innings**

| | | | |
|---|---|---|---|
| D.J. Bell-Drummond | | b Abbas | 0 |
| S.R. Dickson | c Eckersley | b Raine | 59 |
| H.G. Kuhn | c Cosgrove | b Griffiths | 29 |
| J.L. Denly | lbw | b Dexter | 24 |
| S.W Billings * † | lbw | b Abbas | 29 |
| Z. Crawley | lbw | b Abbas | 11 |
| D.I. Stevens | lbw | b Chappell | 6 |
| H.W Podmore | c Eckersley | b Chappell | 6 |
| G. Stewart | c Dexter | b Abbas | 12 |
| M.E. Claydon | c Eckersley | b Chappell | 0 |
| I.A.A. Thomas | not out | | 4 |
| Extras | | 7b 4ln 8nb | 19 |
| **Total** | | 49.2 overs | 10 – 199 |

**FoW:** 1–0, 2–71, 3–109 4–133, 5–157, 6–164, 7–172, 8–185, 9–195, 10–199

| **Bowling** | **O** | **M** | **R** | **W** |
|---|---|---|---|---|
| Mohammad Abbas | 16.2 | 3 | 55 | 4 |
| B.A Raine | 12 | 1 | 47 | 1 |
| G.T. Griffiths | 4 | 0 | 23 | 1 |
| Z.J. Chappell | 10 | 2 | 39 | 3 |
| N.J. Dexter | 6 | 0 | 23 | 1 |
| C.F. Parkinson | 1 | 0 | 1 | 0 |

**Leicestershire second innings**

| | | | |
|---|---|---|---|
| H.E Dearden | not out | | 55 |
| P.J. Horton (c) | not out | | 15 |
| Extras | | 4b 1lb 1w | 6 |
| **Total** | | 15.4 overs | 0 – 76 |

**FoW:**

| **Bowling** | **O** | **M** | **R** | **W** |
|---|---|---|---|---|
| H.W. Podmore | 6 | 1 | 22 | 0 |
| D.I. Stevens | 4 | 1 | 18 | 0 |
| G. Stewart | 3.4 | 0 | 24 | 0 |
| J.L. Denly | 2 | 1 | 7 | 0 |

**Toss:** Leicestershire elected to field. **Umpires:** J. Evans, T. Lungley
**Leicestershire win by 10 wickets**

# Chapter Nine

## The Double Header

Western Storm v Loughborough Lightning
Somerset v Middlesex
County Ground, Taunton
Sunday 29 July

### Part One – Kia Women's Super League

The heatwave that has baked Britain since the middle of June has broken, suddenly and violently, with storms, gales and downpours. After a week of tropically oppressive heat, temperatures have plummeted from the balmy mid-30s to a positively chilly 20, and the parched, straw-coloured ground has tasted its first rain of any note since April. Heavy rain has accompanied me for most of the long drive west to Taunton this morning, and though it has stopped by the time I reach the ground, I am greeted by skies that hang heavy with clouds of battleship grey. "The forecast I saw was 50-50 all day", says the bag-search steward, who is remarkable chirpy despite – or perhaps because of – the sudden absence of hot sun. "I reckon there'll be spits around all day. Still, the wind will dry the outfield – positive thinking, eh?". Another steward shakes her head apologetically when I ask her the way to the Ondaatje Stand, telling me she's never so much as visited the ground before today and doesn't know her way around. She then receives a sudden flash of inspiration, laughs, and points me in the right direction. The huge letters O N D A A T J and E stuck on the front of the stand ahead of us may have helped.

I'm struck by how friendly and cheerful the stewards are here. I blame 2012, myself. There was a time when stewards at any major sporting event would generally be a surly bunch who regarded anyone and everyone as a potential hooligan, or at least someone whose mere presence is a gross outrage. Like those fearsome doctors' receptionists whose role in life is to stop anyone ever actually getting in to see a doctor, so sports stewards had the self-appointed task of withholding as much helpful information as possible in order to maximise inconvenience. "Excuse me, where are the loos?". "Dunno," "Um, do you know where the food stall is?". "Nope." "The shop, then?" "It's closed, now move along, I've a long queue of people to annoy and you're holding things up". It was as if Basil Fawlty had moved on from the hotel business and set up a training college teaching customer service, and these were his star graduates. But then along came the London Olympics and Paralympics and, with them, a revolution. Instead of regarding all fans as trouble waiting to happen, stewards suddenly exuded warmth and friendliness and a desire to be your new best friend. For four unforgettable weeks, the world caught a glimpse of a new Britain, a Britain it had never seen before – a Britain even the British had never seen before. A land in which stranger spoke unto stranger, high fives and smiles were bandied about with reckless abandon, and even smiling police officers danced with happy Games-goers from all corners of the globe. Perhaps the greatest legacy of the London Games is not to be found in stadiums and arenas, or in statistics about participation levels, but at every sporting, musical and cultural event that takes place up and down the land, where friendly stewards make people feel welcome, give out helpful advice to anyone in need, and generally help ensure a pleasant experience. Even at Lord's, where the gatekeepers were once notorious, the stewards are now uniformly welcoming and helpful. Here at Taunton they're like old chums. All this bonhomie may not sit well with the old stiff-upper-lip of old, but it is part of modern, 21st century Britain, and very welcome it is too.

In another pleasant sign of changing times, there are female supporters here aplenty in anticipation of the first of today's matches. The defending Super League champions, Western Storm, are taking on this season's early table-toppers, Loughborough Lightning. It promises, weather permitting, to be quite a match. Attendances for women's cricket have been growing impressively – up 33% last year alone, following England's World Cup triumph – and the 2017 Super League final attracted 3,500 fans, a record for a domestic women's match. As Tanya Aldred wrote in the

*Guardian* a few days ago, there seems to be "an unstoppable surge of interest" in women's cricket. There's certainly evidence of that at Taunton today. Young girls are here with parents and brothers, groups of young women greet each other with hugs, and in one corner of the ground a large group receives last-minute coaching in their Super League flag-waving skills. The more junior ones clutch bright orange All-Star bats, distributed to thousands of children as part of an ECB initiative to get kids involved in cricket. With around 2,000 clubs around the country taking part, and an emphasis on fun, the scheme is growing (last year, 37,000 children took part; this year the target is 60,000). If the enthusiasm shown by the children waving their bats here is any measure, it seems to be working. The news from the middle, though, is not encouraging. The toss has been delayed and there will be a pitch inspection at 12:30, half an hour after the scheduled start time.

At least it gives me a chance to look around. I wander over to the Somerset Cricket Museum, tucked away in a corner of the ground in an ancient barn that was once part of a priory. Unfortunately, on a day when it would have proved a popular hiding place from the weather, it is closed. "Olive", says the sign on the door, "has been laid low by the extreme heat and hay fever". Today's change in climate should hasten her recovery. The 12.30 inspection comes and goes, as does another at 1.00. A third is announced for 1.20, the covers are removed – is there a more gladdening sight at a cricket ground on a gloomy day? – and a distinctly greenish pitch is revealed. The officials are still "hopeful" of some WSL action. I'm not sure if the batters will be, looking at that pitch. But the hopes are not misplaced, and we are to have a six-overs-a-side game. Anyone who thinks Twenty-20 cricket is a slog should look away now. Following the go-ahead, there's time for a quick interview with Heather Knight, who tells us, with fine insight, that "We've got to find a way to score more runs than they do."

As the players emerge, the flagbearers – ten girls and two boys, one of whom is considerably smaller than the flag he's carrying – wave the players onto the pitch, the music is ramped up to 11 and the razzmatazz of Twenty20 cricket is in full flow. The early strike is taken by Smriti Mandhana, a young Indian left-hander who's making a name for herself internationally. She's the first Indian to play in the WSL, and she wastes no time making an impact, hoiking her first ball high and hard for six runs. Music blasts out, flames shoot out of canisters, the youngsters in the crowd wave their boundary placards and there would scarcely be more excitement if aliens landed at square leg. In the next over, Mandhana hits Sophie Devine for another big six that lands only a foot short of the men's boundary. Someone is delighted, as a male voice from the 'alcohol-friendly' stand behind me lets out possibly the loudest cheer I've ever heard for a boundary, even outdoing the blaring music. A ball or two later there is much hilarity and pantomime booing as the ball beats the bat. Devine gets thumped for 19 and Storm are 28–2 off two overs.

Loughborough's bowling is far too short. Ten more runs come off the third over and, against the odds, the sun comes out. Its arrival is greeted by a snatch of that *paso doble* trumpet music without which no Twenty20 match, or indeed any sporting event these days, seems complete. It is followed by the mandatory cheer, and there's another when Mandhana, with a mighty and well-timed swish, belts another six off the next ball. It seems like the game has barely begun – it is, after all, only the fourth over – but already Western Storm, with no time to waste, are on 54. Mandhana is finding the boundary for fun, each stroke greeted by a small sea of bobbing placards. When Priest skies the ball and is caught, Heather Knight comes in to more loud cheers, but, like last month at Worcester, she lasts just three balls. Unperturbed, Mandhana swipes another ball dismissively to the boundary and reaches a remarkable 50, off a mere 18 balls. Forty-four of her runs have come from nine crashing boundaries. She combines a wonderful eye for the ball with exquisite timing, and Lightning have no idea where or what to bowl at her. Taylor ends the innings with another six and Western Storm close on 85–2 from their six overs – a score that would have seemed almost incredible before Twenty20, but which now seems almost regulation. It is as if, to all intent and purposes, Twenty20 has evolved not into a different form of cricket, but has become a different sport altogether.

Between innings, I notice a young girl of about five or six in front of me, intently studying a guide to the WSL. On a series of connected cards, it explains the rules, batting, bowling and fielding, and introduces the teams. It's a nice touch to help children get into what they're watching. Loughborough may be in need of some guidance themselves, needing 86 from 36 balls and facing the medium-fast pace of local hero Anya Shrubsole. Haynes and Devine take 11 off the over, which crazily means they are already they're well off the pace, and Storm are perfectly content to concede the ones and twos that follow. Freya Davies bowls the second over, starting each delivery with a curious skip before bowling a much better length than anything we've seen so far. Only two singles from the first three balls, nine off the over, and pressure mounts. Lightning are not batting as their name suggests, and now need 66 more with just 24 balls left. Knight concedes 16 from the third over as Devine tries to cut loose, but Haynes can't get connect properly and is, at least in Twenty20 terms, mired. Storm have their field set perfectly, Loughborough can't find any gaps, and a mere seven come from the fourth over. Loughborough pass 50 with no wickets down, but are left needing far too many from the final over. Devine wallops a ball from Shrubsole that clears the men's rope, and moves to 46, but with Haynes out of sorts and the openers hitting just five boundaries between them, the visitors can muster only 67. After the strong and vocal support for Storm in their innings, and the frenzy of noise that accompanied each boundary, Loughborough's innings has been an anti-climax, and it's a strangely muted crowd that applauds Storm's win. Still, they have to pace themselves – the second match of the day is yet to come, and this time it will be the full-length Twenty-20.

**Western Storm**

| | | | | |
|---|---|---|---|---|
| R.H. Priest ⵏ | c Jones | b Elwiss | | 25 |
| S. Mandhana | not out | | | 52 |
| H.C. Knight * | st Jones | b Smith | | 0 |
| S.R. Taylor | not out | | | 7 |
| Extras | | 1w | | 1 |
| **Total** | | 6 overs | 2 – | 85 |

**FoW:** 1–71, 2–71

Did not bat: F.C. Wilson, S.N. Luff, N.D. Dattani, A. Shrubsole, A.J. MacLeod, D.R. Gibson, F.R. Davies

| **Bowling** | **O** | **M** | **R** | **W** |
|---|---|---|---|---|
| L.C.N. Smith | 2 | 0 | 23 | 1 |
| S.F.M. Devine | 1 | 0 | 19 | 0 |
| J.L. Gunn | 1 | 0 | 10 | 0 |
| K.L. Gordon | 1 | 0 | 16 | 0 |
| G.A. Elwiss | 1 | 0 | 17 | 1 |

**Loughborough Lightning**

| | | | | |
|---|---|---|---|---|
| R.L. Haynes | not out | | | 18 |
| S.F.M. Devine | not out | | | 46 |
| Extras | | 1lb 2w | | 3 |
| **Total** | | 6 overs | 0 – | 67 |

Did not bat: G.A. Elwiss *, A.E. Jones ⵏ, G.L. Adams, E.J. Villani, J.L. Gunn, S. Glenn, L.F. Higham, K.L Gordon, L.C. N. Smith

| **Bowling** | **O** | **M** | **R** | **W** |
|---|---|---|---|---|
| A. Shrubsole | 2 | 0 | 21 | 0 |
| F.R. Davies | 2 | 0 | 22 | 0 |
| H. Knight | 1 | 0 | 16 | 0 |
| S.R. Taylor | 1 | 0 | 7 | 0 |

**Toss:** Loughborough Lightning elected to field. **Umpires:** M. Burns, I. Gould
**Western Storm win by 18 runs**

## Part Two – Vitality Blast

As the afternoon wears on, and the sun continues to drive away lingering fears of further showers, the crowd grows. Unlike many Vitality Blast matches this season, it's not going to be a full house, but there should still be a good atmosphere for the second match of the day. Perhaps taking their cue from the local rugby side, the Exeter Chiefs, many of the fans are sporting headgear, though unlike the Native American headdress favoured by the Chiefs, these are more modest affairs featuring red hair held in place by a white band. It looks like a convention of Beakers from *The Muppet Show*.

The Somerset mascot, Stumpy the Wyvern, does the rounds, high-fiving eager fans, the big screens cut from an advert for All-Stars cricket to show Middlesex winning the toss, and the players are introduced as the increasingly grandiose music gets ramped up to fever pitch. It's creating the feeling of a big match, and certainly it's one both teams need to win. Gloucestershire top the table on nine points, but they're only two clear of Somerset and just five ahead of the bottom sides, Middlesex among them. Somerset won the reverse encounter at Lord's ten days ago, so will be feeling more confident, and they start well enough, hitting 21 off the first two overs. Every boundary is greeted by a cacophony of metallic clangers and music, as well as frenzied placard waving and bursts from the flamethrowers that shoot shimmering waves of heat into the air, and it's all a million miles away from the gentility of the County Championship. The biggest early cheer, though, is reserved for the Middlesex bowler Tom Barber, who runs in, reaches the crease, slips on the greasy surface and falls flat on his backside. The locals greatly appreciate his mishap, but his revenge is swift. First, Davies skies the ball for an easy caught and bowled, then Myburgh holes out to Fuller two balls later. Hildreth walks to the crease, raises his bat and edges his first ball to the wicketkeeper, and in the space of four balls, Somerset have slumped from 29–0 to 29–3. Their supporters' delight turns to disgruntlement. "What are they doing?", asks one in bewilderment. "Bring on the Storm", cries another. Three Stormers are standing just below where I'm sitting, looking like they'd love to get back onto the pitch.

Somerset have rebuilding work to do, and Peter Trego and Tom Abell set about it. Trego bats with more conviction than the scoreboard might warrant, and plays some lusty drives, but Abell is more cautious and for each over Somerset hit double figures, there's another where they manage only four or five. Realising they need to push on, Trego takes command, plundering the Australian Ashton Agar for 24 in an over. The mayhem prompts a 'Scatterblast', with t-shirts hurled into the eager hands of fans around the ground. Agar wanders disconsolately to his post on the boundary. "Let's have a second, Ashton" shouts a home fan. Agar grins, shakes his head and suggests otherwise.

Scatterblast over, the attention shifts to the big video screens around the ground, which have started showing FlossCam. Cameras pick out fans doing a dance craze, the floss, screening their efforts for all to see. Various youngsters revel in their moment on the big screen and show off some pretty impressive skills; a few parents try too, but some things are best left to the kids, and the adult efforts attract a rather different appraisal from the judges in the crowd. They can probably forget any chance of appearing on *Strictly*… any time soon.

With all this going on, it's easy to forget that there's a game of cricket going on out there somewhere, but Trego reminds us when he reaches a quickfire 50. It's taken him just 26 balls ("What kept you?", one can hear Mandhana ask). Two balls later, the 100 is up, and Somerset, half their innings to come, are back in contention. The returning Agar is greeted with an ironic cheer, but gets his own back when Trego goes for another big hit and is caught. He's made 60 in half an hour, and turned the Somerset innings around after a calamitous start, but his departure boosts the visitors' hopes. As Corey Anderson comes in, the sun is once more replaced by dark clouds. Taunton has no floodlights, but the batters seem to be picking up the white ball without too much difficulty and runs continue to flow. Abell falls with the score on 138, and the *Pink Panther* theme – Middlesex are clad in pink – signals the end of the over, but it's virtually Middlesex's last success with the ball. In the seven overs that remain, Anderson and Gregory put on another 91, not slogging but with fine straight drives and controlled cover drives that find gaps in the field at will. There's more beery chanting from the stands, and a young boy in front of me somewhat nervously asks his parents "Do you think they've been drinking?". "You can guarantee it", replies his mother, "all afternoon I shouldn't wonder". Anderson's 41 takes 24 balls but looks positively laboured against Gregory's inspired 62, which requires only two balls more and ends only when he is superbly caught by a diving Patel in the deep. With a combination of a good eye, strong arm and powerful bat, he's taken the Middlesex bowling apart. From 29–3, Somerset have added a further 200 for three more wickets in 17 overs, and with the light closing in, the odds are firmly in their favour.

Those statistics deserve some reflection. Just a few years ago, the idea of scoring 200 runs in 17 overs would have seem ridiculous, except in one of those contrived innings that used to plague championship matches before they were extended to four days. Now, it is commonplace. There are many still who dislike Twenty20, who think it frivolous and not proper cricket and harmful to the real thing, and they may have some points. Nevertheless, it's introduced a range of new and unlikely strokes to batsmen's repertoires, and transformed how teams approach batting and scoring rates. And, the youngsters, judging by their number and enthusiasm, love it. Not for them the absorbed study of wily spinners bowling maidens to watchful accumulators, accompanied by the occasional sound of someone slurping some tea from a flask. No, they love the frenetic pace, the brashness, the vulgar showiness of

Twenty20, with its music, noise, flames and frenzied hitting. It's a very different game, but it's their game.

Of course, it would be wrong to say that kids only enjoy Twenty20, or that all older people hate it. But it certainly divides opinion, and age is one of the fault lines. Not for the first time this season, I find myself pondering on how cricket mirrors society, sometimes in unexpected ways. The recent referenda on Scottish independence and Brexit have revealed a UK more divided than at any time since the Act of Union. Brexit especially has split the generations, sharply. If you believe, as I do, that cricket reflects the society in which it is played, then here, in Twenty20, is cricket's own Brexit – separating young from old, traditionalists from modernisers, those who find Twenty20 exciting and innovative, versus those who think it is ruining the game and destroying the subtle art of batting in particular. It is the age-old conflict between those who look forward to a new type of game, and those who look back nostalgically at how things used to be. In a society in which the pace of life is getting ever-faster, with instant communications and same-day deliveries and shorter attention spans, fewer and fewer people have the time or patience to sit through a match that lasts three or four days. But give them a Twenty20 match, where it's all over, crash-bang-wallop, in three hours, and it's a different tale.

But now, even Twenty20 is in danger of being deemed too slow, too complicated. The ECB has announced plans for a new tournament, the Hundred, to be launched in

2020 (the irony of which has almost certainly gone over their heads like one of Mandhana's huge sixes). To say it is controversial within the cricket world is like saying Brexit has prompted a bit of a discussion down the pub. For one thing, no-one other than the ECB actually seems to want it, at least if reaction in the media, social and conventional, is anything to go by. For another, it means changing the rules to allow the last over of an innings to last for ten balls. It will also, as things stand, see the Women's Super League terminated just as it's taking off. And, most controversially of all, the ECB propose the men's tournament will be played not by the 18 counties, but by eight city-based franchises, with the women's competition matching them County chairmen worry that, at best, it will put money into the coffers of the already wealthier clubs that own the Test grounds, at the expense of the other counties; at worst, they fear could be the thin end of a wedge that will ultimately lead to the demise of their counties.

For their part, the ECB seem convinced the tournament is needed. Chairman Colin Graves insists that "The younger generation, whether you like it or not, are just not attracted to cricket. They want something different. They want it to be more exciting. They want it shorter." And so he is on a quest to "appeal to younger fans and attract a new audience to the game", mums and kids in particular. Yet looking around, I see plenty of youngsters, plenty of mums and, I suspect, many who are part of the new audience already attracted to cricket by Twenty20. Graves' stance is also hard to reconcile with comments from his organisation proclaiming the huge success of All-Stars Cricket in attracting youngsters. It is a little hard, too, to see why people who aren't attracted to Twenty20 will suddenly take up interest in the Hundred; I, for one, don't buy the patronising idea that an innings of 100 balls is inherently easier to follow than one of 120. While Graves' desire to get young people into cricket is laudable (though again, his own organisation's decision to remove live cricket from free-to-air television has done much to hide the game from that audience), there is also the possibility that he is chasing shadows. The writer Rowland Bowen talked of "half a million people, young people, assembled in a public park to hear a pop group… These young people do not need, nor do they want, cricket". Sound familiar? Bowen was writing in 1969, almost half a century ago. Graves may be right to be concerned about the lack of young people who enjoy cricket; what he should not do is confuse it for a new problem, or one that will inevitably lead to the game's demise and therefore requires drastic action. Just as people's politics are said to move progressively to the right as they get older, so the tastes of a 13-year-old today are no sure indicator what they'll be at 33, 43 or 53. There also seems something inherently patronising in their appeal to 'mums', especially as women have already shown that they enjoy the current product in ever-increasing numbers.

Reaction to the proposal has been, to say the least, unfavourable. In fact, the ECB are looking increasingly like the mad sailor, Captain Rum, in *Blackadder*, who claimed opinion was divided on the subject of whether it is necessary for a ship to have a crew. "All the other captains say it is; I say it isn't." The near-unanimous opposition to the tournament does not mean, of course, that the ECB will change course. I suspect they will plough on regardless. Many cricket fans say they will ignore the new tournament, and the new franchises may find it hard to lure support from those whose allegiance is to their counties. But there is always a chance that the Hundred could be a success – the fact it will be shown on BBC television will help it, as it will get far more exposure than any other form of the game. The immediate fear for the smaller counties is a loss of revenue from the switch to a few city teams; the longer-term worry may be that, one day, all cricket will be played the Hundred way.

In the meantime, the players are back out. Middlesex make a terrible start, when Max Holden is out before a run's been scored. He trudges off, the taunting refrain of *Na Hey Hey (Kiss Him Goodbye)* and a chorus of quacks ringing in his ears. Another Max, Waller, bowls a maiden, as rare as hens' teeth in Twenty20, and his teammates have a positive bounce in their step. In their black and yellow kit, they look like a collection of Tiggers. It takes Middlesex a full ten balls to get off the mark, an unpardonable sin. While the PA announcer greets fans who've travelled from afar or who are watching their very first match, Gubbins smacks a couple of boundaries but then has his stumps rearranged by Gregory, and *Another One*

*Bites the Dust* blares out. One suspects the DJ rather enjoys these gigs. The next man in is no less a personage that the captain of England's limited-overs side, Eoin Morgan. The Dubliner's stay is brief, but memorable. He is beaten twice early on, prompting much glee from the locals, then launches a six towards the outer edges of the atmosphere that rattles the windows of the Colin Atkinson pavilion on re-entry. In the next over he's caught by Taylor off Gregory and departs moodily for 10. Drinks accompany the new batsman, Eskinazi, to the crease (really? It's been about ten minutes since the interval, how can they need drinks?) and it's time for the obligatory rendition of *Sweet Caroline*. It is, I think, enshrined in law that Neil Diamond's classic song has to be played at any professional sporting event. It certainly gets the crowd singing. Some wave their arms, those with small children wave them instead, and it's rather a beautiful sight to see eight-year-olds singing and dancing to a song that was a hit before their mothers were born, and very possibly their grandmothers too.

Play resumes and Middlesex reach 50, 30 of them from a fiery knock from Stirling, but he is then out in spectacular fashion, even by the standards of Twenty20 cricket. Van de Merwe sends down a half-volley that's begging to be hit, and Stirling duly swipes the ball high and far towards long on. Overton leaps and catches the ball, but realising he's going to tumble back over the ropes, he lobs the ball back into the air just a split second before falling back across the boundary. He then steadies himself, runs back onto the playing area and takes the catch a second time. It all happens in a flash, and is quite brilliant. Overton, arms outstretched, races towards his team mates who engulf him, every last man, some of them running, if not faster, then certainly further than Usain Bolt does to win Olympic medals. The crowd are on their feet and even the Middlesex supporters have to acknowledge a wonderful piece of cricket. Within minutes, social media is buzzing; some question the catch's legality (it was, in fact, perfectly fine) but most express delight at Overton's astonishing athleticism and quick thinking.

His catch sums up something that has to be acknowledged, whatever one's views on Twenty20 – that it has enormously improved fielding standards. The improvement started many years ago with one-day cricket, and the need to curtail runs; but Twenty20 cricket, with every run at a premium and batters hitting balls like never before, has taken fielding to new levels. Catches and stops that, 20 years ago, would have been thought of as remarkable are almost commonplace nowadays (the same applies to a few batting strokes). Even so, Overton's catch was outstanding, and everyone at Taunton appreciates it. Not surprisingly, it prompts another Scatterblast. With Middlesex now five down, Eskinazi goes for a big swipe and loses the ball in a stand. It's the signal for the rain to return, and everyone troops off.

With play suspended, people take the opportunity to get a drink, or head to the loos to divest themselves of ones they consumed earlier. They're not the only ones relieving themselves. With what can only be described as malicious intent, a large, angry-looking gull flies past the top of the stand from where I am surveying the scene below, carries on over the concourse and, with precision bombing worthy of the Dambusters, drops his payload onto unsuspecting victims below. Job done, it banks steeply and flies back to base, a satisfied glint in its eye.

The shower is brief and light, though those underneath the gull's flight path may have wished for something heavier to wash away his deposits. The players are quickly back on to the pitch, and even more speedily off again, as, simultaneously, the sun comes out and the rain starts pouring. It's one of those days. This time they run off, Supertramp's *It's raining again* earns a few more pennies in royalties, and umbrellas shoot up all round the ground, sprouting like a field of mushrooms in a time-lapse film. The weather fails, though, to dampen the spirits of the crowd who, being English, accept the summer downpour as an occupational hazard. Very few leave before the players eventually return, the match now reduced to 18 overs. Middlesex's revised target is 213, meaning they need 125 more from 7.5 overs, unlikely even for Twenty20. Simpson, who's never quite got going, departs almost immediately, and there's a review of a run-out that seems to last forever; a clock beat accompanies the growing anticipation, only for a verdict of not out, which is greeted by a loud pantomime groan of disappointment. It's all part of the fun. And it's appropriate too. If Test Matches are Shakespearian productions, and championship matches are chess games, Twenty20 contests are cricket's panto. It's surely only a matter of time before an umpire tells a player he's out and the crowd, seeing them reprieved on appeal, start shouting "Oh no he isn't" in reply.

Eskinazi hasn't given up hope, and he takes on the bowling with gusto, crashing the ball to all corners, but when he's out soon after – another wicket for Gregory, who's romping away with the man of the match prize – the visitors need 72 from 18. A four off every ball will do it, but although anything is possible in this form of cricket, that does seem optimistic. The crowd know the game is won, and start filling in the time until the end with a Mexican wave, which flows through three stands before fading away as surely as Middlesex's hopes. They finish on 174–6, 38 runs short of the target. It's a second home win of the day, and Somerset are now firmly on course to make the next stage. And, inevitably, as we drift slowly out of the ground, we do so under clear, blue skies, with not a raincloud in sight.

**Somerset**

| | | | | |
|---|---|---|---|---|
| S.M. Davies ƚ | | c&b Barner | | 13 |
| J.G. Myburgh | c Fuller | b Barber | | 13 |
| P.D. Trego | c Eskinazi | b Agar | | 60 |
| J.C. Hildreth | c Simpson | b Barber | | 0 |
| T.B. Abell | c Eskinazi | b Agar | | 31 |
| C.J. Anderson | not out | | | 41 |
| L. Gregory * | c Patel | b Harris | | 62 |
| R.E. van der Merwe | | not out | | 0 |
| Extras | | 9w | | 9 |
| **Total** | | 20 overs | 6 – | 229 |

**FoW:** 1–26, 2–28, 3–29 4–112, 5–138, 6–228

Did not bat: J.E. Taylor, J. Overton, M.T.C. Waller

| **Bowling** | **O** | **M** | **R** | **W** |
|---|---|---|---|---|
| R.H. Patel | 4 | 0 | 56 | 0 |
| J.A.R. Harris | 4 | 1 | 40 | 1 |
| T.E Barber | 4 | 0 | 37 | 3 |
| J.K. Fuller | 4 | 0 | 46 | 0 |
| A.C. Ager | 4 | 0 | 50 | 2 |

**Middlesex**

| | | | | |
|---|---|---|---|---|
| M.D.E. Holden | c Abell | b Waller | | 0 |
| P.R. Stirling | c Overton | b van der Merwe | | 30 |
| N.R.T. Gubbins | b Gregory | | | 10 |
| E.J.G. Morgan * | c Taylor | b Gregory | | 10 |
| S.S. Eskinazi | c van der Merwe | b Gregory | | 55 |
| J.A. Simpson ƚ | c Overton | b Gregory | | 29 |
| A.C. Agar | not out | | | 23 |
| J.K. Fuller | not out | | | 8 |
| Extras | | 4b 2lb 2nb 1w | | 9 |
| **Total** | | 18 overs | 6 – | 174 |

**FoW:** 1–0, 2–29, 3–45 4–50, 5–115, 6–156

Did not bat: R.H. Patel, J.A.R. Harris, T.E. Barber

| **Bowling** | **O** | **M** | **R** | **W** |
|---|---|---|---|---|
| M.T.C. Waller | 3 | 1 | 16 | 1 |
| J.E. Taylor | 4 | 0 | 41 | 0 |
| J. Overton | 3 | 0 | 44 | 0 |
| L. Gregory | 4 | 0 | 28 | 4 |
| R.E. van der Merwe | 4 | 0 | 39 | 1 |

**Toss:** Middlesex elected to field. **Umpires:** I. Gould, J. Lloyds
**Somerset win by 38 runs (DLS Method)**

# Chapter Ten

## Lancashire League

Accrington CC v Lowerhouse CC
Property Shop Arena, Accrington
Saturday 4 August

Accrington's ground sits on Thorneyholme Road, nestled in a bowl on the edge of the rolling moorland of Lancashire. Thick banks of coniferous trees give way to open grassy moors that rise steeply on the far side. Just the sort of boggy, windswept landscape that gives rise to tales of malevolent spirits and giant, ghostly dogs that spell doom for lost stragglers unfortunate enough to encounter them on dark winter's nights. But in the bright, clear sun of a lovely summer's day like today, it is glorious, perfect for hikers and ramblers, with views stretching for miles across the half-wild, half-industrial landscape of England's northwest.

The ground has a new name this year, courtesy of a sponsorship deal with local estate agents launched just a few weeks ago by one of the town's favourite sons, David Lloyd. It was here that Bumble cut his cricketing teeth, and he's still a popular figure round these parts. I park my car but delay getting out, as my arrival has coincided with the climax of a thrilling Test Match, 120 miles south at Edgbaston. After three and a half days of ebb and flow, England have beaten India in a gripping finish, the visitors falling 31 runs short of their target of 194, despite a valiant half-century from Virat Kohli. Game over, I turn off the radio, get out and instantly all those old clichés about northern friendliness compared to southern reserve come to the fore. "Y'awreet?", asks a youngish man on crutches, who looks like he might be an injured player. I ask him how he is. "I'm fine", he says, and hobbles away. As I wander over to find a seat, I am greeted by a succession of strangers as if I were an old acquaintance they last saw yesterday afternoon. Some nod and smile, others say "ayup" or "'owdo". It's all very warm and very friendly, and I'm taking a shine to Accrington. Seats are dotted around the ground, enough for a couple of hundred spectators, and there's a club house that looks like it really was a house once, but now has rows of benches in front. The flags of the club and of St George flutter above. There is a café too, which I shall frequent later, as well as a rugby pitch and some tennis courts, which I'm pleased to see are in use. The two teams are on the ground doing their warm-up exercises – cricket skills for one, football for the other. Well, it is the opening day of the football season, so they can be forgiven.

The new sponsorship deal seems to be putting some fresh life into a club that has had its share of financial difficulties. "Ay, we've new covers and a sight screen" one old stalwart tells me. Warming to his theme, he adds, with deadpan face, "and a centrally heated pitch". Somehow, I doubt that the sponsor's largesse, generous as it clearly is, quite stretches that far, but I go along with it. "Should be a decent crowd in today, they're bringing 80 guests", someone says. "England 'ave won", says another. 'Ave they?" "Aye. They wouldn't've won it if Kohli 'ad stayed, 'e'd 'ave got 'em."

Exercises finished, the players make their way to the clubhouse, and are replaced by a black collie, who shows off his own considerable fielding skills, retrieving a succession of balls with admirable agility. While that's going on, two old boys near me reminisce over past encounters with Lowerhouse. "I remember a player called, Danny Wardy, now that's going back a bit. We needed five wickets, they needed one run – and they got it off t'last ball to win by one wicket! That were Danny Wardy's doing – 'e took 2–2, missed his hat trick, then took 2–2 again and they got t'run off t'last ball!" (Later on, back home, I check on the club website's history page and he was going back a bit, if the player of his memory was the one I find details for. Sayajirao (Danny) Dhanwade was a pro here in the 1950s. There's no mention of him taking four wickets in the last over, but he did take four in four balls and five in the over against Lowerhouse in 1956. Tragically, within two years he was dead, killed by a brain haemorrhage following a blow to the head in the nets).

The trip down memory lane is interrupted by a sharp cry of "get off the field", though it's not entirely clear whether it's aimed at the collie and his owner or the umpires, who have begun making their way to the middle. Lowerhouse have won the toss, and have elected (is there any other game in the world where a side elects, rather than chooses?) to bat. The Accrington supporters will be hoping their opponents have at least one eye on tomorrow, when they take on their hometown rivals Burnley in the final of the Worsley Cup. Remarkably, it will be the first time in the local tournament's 93 years that the two neighbours have met in the final. All around me, meanwhile, is the excited chatter of spectators recalling past games ("Remember that game at Rawtenstall? It were lashing down, it were more like a lake") or checking on current players ("Ow many runs has Grimsy got this season?" "500ish." "What's the record for an amateur?" "Ooh, 900 odd…"). The passion of the spectators for cricket, and for Accrington cricket in particular, and what it means to them, is palpable. It's uplifting to see, but then the Lancashire League has always been more than just another competition. They have a proud history here, and, far from London, not even the long arm of the game's rulers always reaches this far. When the newly formed ECB tried, in 1987, to restructure club cricket, they received short shrift in this neck of the woods. "This is the Lancashire League", said the league's chairman, "an historic league. We don't need a Premier League." And the Lancashire League it remains.

Meanwhile, more fans are arriving and greeting old mates with 'Owdo" and "y'alright" and the odd "No thanks, I've just had a brew", which makes me wish I was going on to the club in *Phoenix Nights* for post-match entertainment later. Accrington's bowlers start well, Clarke and JE Hayhurst bagging three maidens in the first four overs. There's exasperation from Clarke, though, when a catch is dropped, and choice words follow. "Stop swearing, foul mouth", shouts someone reproachfully from the seats. Another spectator seems to be making precautions in case of rain, which seems unlikely but can never with certainty be ruled out in these parts. He waves a booklet at his companion. "'Ere, Barry, ever read this – the Duckworth-Lewis thing? I've read it right through, and I still don't understand it!". I dare say he's far from alone. Suddenly, and without warning, he turns to the pitch and, in a voice suggesting a possible career as a town crier, sings "It's coming home, it's coming home, the Worsley Cup is coming home." I have no doubt the players all heard it; I shouldn't be surprised if Lowerhouse's loved ones nine miles down the road in Burnley heard it. Not to be outdone, the Accrington players become increasingly vociferous. "Come on boys, we're winning every ball here… On top boys, keep it going". There's even a bit of the mildest of sledging as another ball whizzes past an outstretched bat: "Not convincing boys, not convincing". Progress for the Lowerhouse openers, Heap and Martin, is painstaking, and after ten overs they have made just 20. This is old-fashioned cricket, opening bowlers pinning the batsmen down with quick bowling on a lively pitch, while the batsmen aim to survive, see off the new ball and grind out a platform.

There's a second big shout for leg before, prompting another outburst from the town crier. "Settle down Accrington, it's only a game!". Soon after, the youthful, wiry Clarke, whose countenance betrays a severe distaste for batsmen, breaks through. Heap edges a lively delivery that nips away from him, two Accrington slip fielders juggle the ball between them, and eventually the older of the Hayhurst brothers keeps hold of it. Heap is replaced by a burly fellow who'd be a shoo-in for the role of big-hitting blacksmith in a period film about a village team. He looks remarkably familiar, and I try to think who he reminds me of. I cast my mind back to other matches I have seen this season, and eventually settle on Canterbury, as I realise he looks uncannily like Leicestershire's Mark Cosgrove. I had thought Cosgrove was a fairly unmistakeable figure in the modern game, but according to the Lancashire League's rather useful online, real-time scorecard, this is Lowerhouse's pro, Ockert Erasmus.

With the opening bowling seen off, Lowerhouse start to settle. Clarke and Hayhurst are replaced by Vimukhti, Accrington's Sri Lankan pro, and Brown, who together pose considerably less threat. Vimukhti concedes six off an over and gets an encouraging pat on the back, while Brown's off-breaks start to prove costly. Erasmus looks solid, as you'd expect, and the batsmen make steady progress until Martin is out caught off Grimshaw. There's no appeal, and a slight air of surprise when he walks off. The tall Haasbroek, who's played first-class cricket in his time, strides to the crease, looking like the sort of batsman who will swipe the ball away as if it were a fly; his looks, though, are deceptive. He scratches around for a few overs before rather weakly sending the ball to the safe hands of Hayhurst. Lowerhouse are 109–3, Accrington very much in the game. Two spectators behind me seem nonplussed. "How was that last man out?", asks one. There's a pause before his neighbour replies. "I'm not sure. To be honest, I didn't realise he was out". "Aye, that were Frankie Haasbroek." Another pause. "I thought he were at Rishton?"

As the sun gets hotter, the smell of chips and the distant sound of cheers from the football stadium, where Accrington Stanley have kicked off their season, drift across the ground. There's yet another loud LBW appeal, and the inevitable riposte from the town crier: "Calm down Accy, steady on – 'ave a word, umpire!" Erasmus looks determined and reaches the 40s. As he approaches his 50, he survives a stumping appeal ("Get a grip Accy – 'ave a word umpire!".) Unruffled, he strikes an off-drive right off the middle and reaches his half-century. "Bish bash bosh", shouts the crier, who may well be imbibing some lubrication to keep his voice strong. "Jesus wept", utters an Accrington fan, wearily, "What the 'ell's he going to be like tomorrow?".

Clarke is recalled and the lively youngster makes another breakthrough, with the extravagantly initialled PTBM Martin out for 11. A bucket is brought round the ground by two teenagers who call out "Donations for Cosgrove's 50". "Did you say Cosgrove?", I ask. "Aye", replies one of them, “Mark Cosgrove, ‘im wot’s got 50”. “I thought the pro was Erasmus?” “Oh, ‘e’s injured, they’ve signed this lad from Leicestershire for t’weekend.” So it is our old chum, after all. His identity out in the open, he increasingly looks the part of club pro. Of course, the Lancashire League has a long history of employing professionals, decades before the practice caught on in the south. And not just any old professionals either. A quick look at some of the names who have graced the Lancashire League testifies to the love of cricket in these parts, and its quality: Sydney Barnes, Allan Border, Learie Constantine, Charlie Griffith, Allan Donald, Dennis Lillee, Kapil Dev, Wes Hall, George Headley, Michael Holding, Clive Lloyd, Viv Richards, Andy Roberts, Shane Warne, Steve Waugh… The three W’s, Fran Worrell, Everton Weekes and Clyde Walcott all played here; what displays they must have put on for the factory workers and office clerks in the grey and smoky 1950s. (Seeing that roll-call of great West Indian names on that list, one cannot help but feel a twinge of sadness at the complete absence of anyone of African or Caribbean heritage on the pitch today, or indeed off it).

It was this rich litany of legends that led me, as a child growing up far from the moors and mill towns of the northwest, to think of the Lancashire League as something very exotic and exciting. Tales of the League seemed to me like stories from *The Arabian Nights*. It was a land where giants of the game would turn out for towns with strange-sounding names like Rawtenstall and Todmorden and

Ramsbottom, Gods coming down from Mount Olympus to show off their divine skills to the mortals. The grounds, in my child's mind's eye, all looked like Old Trafford and were packed to the rafters every weekend. In reality, I later discovered, they were somewhat less grand, but crowds were certainly bigger than these days, as an elderly spectator sitting near me confirms. "I remember a £300 gate when Everton Weekes was playing for Bacup, and in those days you could buy a house for £300 round there." I suspect today's takings would more likely be in the range of a garden shed, rather than a house, even if prices are considerably lower here than down south.

Mark Cosgrove may not quite be in the same exalted company as some of his predecessors, but he's earning his weekend's corn. As Accrington's bowling flags, they become profligate with extras, wide after wide keeping the scoreboard ticking over, and Lowerhouse push on in search of a testing target. Cosgrove drives with increasingly lusty blows, moving swiftly through the 60s, 70s, 80s. By the time he reaches the 90s he's picking off the bowling at will, every ball flying off the middle of his chunky bat. His century seems inevitable, but he swings the bat again and for once just mistimes his stroke. It still needs a decent catch, but he's out for 94. The rest of his team's runs come mainly from Cottam, who plays a steady cameo, and Lowerhouse wrap up their innings on 243–7. Only Cosgrove has passed 50, but Accrington have gifted them a costly 41 in extras.

The players tuck into their tea, and I wander into the café. It's small, but serves a good variety of food and drinks. A plate of chips is a bargain at £1, and these, together with steaming mugs of tea – brews – are selling well. Even the beer is only a little over £2 a pint. I won't mention to the locals what I'd have to pay for that in Cambridge, they'd laugh me out of town. Tea consumed, Sneddon and the younger Hayhurst brother open the batting for Accrington, while Hussain and Cosgrove – from whom Lowerhouse will get their money's worth over the weekend – lead the bowling. The crier, fortified by more beer, quickly gets to work. "Wicket in a minute, there'll be a wicket in a minute" he sings. I say sings, though I used the word in the loosest sense. Annoyingly for the home fans, though, he's proved right, as Cosgrove, as if on cue, sends down a ball that leaves Sneddon bewildered and his stumps scattered. He strikes again in his next over, removing Hayhurst, and when Grimshaw comes and goes without scoring, the home side are reeling on 16–3. It's a stark demonstration of the difference between even very good club players and a professional. It also delights the crier, whose increasingly drunken chants finally snap the patience of a home supporter. "SHUT UP, YOU NOISY SOD!", he bellows, only to be met with an enigmatic "Bish bash bosh" and a verse of "You are my Lowerhouse, my only Lowerhouse", vaguely to the tune of *You are my Sunshine*.

A fourth-wicket stand stems the flow of wickets until, on 45, Clarke is given out caught, much to his displeasure.

He lingers just a little longer than is wise, before turning and trudging off with the speed of a tortoise dragging a ball and chain. He emits a loud grunt of dissatisfaction as he goes, and his mood isn't helped by yet another cry of 'bish bash bosh' as he reaches the clubhouse. He shows admirable restraint in not finding further use for his bat as he walks up the steps. As afternoon turns into early evening, and the beer takes effect – and at these prices, plenty will be consumed – the banter turns into football songs, the language gets a little riper, and there's an exchange in front of the clubhouse between the crier and an Accringtonian that just about manages to stay the right side of the ledger between amiability and a punch on the nose. Perhaps the crier's friends have a word, as things do quieten down. In the meantime, the home side are giving their supporters some cheer, as they remain ahead of where Lowerhouse were at the same stage, but they do have four wickets down. Vimukhti is keeping them in the contest, but his innings is neither fluent nor dominant. Sadly for him, and like so many batsmen, the drinks interval proves his downfall, and no sooner does play resume than he is gone. Within minutes, Accrington are surveying the tattered remains of their innings. Ramiz is out to the first ball of the next over, and JE Hayhurst is bowled to put the wily Finch on a hat trick. Three wickets have fallen for no runs, Accrington are still a dozen shy of a 100, and Lowerhouse are romping away. "Oh dear me", says a resigned voice behind me. "Alright Jeff?", enquires a friend. "Aye, fine", he replies, "living the dream".

The crier, meanwhile, is now as unstoppable as he is indecipherable. A small group of people regard him with pity. "He's always like this when he's had a few beers, he never shuts up. There's no malice in him." It's said with the air of one who's seen it all too many times before.

Accrington pass 100 but Greenwood departs soon after, and they are down to the tail. Bancroft walks virtually all the way back to the clubhouse to greet the incoming Brown and gives him a lengthy talking to, which can only be either a level of instruction likely to be lost on any self-respecting tailender, or a very convoluted story that he started in the dressing room and has been itching to finish ever since. Either way, it's to little avail as two runs later he has to make the walk all the way back again, this time not stopping when he reaches the ropes. Brown plays a defiant, and rather attractive, straight drive and Kasser manages to avoid being bowled for seven balls, until the next one gets him, and Accrington are all out for 115. They came into the match as underdogs, and conceding 41 extras and losing three early wickets did nothing to help their cause. Lowerhouse, meanwhile, will march on with confidence into tomorrow's cup final. As the spectators pack up their belongings and say their goodbyes, a distant voice trails across from the car park. "One team in Burnley, there's only one team in Burnley…". What, indeed, will he be like tomorrow?

**Accrington C.C.**

| | | | | |
|---|---|---|---|---|
| B. R. Heap * | c JE Hayhurst | b Clarke | | 7 |
| J. Martin ŧ | c JE Hayhurst | b Brown | | 39 |
| M. J. Cosgrove | c Hussain | b Grimshaw | | 93 |
| D. F. Haasbroek | c JE Hayhurst | b Brown | | 3 |
| P.T.B.M. Martin | c Bancroft | b Clarke | | 11 |
| C.R. Cottam | not out | | | 36 |
| C.J. Bleazard | b Brown | | | 1 |
| J.M. Hawke | b JE Hayhurst | | | 11 |
| J.A. Finch | not out | | | 1 |
| Extras | | 5b 1lb 35w | | 41 |
| **Total** | | 50 overs | 7 – | 243 |

**FoW:** 1–32, 2–82, 3–109, 4–147, 5–216, 6–219, 7–242
**Did not bat:** T. Hussain, B.N.M. Uttley

| **Bowling** | **O** | **M** | **R** | **W** |
|---|---|---|---|---|
| J. Clarke | 15 | 3 | 44 | 2 |
| J.E. Hayhurst | 9 | 1 | 38 | 1 |
| Vimukhti | 8 | 0 | 35 | 0 |
| R.L.E. Brown | 13 | 0 | 74 | 3 |
| K. Grimshaw | 5 | 0 | 46 | 1 |

**Lowerhouse C.C.**

| | | | | |
|---|---|---|---|---|
| G.L. Sneddon | b Cosgrove | | | 3 |
| J.N. Hayhurst | lbw | b Cosgrove | | 8 |
| K.L.J. Vimukhti | lbw | b Haasbroek | | 38 |
| K. Grimshaw | | b Cosgrove | | 0 |
| J. Clarke | c Finch | b Hussain | | 19 |
| Ramiz Hussain | lbw | b Finch | | 14 |
| A.M. Greenwood | c P.T.B.M. Martin | b Heap | | 10 |
| J.E. Hayhurst | | b Finch | | 0 |
| S. Bancroft ŧ | | c&b P.T.B.M. Martin | | 5 |
| R.L.E. Brown * | not out | | | 7 |
| R Kasser | | b Heap | | 0 |
| Extras | | 6lb 5w | | 11 |
| **Total** | | 36.1 overs | 10 – | 115 |

**FoW:** 1–12, 2–14, 3–16 4–45, 5–88, 6–88, 7–88, 8–107, 9–109, 10–115

| Bowling | O | M | R | W |
|---|---|---|---|---|
| T. Hussain | 8 | 2 | 27 | 1 |
| M.J. Cosgrove | 5 | 0 | 15 | 3 |
| D.F. Haasbroek | 8 | 3 | 14 | 1 |
| J.M. Hawke | 1 | 0 | 5 | 0 |
| J.A. Finch | 7 | 1 | 38 | 2 |
| P.T.B.M. Martin | 5 | 1 | 7 | 1 |
| B.R. Heap | 2.1 | 0 | 3 | 2 |

**Toss:** Lowerhouse elected to bat. **Umpires:** T. Bartley, S. Beswick
**Lowerhouse win by 128 runs**

# Chapter Eleven

## Second Test Match

England v India
Lord's, London
Thursday 9 – Sunday 12 August

**DAY 1**

Anyone arriving at St John's Wood Underground Station this morning unaware of the Test Match taking place down the road would soon be put right. The faces of Joe Root and Virat Kohli smile disarmingly from a hundred posters, their gazes following the thousands of spectators who are carried up the escalators that groan under their weight. Outside, touts have gathered in force and everyone leaving the station is forced to run, or at least crawl, the gauntlet between them. Those who have made it form an eclectic army snaking its way along Wellington Road. There are young men and woman in smart suits and dresses, taking a break from making money in the City; families up from the country for the day; middle-aged, Middle England types in floppy sunhats, lunch carried in holdalls; business colleagues clutching hospitality tickets and greeting each other with the eager delight of children allowed out of school for the day;

and, of course, the MCC Members, in regulation navy blazers, egg and bacon ties and Panamas. Along the way, elegant woman of a certain age attempt to part people from their loose change for whatever charity they are collecting for, while a few locals struggle bravely against the flow, their faces suggesting an ordeal they'll be lucky to get through in one piece.

A full house is expected, though rain has arrived overnight and, under leaden skies, prospects for an 11am start are decidedly gloomy. It is humid too, a muggy, clammy morning, the sort of morning on which England's bowlers will be champing at the bit. India come into the match as the world's highest-ranked Test side, but England's confidence has been boosted by victory in a thrilling first Test (the first, of five, in August – has a series ever started later? What crammed, compressed schedules teams have to contend with these days), and conditions like this are tailor-made for them. However, since that match at Edgbaston, they have lost the services of talismanic all-rounder Ben Stokes, unavoidably detained by a court case in Bristol where he is defending himself against a charge of affray. The general view is that he'll be badly missed.

The big screens inside the ground are busy relaying adverts for the MCC Foundation ('Changing lives through cricket'), players' dining room experiences, the Lord's 2018 clothing range and, of course, the museum. With no likelihood of play any time soon, I head for the last of those attractions, which is, not surprisingly, crowded. Among the usual collection of bats and balls, caps and blazers, kit bags and gloves, are exhibitions on women's cricket through the ages – with tales of early women's teams forced to use chaperones and pseudonyms for fear of disgrace – Aboriginal touring sides and, celebrating today's visitors, Indian memorabilia. But like the *Mona Lisa* at the Louvre, the biggest crowd is to be found milling around the glass case containing the little urn that holds the Ashes. Some jostle to get a better position for selfies with it, though most just gaze at it in quiet, respectful awe, like worshippers kneeling in adoration of the Sacred Host. For years, now, the MCC has adopted the soubriquet 'the home of cricket' to describe Lord's. Clever, harmless marketing, perhaps, but it runs deeper. The ICC may be based in Dubai these days, and the real power found in Mumbai rather than NW8, but Lord's retains a mystique that still draws cricket lovers from every corner of the globe. And if Lord's remains the spiritual home of the game, its greatest cathedral, then here, in this small glass case, is its *sanctum sanctorum*, a place of pilgrimage where cricket's holiest relic is to be found and knelt before in awe. The Australians, of course, protest at the MCC's refusal to let them have it in Australia when they hold it, but the club is not for turning on the issue. Officially, the reason is the fragile state of the urn. Perhaps, though, the real reason is a fear that, like the ravens at the Tower of London, Lord's, or even England itself, would fall should the Ashes depart.

The urn aside, the museum is, of course, full of memories of Test cricket's great history. Perhaps, though, there should be a section on its future. India and England may come into this match in good shape, but Test cricket does not, or so runs the perceived wisdom. For years, the media has been full of stories of the decline of Test cricket, but in recent months it has become a cacophony, with a litany of dramatic headlines: "Why Test cricket is a game in decline"; "Slow, boring, unseen: it's no wonder Test cricket is dying."; "How much dying can Test cricket do?"; "Young people don't care for Test cricket anymore, say sports fans in Sky poll". Even the *Chicago Tribune*, not renowned as a bastion of cricket coverage, got in on the act when Ireland played their inaugural Test in May: "Ireland is spending a small fortune to stage a sporting match that takes five days to play, has a dwindling fanbase, and is often labelled impenetrable. The country's national cricket team is in the middle of its first-ever Test match – the five-day event considered the pinnacle of the sport – against Pakistan, at a time when ever-fewer fans have the stamina to tune in or show up to watch the storied version of the game, let alone actually pick up a bat and ball."[7] At times in the last year, one could have been forgiven for thinking that by 2025 Test cricket would itself be no more than a museum piece, a relic of a bygone age, the dodo of the sporting world.

---

[7] www.chicagotribune.com/sports/breaking/ct-spt-cricket-declining-popularity-20180514-story.html+&cd=1&hl=en&ct=clnk&gl=uk

It's not all doom and gloom though – well, not quite all. Just two days ago, a *Guardian* story proclaimed, "Test cricket is not dying", arguing that, at least in England, there are grounds for optimism. The article points out that, rather than falling, Test match crowds in this country have been steadily increasing for decades, up from an average of 52,851 in the 1980s to 77,418 in the current decade[8]. England is, though, bucking the trend and generally crowds around the world have dwindled, almost to nothing in many cases. Plenty of reasons are offered for this decline – the time and cost of attending, especially in countries where most workers are on low incomes; the slowness of Test cricket, especially with its absurdly unhurried over rates; the short attention spans and demands for immediate gratification by today's audiences, fed by the rise of Twenty20; the trend towards dominance by home sides; and the disappearance of live Test cricket from free-to-air TV, thus cutting off Test cricket from a large swathe of the potential audience (though in England, at least, where live Test cricket departed free-to-air channels thirteen years ago, this is hard to reconcile with the evidence of increasing crowd numbers). There are as many proposed solutions, too, from a Test championship and day/night matches to reducing Tests to four days. That suggestion has prompted an inevitable outcry from those defending the traditions of Test cricket, though they conveniently forget that matches were often played over four days up until the early 1970s,

[8] England: the Biography, Simon Wilde (Simon & Schuster, 2018)

and other traditions, like rest days, have been changed with no ill-effects. Besides, the proportion of matches going to a fifth day has fallen from around three-quarters to barely more than half last year, so four-day Tests are introducing themselves.[9]

But, regardless of the *Guardian's* grounds for optimism, the widespread belief for many is that Test cricket's days are numbered. And when enough people start to believe something, it can become true, a self-fulfilling prophecy that steamrollers any evidence to the contrary through the force of its own momentum. The fear is that, with Test cricket, the perception of its demise might become so widespread that the reality is not properly investigated, and 'innovations' put in place to rescue it that do not actually address the right issues. That's not to say that Test cricket does not face some serious challenges – not even the proverbial ostrich with its buried head could think otherwise – but I hope whatever decisions are taken are based on careful analysis, not knee-jerk reactions to the latest faddish thinking.

Back outside, prospects for play are receding faster than the UK's hopes of winning the EU Member State of the Year award. A group of hardy souls huddles together underneath the media centre, like penguins sheltering from the Antarctic winter. It's a different story in the covered areas, where there is much catching up with old friends over wine and champagne and Pimm's. The TV screens helpfully

[9] www.telegraph.co.uk/cricket/2017/08/08/time-reduce-test-matches-four-days/

remind us that play is delayed, but the gloom starts to lift, there's a hint of the rain easing, and broom-wielding ground staff in shorts and wellies scurry round with purpose. There's a cheer when the two umpires walk out to inspect the pitch, and a larger one when Aleem Dar's umbrella blows inside out. Nevertheless, the drizzle persists, and they retreat to the comfort of their room.

As the afternoon wears on, there are bigger cheers still when two spectators, having perhaps taken a little too much advantage of the opportunity for drinking, catch the stewards off-guard, run onto the ground and dive, Jurgen Klinsmann style, onto the covers. They are quickly escorted off, though it would be more appropriate to say manhandled for one of them, who is more or less thrown by a steward over an advertising board, prompting a loud collective reaction from the inhabitants of the Mount Stand, who think it too heavy-handed. It is, though, the last excitement of the day. As 5.00 approaches, rain still falling, play is abandoned for the day. It is, apparently, the first entire day of a Lord's Test to be lost in 17 years, which comes as a surprise. As the thousands who have gamely stuck it out all day in good humour shuffle their way slowly back to the underground station, all looking like penguins now, there are loud thunderclaps overheard, the heavens open and there is a monsoon. We can only wish for better tomorrow.

~~~~~~~~~~~~~~~~~~~~~~
~~~~~~~~~~~~~~~~~~~~~~

## Day 2

After yesterday's false start, it is time for business. Lord's is buzzing this morning, activity everywhere, with players practising, former players offering up their thoughts and TV crews broadcasting them, people with ID badges and clipboards walking around and looking important, and ground staff making final preparations with strips of tape and buckets of whitewash. Amidst all this, Joe Root wins the toss, and England will bowl. Was that a hungry roar from Anderson in the dressing room? As the stage clears, Ollie Pope, a club cricketer just two years ago but averaging over 85 for Surrey this season, receives his England cap from Alec Stewart, and Marais Erasmus is presented with a trophy to mark his 50$^{th}$ Test as an umpire. It's all very pleasant, until someone remarks loudly "There's a 70% chance of rain at 2pm". Despite this, both sides have brought in a second spinner. The bell is rung, 'Lord' Ted Dexter doing the honours in what has become a delightful Lord's tradition, the umpires walk to the middle, and we're finally underway in what is now a four-day Test.

Vijay runs out, long hair flowing beneath his helmet; behind him, Rahul makes an altogether more sedate approach to the crease. Anderson prepares to open the bowling, and my neighbour immediately opens his *Daily Telegraph* and settles down to the crossword. It takes Anderson all of five balls to remove Vijay, who plays a truly terrible shot and has his stumps spread-eagled. He turns mournfully and makes his way back at a considerably slower pace than when he walked out. Broad draws Rahul forward but just misses the edge of his bat, and not until the fourth over do India get off the mark. Not long after, the clock still short of 11:30, the floodlights come on. Rahul plays and misses some more and then nicks a ball from Anderson to Bairstow; India are 10–2, their prospects as gloomy as the sky. Kohli comes in to enthusiastic applause from the crowd, but it's probably with considerable relief that he is soon off again, as the rain returns early. Anderson and Broad have been at their meanest in the little play we've seen, and India will welcome the sanctuary of the changing room.

When play resumes, lunch has been consumed and we are well into the afternoon. Above us is blue sky to one side, thunderous-looking clouds to the other, and the floodlights remain on. Ten balls later – enough for Kohli to play and miss several deliveries from a fizzing Stuart Broad – the players are marched off again, only to be recalled before the scurrying Indian batsmen have reached the pavilion (the England players, for whom this is a much more familiar ritual, merely stroll back casually). Play starts again and if the umpires are confused, it's as nothing compared with the batsmen. Poor old Pujara, who's been in for 41 minutes for a solitary run, prods at the ball, which runs down to point. He starts running, as does his skipper, but Kohli changes his mind – captain's prerogative, he'll argue – and Pujara might as well be back home in Gujarat, so far from the crease is he. He departs with the air of a man bewildered by the madness around him. It doesn't help that the rain immediately returns with a vengeance, a cloudburst drenching everyone before they've had time even to say umbrella, let alone find and hoist one. Thunderclaps boom across St John's Wood, and when the downpour ends, things do not look good. There are puddles everywhere, but the area in front of the Mound and Tavern Stands looks like the Roman Colosseum when emperors staged recreations of great naval battles.

Next to me, a steward sweeps water from a doorway. I suggest he's fighting a losing battle and point to the lake. He turns and his jaw drops. "Christ!" he replies. When he recovers, he thinks there's still a chance of play. "The drainage is wonderful here these days – a few years ago rain like that would have been the end of the day's play, but they do wonders now." Let's hope he's right. The Lord's drainage is indeed hugely improved these days, despite the ground sitting on a thick layer of impermeable London clay, as a result of a huge investment in a sophisticated system installed at the start of the century. Thanks to that – and the efforts of ground staff with brooms and buckets – the lake recedes with remarkable speed. At a little after 5.00, there's an enthusiastic cheer from the still sizeable, ever-patient crowd – ah, the stoicism of the English at a summer event – and Rahane and Kohli emerge to take guard against the still-fresh England bowlers. By day's end, they'll be cursing the Lord's drainage and wishing the rain had fallen all afternoon.

Kohli, far from the imperious centurion of the first Test, is looking out of sorts. He plays another loose shot,

Root puts down a chance from one ball, and the slips leap in the air in a collective leg-before appeal after another. The ball, though, isn't doing as much as earlier, and the two batsmen settle down to build a recovery. Kohli and Rahane scamper to and fro, keeping the scoreboard ticking over, but when Woakes is brought on, there's an immediate change of atmosphere. He is magnificent from the off, bowling a beautiful length and drawing the batsman with every ball. Kohli survives a chance, edging a ball that flies between Root and Cook, but Buttler makes no mistake with the next ball. Pandya and Karthik fall in quick succession, the latter to a ball from Curran that curves like a banana. Anderson replaces Woakes, who has not received the rewards in wickets his bowling has deserved, and, roared on by the crowd in full voice, wreaks havoc with the tail. Rahane has resisted stubbornly for well over an hour and a half, but when he departs for 18 the scent of wickets hangs heavy in the air. Yadav is beaten by three beautiful out-swingers from Anderson, then trapped plumb leg before to one that comes in; Ashwin goes the same way to Broad, who's not finding swing but bowls directly at the stumps. Shami lashes out and takes India into three figures, but Anderson is like a cat playing with a mouse. Having let the number 10 have his fun, he pounces with devastating effect, another delivery swinging in and leaving the batsman groping in vain as the ball thumps into his pads. India are all out for 107. We may have had only half a day's play, but England have made the most of it, while India, taking the earlier view from the balcony literally, have looked all at sea.

## Day 3

There is nothing in cricket quite like the Saturday of a Lord's Test. It is cricket's summer fete, a holiday of games and feasting. I've yet to experience Boxing Day at the MCG, but in England at least, today is one of summer's highlights, like Derby Days of old, or the Wimbledon finals. In my mind's eye, at least, it is always a day of glorious, hot sunshine beaming down from a cloudless sky, happy summer music drifting from a thousand open windows, carefree throngs enjoying enforced idleness, dogs lying dreaming in the shade, escaping the heat of the day. In reality, of course, it is rarely so. But today, it is doing a fair approximation, and after two days of gloom and rain, the sun does indeed shine from a bright, blue sky. By 10am, it is already verging on hot, Lord's looking resplendent in its finest summer clothes. Flower beds and planters are full of vivid displays in the club's red and yellow colours; prosecco and Pimm's are flowing, and picnic hampers are spread out in the Harris Garden, places bagged early for lunchtime socialising. Outside the new Warner Stand, visitors pose for photos alongside the statue of WG Grace. After battling through the crowds that fill the narrow avenue behind the Grandstand, I reach the 'Activation Area' alongside the Nursery Ground, where a long line of fans queue to have their fielding skills tested by a firm of opticians who've rigged up a catching contraption. Nearby, the concourse joining the main ground to the Nursery is thronged with those hoping to get a selfie with one the England players as they make their way to the nets. Johnny Bairstow, all smiles and jokes, obliges for a group of young women, who look like they've had their ticket's worth of excitement before play has even begun. Some of his teammates are going through their paces in the nets; others are earnestly discussing technique with coaches, or warming up with a game of football. Back in front of the pavilion, Mark Nicholas and Mike Atherton, smartly suited, mics in hand, analyse the state of the match. A few yards away, David Gower, *sans* golden locks these days but still youthful, and his old colleague Ian Botham discuss plans – possibly for filming, more likely for this evening's dining – with their TV crew members. There's another presentation, this time to head groundsman Mick Hunt, who's retiring one year short of his half century. He's swapped his customary shorts for trousers in honour of the occasion, and runs the risk of not being recognised. "What have you done with the real Mick Hunt?", asks one jovial wag.

As the start gets closer, the stands fill and there is not a spare seat in the house. Lord's is a glorious sight when packed, full of colour and chatter and anticipation. Unlike the other English Test grounds, there's no-one to lead the crowd in community singing of *Jerusalem*, the adopted English anthem – they don't do that kind of thing here – but the large video screens show clips of the England playing, superimposed with Blake's famous words should anyone wish to sing along gently to themselves. This corner of England is certainly a green and pleasant land today. The guest bell-ringer, Sanjay Manjrekar, sounds the bell and the Lord's hum rises eagerly in prospect of a full day's entertainment. Truly, it's for days like this that we suffer days like Thursday and Friday.

Alastair Cook, England's record run-scorer, walks out purposefully, while Keaton Jennings wiggles and jiggles to loosen his limbs. He's under pressure, like all of Cook's partners have been since Andrew Strauss retired in 2012. Jennings is the 11th man to partner Cook in those six years, a statistic that tells a tale, and his place is by no means assured. He made a century on his debut, also against India, in 2016, and a 50 in the next match, but has struggled since, garnering just over 200 runs in 11 innings. He needs a big score or two if he's not to be sent back to the county circuit like all the others.

Sharma opens the bowling, gives Cook a generous half-volley and England are off the mark to a loud cheer. Like the clouds, yesterday's swing is all but gone and the openers make an untroubled start. Jennings settles quickly and plays some nice strokes off the front foot, Cook clips crisply off his legs for early boundaries. Cook is not a showy batsman; he does not have the languid grace of a Gower, or the flamboyance of Kevin Pietersen; he accumulates rather than dazzles, but he has more resilience, born of a strength of mind that can veer towards stubbornness, than any England batsman of his generation. He has broken one record after another – and his leg, too, though even that didn't stop him scoring a hundred the next day – and if

England can't find one opener to form a partnership with him, one wonders how they'll ever find two when he retires.

Finding nothing over the wicket, Sharma moves round to the two left-handed batsmen. It works, too. He gets just a hint of movement and the hitherto comfortable Jennings is struck on his pads right in front of middle stump. It's a wicket from out of the blue, which may explain – though not excuse, for it is a shocking waste – why Cook persuades Jennings to call for a review. The decision does not take long, and confirms what everyone else in the ground knew. The Lancashire batsman makes a long, sad walk back to the changing room, and there are what sound like boos, but are in fact the guttural cries of 'R-o-o-t, R-o-o-t' that herald the arrival of his replacement. Cook welcomes his successor as captain with a magnificent cover drive but is then undone by a superb ball from Sharma and England are 32–2. Oliver Pope, a mere 20, runs out to play his first innings in Test cricket. He receives a word of encouragement from the departing Cook, falls to his knees, looks to the sky, then gets up and trots to the crease. He's never batted as early as this in a first-class innings – we're still only in the ninth over, and he bats at six for Surrey – but he plays his first ball confidently to square leg. It's not quite a Goweresque boundary from his first ball in Test cricket, but he's only one behind as he flicks his second ball beautifully off his pads to open his account. Social media is immediately buzzing, though the most frequent comparisons being made are not with Gower but with Ricky

Ponting, no less. Two balls into his career, and the young man already has a lot to live up to – but then, if anyone can bat as if divinely inspired, surely it's a Pope?

Root is beaten several times in a torrid over from Shami, who's working up a fair pace, and goes for a walk to compose himself. What looked ten minutes ago like a stroll in the sun for England has suddenly become an ordeal, and the chatter level from the Indian slip cordon intensifies. Pope, meanwhile, compact and composed, continues his impressive start, despite his tender years. In fact, he's the third 20-year-old picked by Ed Smith since he became national selector in April, suggesting he's been reading Terry Pratchett, whose character Leonard Da Quirm once requested apprentices rather than seasoned craftsmen: "I have no use for people who have learned the limits of the possible." How much has Pope not yet learned? India, meanwhile, slow the bowling rate down to an inexcusable 12 overs an hour (if the ICC wants to revive the fortunes of Test cricket, they could do a lot worse than by starting with proper action to improve over rates). It is Pandya who finally ends Pope's impressive debut, another LBW to a ball that angles in, and another wasted review too. On the stroke of lunch, Root goes the same way, trapped by a ball from Shami that keeps low, and England head off for their grilled chicken or braised halibut at 89–4. They're only 18 behind India, but on a fine morning they'll be disappointed to be four down. Not surprised, though. England's top order, despite the presence of two world-class batsmen in Cook and Root, seems incapable of building strong platforms. This is, by my reckoning, the 29th time in their last 60 innings that England's fourth wicket has gone down with fewer than 100 runs on the scoreboard. If it wasn't for their much-vaunted middle order, heaven knows how many more of those Tests they'd have lost. But why does this keep happening? Many blame Twenty20 cricket, with batsmen forgetting how to play a straight bat and focusing always on attack, and on the evidence of England's performances in recent years, it's hard to argue against the theory. Of course, scoring rates have improved out of all recognition, and it's undoubtedly made for more exciting cricket, but not necessarily more successful cricket. The England mantra of recent years has been "positive cricket", but they need to understand there's more than one way to be positive. Trying to hit every ball to the boundary might seem positive, but ultimately it has to be about winning, and scoring more runs and losing fewer wickets seems a much better way to go about doing that, even if it takes longer. Which is actually more positive – scoring 4.5 an over and being 90-4, or making 3 and over and reaching 200–3? Sound defence may not be sexy, but that doesn't mean it is negative – sometimes it's the best form of attack

Lunchtime passes with a performance from the band of the Royal Marines and the now-customary locating by the cameras of spectators in fancy dress. Some would say the cameras just need to linger on the members' pavilion to spot outlandish garb, but instead the honours go to a group of nuns, two Edwardian gents, and Chewbacca, taking time off from helping the Rebel Alliance to take in some cricket at Lord's. Lunch over, Bairstow and Buttler take up the cudgels for England, though Buttler soon departs. Ashwin finally joins the Indian attack, though there's little in the pitch for the spinners, and despite some uneven bounce and the occasional shooter, the Indian bowling is losing its bite. Bairstow, with a mix of accomplished strokes and occasional luck, keeps the runs coming and grows in authority, while Woakes picks up with the bat where he left off with the ball last night, which is to say superbly. As the two batsmen start to take control, the Indians' body language increasingly suggests resignation to a big deficit. Kuldeep comes on, lasts two ineffectual overs – India are in desperate need of a fourth seamer they don't have – and is taken off again, and Woakes starts to catch up with his partner. He pulls, cuts and drives, looking every inch a Test batsman, though plays his streakiest shot – and nearly plays on – to bring up his half century. As teatime arrives, Woakes trails Bairstow by only 7, India trail England by 123, and it's looking increasingly easy for the batsmen.

The crowd is surprisingly quiet after tea. The pre-interval football chants have died down, perhaps as people snooze off the effects of beer and sun, though clouds have gathered and there are rumours of rain on the way. Woakes, meanwhile, continues to delight. It's not often that Bairstow's batting is eclipsed, but it is today, Woakes looking full of confidence and timing his strokes with the precision of the finest Swiss watch. He moves serenely through the 70s in a single over, overtaking Bairstow in the process, and three overs later is in the 90s. He's made centuries before, but never one for England. If he feels nerves – as he must, if he is at all made of flesh and blood – he controls them well. On 94 he is beaten by a ball he'd have been better off leaving alone, and Ashwin's spin keeps the next over tight, but Woakes pulls a ball from Pandya over mid-wicket for three runs and his maiden Test century. The crowd rises as one, and Woakes removes his helmet to reveal a smile as wide as the media centre behind him. In and out of the England side, injuries have restricted Woakes to something of a peripheral figure in recent years. Despite the setbacks, he's never given up his dreams and the bear hug he receives from Bairstow, and the warm applause from the players' balcony, show just how popular a figure he is in the dressing room.

The crowd's hopes of a repeat celebration are dashed, though, when Bairstow falls 15 minutes later, caught behind after flashing at a ball from Pandya for 93. He's missed his century, but has done his job. He and Woakes have restored England's fortunes and the lead is well over 200. Many now expect Root to declare and give his fresh-as-a-daisy bowlers a few overs at the tired Indian batsmen, but in increasing gloom England press on. Discussions flare up around the ground, fuelled by a similar debate on the ever-wonderful TMS, to which thousands, me included, are listening via earphones. Some, led by Jonathan

Agnew, feel England, with terrible weather forecast for Sunday, should put India in and try to make inroads; others fear the umpires will call a halt for bad light and with the current batsmen's eyes accustomed to the gloom, England should press on. The one decision that matters is Root's, and he presses on. As does Woakes, who plunders more runs. Pandya has a tantrum when Shami fails to take a catch he was nowhere near, and between overs vents his feelings on an unfortunate advertising board. Soon after, he runs all the way to square leg to field off his own bowling and hurls a furious, if rather inaccurate, ball at the stumps, before getting into a debate over something with umpire Erasmus. India take the new ball, but as the light fades further the umpires draw stumps early, with England in command on 357–6. Though play has not been officially ended for the day, the crowd know better and drift homeward. At a crowded tube station, the debate over the non-declaration is still going on. One man, a BBC Sport lanyard round his neck, is firm of view. "If this were Australia v India", he says, "Australia would be bowling by now and India five down. England are far too conservative." He's not the first to level such a charge at England, and with heavy rain forecast – and even the prospect of another largely washed-out day – he may yet be proven right.

~~~~~~~~~~~~~~~~~~~~~~
~~~~~~~~~~~~~~~~~~~~~~

## Day 4

The rain falls steadily until well past 9 o'clock this morning. My weather app seems undecided as to how much more we'll get and when, but the rain relents sufficiently for play to start on time. It is overcast, but the clouds are high and there's even a hint of sun, enough to tempt a decent-size crowd to take their chances. That and the prospect of Indian wickets on a humid morning. Virat Kohli will have opened his hotel curtains with a sinking heart this morning. If India are somehow to claw their way back into this match, they're going to have to do it the hard way.

The expectation – nay, assumption – is that England will have declared overnight, but as Anya Shrubsole rings the bell for the morning session, it is Curran and Woakes who walk out to the audible surprise of the crowd. England's lead is already more than double India's first innings total and England may need all the time they can get to bowl the visitors out before the heavens open again. Too conservative? Few are arguing otherwise this morning. The decision looks even more bizarre when Shami and Sharma move the new ball like a banana. Woakes, whose bat was three feet wide last night, can't get anywhere near ball this morning and is repeatedly beaten all ends up. To compound things, Kohli is laid up on the physio's couch with a sore back, leaving a gaping hole in India's batting. When news comes via TMS that rain is forecast at 11.30am and will last until tomorrow, England's decision shifts from conservative to perverse, but Root's hands remain firmly in his pockets. Woakes and

Curran try some outrageous shots to force matters, but when Curran rides his luck once too often the catch is taken and England finally declare, 289 ahead.

The 11.30 rain deadline passes without a drop, and the Indian openers, Vijay and Rahul enter the arena with the air of men being fed to the lions. The beasts in question, Anderson and Broad, are straining at the leash and when it is removed, the result is predictably brutal. Anderson, fire in his eyes, strikes the first blows, removing both openers with just 13 on the board, and the crowd, hungry for blood, roar their delight. Vijay becomes his 100th wicket on this ground, and for his second duck of the match at that. At 36, Anderson's hunger for batsmen seems unsated, despite a decade and a half of feasting upon them. His record now is such as that every innings in which he bowls brings new records and milestones, and he has no thoughts of retirement just yet, it seems. Rain, and an early lunch, eventually come to the Indians' rescue, but it is a temporary reprieve. Play resumes a little before 2 o'clock. Pujara and Rahane bat sensibly, but like Canute's tide, England's bowling cannot be held back and Broad strikes, removing first Rahane and then Pujara, whose wicket is as broken as his side's hopes. Kolhi winces and grimaces his way to 17 until Broad, as irresistible in this innings as he was ineffective in the first, forces him back and he glances a catch by Pope at short leg. The crowd roaring the bowlers on, Karthik comes in, is hit on the pads by his first ball and Broad is on a hat trick. Root brings everyone in close and Broad sends down an unplayable in-swinger, but it's uncatchable too, as it races to the boundary for anti-climactic byes. There's a pantomime groan from the crowd, but they know the result is in no doubt. The rain comes back, the covers go on, and India retreat for an early tea on 66–6. It's an appropriately devilish score for the day they're having.

The break is short, and when play resumes the only question is when, rather than if, England will wrap up this match. Pandya and Ashwin bat with surprising comfort, despite a nasty blow to Pandya's hand that needs attention, but when Anderson and Woakes return to the attack the end is swift. Woakes takes his performance to Bothamesque levels, removing Pandya with his first ball, and Anderson bowls Kuldeep Yadav, who joins Vijay with a Lord's pair. Shami has some fun, but fittingly it's Woakes who seals the victory, Sharma caught in the slips. India have been bowled out twice in fewer overs than a full day's play, and it's no surprise when Kohli says he is "not very proud of the way we played."

It's been a crushing victory for England, and they will rightly celebrate. At moments like this, it seems churlish to think that there are still question marks over their top order, not to mention their away form, and the conditions throughout this match could scarcely have favoured them more. But for now, they can rejoice in an outstanding performance, the rediscovery of Woakes as a Test all-rounder, and a 2–0 lead over the world's top side.

**India first innings**

| | | | | |
|---|---|---|---|---|
| M. Vijay | b Anderson | | | 0 |
| K.L. Rahul | c Bairstow | b Anderson | | 8 |
| C.A. Pujara | | run out | | 1 |
| V. Kohli * | c Buttler | b Woakes | | 23 |
| A.M. Rahane | c Cook | b Anderson | | 18 |
| H.H. Pandya | c Buttler | b Woakes | | 11 |
| K.D. Karthik ƚ | b Curran | | | 1 |
| R. Ashwin | lbw | b Broad | | 29 |
| Kuldeep Yadav | lbw | b Anderson | | 0 |
| Mohammed Shami | not out | | | 10 |
| I. Sharma | lbw | b Anderson | | 0 |
| Extras | | 5lb, 1nb | | 6 |
| **Total** | | 35.2 overs | 10 – | 107 |

**FoW:** 1–0, 2–10, 3–15, 4–49, 5–61, 6–62, 7–84, 8–96, 9–96, 10–107

| **Bowling** | **O** | **M** | **R** | **W** |
|---|---|---|---|---|
| J.M. Anderson | 13.2 | 5 | 20 | 5 |
| S.C.J. Broad | 10 | 2 | 37 | 1 |
| C.R. Woakes | 6 | 2 | 19 | 2 |
| S.M. Curran | 6 | 0 | 26 | 1 |

**England first innings**

| | | | | |
|---|---|---|---|---|
| A.N. Cook | c Karthik | b Sharma | | 21 |
| K.K. Jennings | lbw | b Mohammed Shami | | 11 |
| J.E. Root * | lbw | b Mohammed Shami | | 19 |
| O.J. Pope | lbw | b Pandya | | 28 |
| J.M. Bairstow ƚ | c Karthik | b Pandya | | 93 |
| J.C. Buttler | lbw | b Mohammed Shami | | 24 |
| C.R. Woakes | not out | | | 137 |
| S.M. Curran | c M. Shami | b Pandya | | 40 |
| Extras | | 11b, 10lb, 1nb, 1w | | 23 |
| **Total** | | 88.1 overs | 7 – | 396 dec. |

**FoW:** 1–28, 2–32, 3–77, 4–89, 5–131, 6–320, 7–396, 8–96, 9–96, 10–107

Did not bat: A.U. Rashid, S.C.J. Broad, J.M. Anderson

| **Bowling** | **O** | **M** | **R** | **W** |
|---|---|---|---|---|
| I. Sharma | 22 | 4 | 101 | 1 |
| Mohammed Shami | 23 | 4 | 96 | 3 |
| Kuldeep Yadav | 9 | 1 | 44 | 0 |
| H.H. Pandya | 17.1 | 0 | 66 | 3 |
| R. Ashwin | 17 | 1 | 68 | 0 |

**India second innings**

| | | | |
|---|---|---|---|
| M. Vijay | c Bairstow | b Anderson | 0 |
| K.L. Rahul | lbw | b Anderson | 10 |
| C.A. Pujara | b Broad | | 17 |
| A.M. Rahane | c Jennings | b Broad | 13 |
| V. Kohli * | c Pope | b Broad | 17 |
| H.H. Pandya | lbw | b Woakes | 26 |
| K.D. Karthik † | lbw | b Broad | 0 |
| R. Ashwin | not out | | 33 |
| Kuldeep Yadav | b Anderson | | 0 |
| Mohammed Shami | lbw | b Anderson | 0 |
| I. Sharma | c Pope | b Woakes | 2 |
| Extras | | 6b, 6lb | 12 |
| **Total** | | 47 overs | 10 – 130 |

**FoW:** 1–0, 2–13, 3–35, 4–50, 5–61, 6–61, 7–116, 8–121, 9–125, 10–130

| **Bowling** | **O** | **M** | **R** | **W** |
|---|---|---|---|---|
| J.M. Anderson | 12 | 5 | 23 | 4 |
| S.C.J. Broad | 16 | 6 | 44 | 4 |
| C.R. Woakes | 10 | 2 | 24 | 2 |
| S.M. Curran | 9 | 1 | 27 | 0 |

**Toss:** England elected to field. **Umpires**: A. Dar, M. Erasmus
**England win by an innings and 159 runs**

The floodlights shine brightly on one of the few dismal days of 2018 – thank goodness for the Lord's drainage system

Captain Joe Root has last-minute discussions with Jimmy Anderson before play starts against India in the Second Test at Lord's. Anderson will feast on Indian batsmen before the day is done.

Cricket under a sky John Constable could have painted. Has any activity ever captured the essence of a country in the way cricket does in England?

# Chapter Twelve

## The Village Match

Barley CC v Buntingford CC
Smiths End Lane, Barley, Hertfordshire,
Saturday 25 August

Barley Cricket Club nestles contentedly in the rolling Hertfordshire countryside. It is reached by a narrow, winding lane, along which stand whitewashed dwellings with roses round the door, large houses with larger driveways, thatched cottages painted in the deep pink favoured round these parts, and farms with flint walls and smart barn conversions. The ground itself lies between two halves of the village, in open country atop a hill. It means there is no village green, duckpond or pub to provide a quaint, picture postcard backdrop, but the location does offers views of English countryside that stretch for miles. Gaze across from the compact, clapboard pavilion and the eye sees farms and spires and villages far below, cosily wrapped up in a patchwork quilt of fields, all full of bales of hay that vie to catch the golden sunlight of late summer.

In short, Barley is the sort of place where village cricket has been played for centuries, as deeply rooted in life here as the oaks and beeches and sycamores that line the ground. Even the names of the two villages meeting today are unmistakably English, conjuring up images of summer crops and wild birds and babbling brooks. When a biplane, presumably from the nearby Duxford Air Museum, flies over, you really could be forgiven for thinking that Miss Marple lives in one of those thatched cottages down the lane and the adjoining fields were harvested by men with pitchforks and shire horses and flagons of cider. It's a place to warm John Major's heart.

The trees that border the ground are just starting to lose their summer lustre, giving way to the first hints of autumn. After a long, fine summer, it seems hard to imagine that, suddenly, the cricket season, at least for amateurs, is nearly at an end. For the professionals, there is a long way to go – there are two Test matches to be played, and we have a full third of the Championship to go. But for many club and village teams, next weekend will see them pack away their bats and pads, hang up their helmets, and ponder the prospect of the coming winter. Already, many will be shuddering at the thought of rooms to be painted, shelves to be put up, gadgets to be repaired and a myriad of other tasks that they've been able to avoid since April. But for now, like the farmers who work the neighbouring fields, they can make hay while the sun shines.

Of course, no self-respecting English village is without its peculiar little quirks, and one is immediately apparent. Barley and Buntingford, despite being deep in Hertfordshire, play in the Cambridgeshire and Huntingdonshire Premier League – in CCA Senior League Division 2, to be precise. They could both do with a win today as well, to ease any lingering fears of playing in Division 3 next season. Buntingford bat first, the opening batsmen eschewing helmets for traditional caps. In another fine nod to tradition, they've arrived with only ten men, and anxiously await the arrival of the missing colleague. The only clue to the existence of the 21st century is the glove punch the openers swap before taking guard.

The Barley bowler, de Souza, is given the unwelcome task of bowling up the hill – no Lord's-like slope but a serious climb – and his first ball is crashed away for four, beating not just the fielders but the trees as well, escaping into the field beyond. A search party eventually retrieves it, the bowler runs in again and the batsman takes a wild swing at his next delivery, accompanied by a loud cry of "Ya-oow" as it hares past him. There's plenty of clapping and words of encouragement from the Barley skipper, and the sudden activity attracts the interest of a pony in the adjacent paddock. He wanders idly up to the fence, swishes his tail and considers proceedings before deciding, Eeyore-like, that there's nothing to see here. "We can't all", I hope he says to himself, "and some of us don't".

Buntingford's opener, Caine, is scoring almost exclusively in boundaries. A huge six briefly threatens to endanger the safety one of the succession of small aeroplanes flying over the ground, before landing in the next field, prompting an exasperated cry of "Come on, keep it up!" from a fielder in wraparound sunglasses. While that's going on, the missing eleventh player finally arrives and heads to the pavilion as fast as his heavy kitbag will allow. "Who brought you?", he's asked. "Rachel Riley". "Ha, you wish!" The first wicket falls, and there's a nervous exchange of "yes…no…yes…come on" as the partnership finds its feet. De Souza is toiling with his burden but bowls a succession of full tosses, all summarily despatched by Caine before a huge six lodges the ball firmly in one of the trees. While a lengthy search and rescue exercise ensues, one of the Barley players takes some rest. "Getting in the sun are you Tommy, you cheeky bugger?" The recumbent Tommy replies that he's just got back from Cornwall and needs to top up his tan. "You not here for the dinner dance?", his colleague enquires. "Why's that – you on tour?". The ball finally located, play resumes. There's another big heave and this time the boundary is cut off, just inside the ropes, only for the fielder to be advised the batsmen have run five anyway.

In front of the pavilion, the players have other matters on the mind. "I see a new swingers' club has opened. Thursday nights is ménage-a-trois". "You going then?" "Dress code says 'no ripped jeans' – I thought they'd be down to less than that! Though what threw me more was it's just off the A1".

The adventurous world of the Great North Road uncovered, there's a change of bowler, as Barley look to slow the run rate. "'Owzat?", cries the new bowler. "Not out", replies the umpire. The Barley fielders stick their hands back in the pockets and walk back to their marks, only to hear the bowler, arms still aloft, cry out "Owzat?" once more. The second appeal is no more successful than the first, and was never likely to be, given that the umpire is one of the Buntingford players. The two batsmen are flying along, and while the scoreboard lags behind play a bit, depending on which player gets roped into updating it, they've reached well over 60 after 20 overs. "We'll have taken this start" says one of their colleagues.

When another mighty pull by Chambers deposits the ball once more into the upper branches of a tree, there's much staring and scratching of heads, before someone eventually clambers up and dislodges it, to a deserving round of applause from those on the ground. The pavilion discussion, on Arsenal's prospects for the forthcoming season without the departed Arsene Wenger, is disturbed when Caine strikes a fine on-drive, and the scorer announces he has reached his 50, prompting applause and encouragement. Drinks are taken, but despite Caine's best effort, they do not produce a wicket as the fielder drops a straightforward catch, and the silence that follows speaks volumes. Finally, though, Barley's skipper tempts Caine to try another hoik and he mistimes his shot. Doggett takes the catch, Wakeel skips down the pitch doing a passable Irish jig and Buntingford are 112–2. "Interesting pitch out there",

Caine declares on his return to his colleagues. “Testing.” Well, he’s made 63, so he’s come through the test pretty well. Ominously, though, to the southwest, dark, heavy clouds are gathering, like an army assembling before a battle. Rumours circulate of thunderstorms on the way, the branches in the trees start swaying in a sudden stiff breeze, and heavy rain falls in the distance, though thankfully skirts the ground. Chambers is picking the ball off his legs for fun and he too soon passes 50. Another ball is lost, deep in the undergrowth, and this time a posse of children in the pavilion are despatched to find it.

The rain continues to lurk menacingly, but its threats prove empty. Soon, though it is raining wickets instead, as Barley suddenly seize the initiative. In the space of six balls, three wickets fall, two of them to de Souza. Among the casualties is Chambers, who’s played a fine innings. “Great knock Chippy – shit ball”, says a teammate in sympathy, but Barley are cock-a-hoop. Flaherty and Garner stop the collapse and make steady, if sluggish, progress until the latter goes for an agricultural swing and his stumps are spread-eagled behind him. The new batsman, Coote, is the youngster of the side, and receives plenty of advice. “Keep it straight George”; “Proper shots George, keep ‘em working, mate”. Whether he’s heeding their advice or just playing his own game, he does indeed play some proper shots, and he and Flaherty take their side past 200, Coote eventually reaching a well-made 23. He’s warmly received as he walks back, his colleagues perhaps mindful of the high teenage drop-out rate in club cricket and keen to encourage him to stay. A few minutes later Buntingford complete their allotted overs, setting Barley 230 to win. There are plenty of boundaries to be had, at least on one side of the ground, but the bounce is uneven. Both sides will still fancy their chances.

As tea is taken, I look around and think about the number of towns and villages where this scene is being repeated at this very moment. Sadly, the answer is a lot fewer than used to be the case. Cricket on the green may evoke a timeless image of England, but time may, in fact, be running out for it. The sad fact is that all around the country, clubs are folding at an alarming rate. An ECB survey four years ago showed an alarming decline in the number of people playing cricket, from 908,000 in 2013 to 844,000 a year later[10]. Perhaps more worryingly, only 247,000 of those were what were described as 'core' cricketers, those willing and able to play at least 12 weeks across the season. The figures from Sport England's Active Lives survey were scarcely better, showing a decline in the number of people playing the game at least twice a month, from 364,600 in 2016, to 291,900 in May 2018[11].

Of course, it's easy to make too much of one survey, or one season's figures, when things like bad weather can skew results. But anecdotally, the picture looks grim. Not only are fewer people playing the game, but there are fewer

---

[10] www.espncricinfo.com/england/content/story/801645.html

[11] www.sportengland.org/research/about-our-research/active-people-survey/

teams for whom they can play, as clubs fold or merge. In 2008, 380 teams participated in the National Club Championship. This year, just 220 have entered. So what is behind this trend? Perhaps the most obvious answer is that people today are time poor. Not so long ago, many people could easily give up a whole Saturday or Sunday every week to play cricket, but today, that's a luxury far fewer can afford. For most couples, both partners now work, which means weekends have to be filled with shopping, DIY and other household chores, things that previously could have been done in the week by a non-working partner. And with children's social lives far more crowded than a generation ago, many parents become taxi services at the weekend, ferrying their offspring from football match to riding lesson, music class to sleepover. The one thing they don't seem to be doing is taking their children to play cricket. The ECB All-Stars campaign might be getting five to eight-year-olds to pick up bats and balls, but when they get to their teens, they're dropping them again. The teenage drop-out rate at cricket clubs is a particularly serious problem. The ECB's National Playing Survey in 2013 calculated that 40% of 16–19-year-olds who play more than 12 weeks a season quit playing by 19[12]. And that's on top of a more general decline in participation – another survey suggests only about one in eight 11–15-year-olds plays any cricket at all, let alone for a club[13]. All-Stars Cricket may be

---

[12] http://nsscpcl.org/wp-content/uploads/2014/08/StayInTheGame.pdf
[13] www.statista.com/statistics/421078/cricket-sport-involvment-children-england-uk/

proving successful with younger children, but unless it's followed up with older kids, it could well prove, ultimately, to be a wasted opportunity.

On top of that, there are social and cultural changes within the game. Fewer clubs run friendly teams nowadays, but there are plenty of players, or potential players, who just want to enjoy a game with mates and a few laughs, and not have the pressure of competitive league cricket. And, for a host of personal, social and cultural reasons, there are more players today for whom the traditional boozy after-match session in the pub does not appeal, and so that aspect of the game is changing too. That may not be a bad thing, in this case, but it is another chip in the tradition of club cricket that the game must overcome. Faced with all these pressures in a changing society, what can clubs do about it? Many now play Twenty20, at least in midweek, which can help players squeeze cricket into their schedules, and many clubs are trying hard to maintain active youth sides. But with no prospects of people gaining more spare free hours in their lives any time soon, the traditional weekend game, starting around midday and finishing in the early evening, then carrying on over beers in the village pub, may well be doomed.

I try to put such depressing thoughts to one side, and focus on the game in hand. Some of the Barley players have gone to the pitch with a large brush with a long-curved handle that looks like it should have Nimbus 3000 in gold lettering down the side. An impromptu game of Quidditch fails to materialise, however, and, pitch repaired,

Buntingford take to the field. Without wanting to cast doubts on Barley's abilities, the visitors, it has to be said, look considerably the trimmer and more athletic of the sides. The umpires come out, one clad in the sort of long, old-fashioned lab coat that I've not seen in years, the other fighting, not altogether successfully, to get into a more modern jacket that's several sizes too small for him. Buntingford set an attacking field: three slips, a gully and a silly point. Chambers, recovered from his exertions with the bat, opens the bowling, Edward Whybrow and Tom Doggett doing the batting honours for Barley. The innings is less than an over old before confusion sets in as the umpires, more used to playing, lose count. "How many balls to come?", they ask the scorers. Buntingford strike in the next over, when Doggett is bowled for 4, and more confusion follows. "What's the score?", ask the batsmen. "13–1", comes the reply. Minutes later the request comes back. "What's the score – scoreboard please!". "We just did it" protests one of the Barley players, who's reluctantly on scoreboard duty. "It says 33–1, we haven't got that many". He surveys the scoreboard glumly and realises the error. "Alright", he shouts back, "leave me alone".

The score, whatever it is, matters little to the players with their feet up on the pavilion balcony, where one is being quizzed on his domestic affairs. "How long have you been engaged then?", he's asked. "Eight years." "Eight years?!" his teammate replies, shaking his head in disbelief, "eight years and you haven't set a date yet?".

Seven overs in and the second wicket goes down as the captain, Wakeel Shah, departs. Jameel Shah quickly follows and Barley are 43–3. Buntingford looking chirpy and Chambers, who's dismissed both the Shahs, stands menacingly at the end of his run. Whybrow decides attack is the best form of defence and drives a huge six over the bowler's head, to the evident delight of the umpire who raises both arms aloft not once but three times, each time higher than previous effort. When Whybrow is joined by Shafi Ullah, the pair quickly take control and the Buntingford bowling, which had made such a promising start, is plundered. The batsman match each other with one lusty blow after another, Buntingford spread their field, and one of the umpires comes over to speak with some of the players watching from the boundary. Gloomily, he informs them his team are unhappy with the quality of umpiring and have requested a change, but no-one rushes to relieve him.

It matters little, as runs flow and Buntingford see the game disappearing, like the far side of the ground. over the hill and far away. No matter where Buntingford position their fielders, Barley find the gaps. One mighty blow strikes a tree directly, showering a fielder standing nearby with leaves, and the scorers remind the chuckling umpires to signal a six. Eventually, with the score on 151, Whybrow is undone, bowled while going for another big strike. He walks off with the air of a man who has blown his entire fortune on the wrong call at a roulette table. There was certainly a century there for the taking, but he and his partner have done enough to secure the game. With ten overs to go, Barley need only 46 more. "Come, on", cries a Buntingford fielder, rallying his troops for a doomed mission, "to the end". With more objects flying through the skies between midwicket and deep square leg than over Duxford, the end will come soon.

As afternoon turns into early evening, the clouds give way to sunshine, and the fields beyond take on soft, golden hues that matching the colour of the ancient church in the next village. It forms a timeless backdrop to the figures in white running around on the hilltop. For all the changes in society, and in cricket, there are some images that endure through the ages. Were Mary Russell Mitford, who wrote such a memorable description of a village match in her book *Our Village*, to stand here today and gaze on this scene, there is little she would find unfamiliar, save for the helmets (though whether she would still write, as she did in 1824, of sobriety being one of the chief habits of a cricketer is another matter).

My drifting thoughts are interrupted by the cries of one of the batsmen, who has ventured to within earshot of the scorers. "Shafi wants to know his score", he says. "No he doesn't", they reply. "Er, he does", argues the puzzled batsman, "he's just asked." The reply is firm; "No, he really doesn't, we know what he's like". Shafi is, it transpires, on 93, and Barley need ten. When he adds a mere single and de Souza strikes a four, the equation is simpler – six to win, six for a century. He drives through the covers in search of another boundary, but the ball is stopped by a fielder. His return, though, is wild, well wide of the wicketkeeper, and the ball runs away for four extras. “Shambolic”, says a disgruntled colleague. There’s a rare forward defensive stroke to the next ball, before Shafi drives the next. This time it reaches the boundary and Barley have the win, but Shafi is left on 98. He’s played beautifully, and deserved a hundred, but he has helped take his side to a win that takes them to safety. For Buntingford, the result leaves them too near the bottom for safety. Many nails may yet be bitten between now and the end of the season.

Barley Cricket Club presents a timeless scene of rural English life, yet one that has disappeared from many villages.

**Buntingford CC**

| | | | | |
|---|---|---|---|---|
| A. Williams | c Whybrow | b Wakeel Shah | | 8 |
| S. Caine | c Doggett | b Jameel Shah | | 63 |
| C. Chambers | c Ullah | b Doggett | | 75 |
| M. Townsend * ŧ | | b de Souza | | 5 |
| M. King | lbw | b de Souza | | 4 |
| T. Faherty | | b Doggett | | 16 |
| G. Garner | | b de Souza | | 11 |
| G. Coote | | b Doggett | | 23 |
| A. West | not out | | | 6 |
| O. Garrett | not out | | | 1 |
| Extras | | 14b 1lb 1nb 1w | | 17 |
| **Total** | | 45 overs | 8 – | 229 |

**FoW:** 1–29, 2–112, 3–153, 4–157, 5–157, 6–188, 7–216, 8–226
Did not bat: O. James

| **Bowling** | **O** | **M** | **R** | **W** |
|---|---|---|---|---|
| W Shah | 9 | 3 | 31 | 1 |
| De Souza | 9 | 0 | 58 | 3 |
| J Shah | 9 | 2 | 18 | 1 |
| S Ullah | 9 | 1 | 48 | 0 |
| T. Doggett | 7 | 0 | 38 | 3 |
| B. Symes | 1 | 0 | 14 | 0 |
| E. Whybrow | 1 | 0 | 7 | 0 |

**Barley CC**

| | | | | |
|---|---|---|---|---|
| E. Whybrow | | b James | | 77 |
| T. Doggett | | b Garner | | 4 |
| W. Shah | c Caine | b Chambers | | 8 |
| J. Shah | c West | b Chambers | | 4 |
| S. Ullah | not out | | | 98 |
| J. de Souza * | not out | | | 37 |
| Extras | | 4w | | 4 |
| **Total** | | 41.5 overs | 4 – | 232 |

**FoW:** 1–12, 2–29, 3–43, 4–151
Did not bat: B. Symes, D. Ambrose, N. Butler, K. Markham, A. Pattison ŧ

| **Bowling** | **O** | **M** | **R** | **W** |
|---|---|---|---|---|
| Chambers | 9 | 1 | 45 | 2 |
| Garner | 8 | 0 | 49 | 1 |
| West | 3 | 0 | 27 | 0 |
| James | 9 | 0 | 50 | 1 |
| Caine | 9 | 1 | 31 | 0 |
| Williams | 3 | 0 | 26 | 0 |
| Faherty | 0.3 | 0 | 4 | 0 |

**Toss:** Barley CC elected to bat. **Umpires:** Various
**Barley CC win by six wickets**

# Chapter Thirteen

## The Disability Cricket Super 9s final

Derbyshire Merlins Disability CC
v Essex Disability CC
Kidderminster Cricket Ground
Sunday 2 September

Kidderminster Cricket Club's ground is abuzz with activity as I arrive. Groups of players are practising, the pitch is being thoroughly attended to, and spectators are milling around, chatting and laying claim to the benches that ring the playing area. The pretty, black and white timbered pavilion, with its hanging baskets of brightly coloured petunias and lobelia, looks a picture in the sunshine. Despite the gentle breeze that takes the edge of the late summer heat, the tall beeches and sycamores that edge the ground stand still and serene. They used to play Championship cricket here, though not since 2007, and only then because the New Road ground was undergoing its annual springtime transformation into a lido. The same year, Loughborough's students pulled off a rare win over the professionals, but were less successful in 2008 in the final first-class match at the ground.

I have not seen a game of disability cricket before, and if I'm being honest, I'm not sure what to expect. Like many, my eyes were opened to disability sport during the 2012 London Paralympics. The Games did so much to alert people to the high quality of disability sport, and the realisation that it is played by top-class athletes who just happen to have a disability alongside a huge amount of ability. Even so, disability cricket has largely remained off my radar. While the likes of David Weir, Jonnie Peacock, Tanni Grey-Thompson and Hannah Cockcroft have become household names, cricket, not yet a Paralympic sport, has had a lower profile. But things may be changing. Earlier this summer, while listening to a Twenty20 match on BBC Five Live, I heard an interview with Ian Salisbury, the former England leg spinner and now Head Coach of the England Physical Disability Cricket team. The interview came ahead of the England disability side's triangular series against Pakistan and Bangladesh. I was out of the country at the time of the tournament, and so find myself here today instead.

I find a bench and am soon joined by a couple who introduce themselves as George and Mary, down from Derbyshire for the match. They ask me which team I'm supporting, and seem surprised when I say I'm a neutral. There's a tangible sense of a community here today – everyone seems to know everyone else, with many greetings of old friends – and as a new face I am an object of slight, albeit friendly, curiosity. George, it transpires, was a player himself and, I think he's rather itching to be playing today. He introduces me to Bill Higginson, who is sporting an ECB shirt. Bill is involved in the British Association for Cricketers with Disabilities (modestly, he does not mention that, as I later discover, he is actually the President and played first-class cricket for Middlesex). The BACD has overseen the growth of disability cricket in this country, but this year it is handing over the reins to the ECB. It is the first time a national governing body has taken on responsibility for the disabled game, which I hope is a sign of its progress rather than a lust for power. From a handful of teams twenty years ago, there are now 31 active counties, with the county cricket boards doing much to drive the growth. The game is rapidly growing at international level too, where there are four impairment groups, for those with visual impairments, hearing difficulties, physical disabilities and learning disabilities. That said, George tells me the level of commitment varies from one county to another. Essex CCC have sent a whole posse of coaches, who are striding around purposefully in official County kit, and a look at their website and social media output reveals the strength of their commitment to disability cricket. The lack of coaches sent by Derbyshire, in contrast, is, I am told, "a disgrace", and there are murmurings of some counties doing enough to tick the boxes without really being committed. That's clearly not a charge that can be levelled at Essex County Cricket Club, and congratulations to them for it.

Today's contest, the Super 9s, is an 'entry level' for those looking to play or coach competitively. To my surprise, it features players with a mix of disabilities, some physical, others learning-related. The Super 9s has been around since 1999, when Lancashire were the dominant side, winning five of the first six championships. This year's tournament featured 14 counties split into four groups. Essex, the defending champions, saw off Shropshire in their semi-final, while Derbyshire, winners in 2015 and 2016, defeated Somerset to set up today's encounter. There are, of course, some variations to the laws of the game for Super 9s cricket. The ball weighs the same as a regulation ball but is not quite as hard, and there are options available to teams such as the length of a game, the distance to the boundary, and the number of players in a team – today's match will have eight wickets a side. There are restrictions, too, on the number of runs and wickets players can make or take before they have to retire, in order to ensure one or two players do not dominate, but for the most part, the actual play follows the regular laws.

Derbyshire win the toss and put Essex in to bat. The Merlins open the bowling with Chamath Wickramarachchi, an IT specialist with one arm and a relentlessly accurate line and length that immediately causes problems for the Essex batsmen. Saville is quickly out leg before for nought, and runs from Wickramarachchi's bowling are few and far between. George tells me the impressive bowler is in his first season with Derbyshire, having been signed from Yorkshire where he lives, and they're very keen to keep hold of him. I can see why. At the other end, a couple of boundaries off Gillott steady the nerves, and there's nearly a third from a beautiful off-drive by Joe Freestone. A Derbyshire fielder gets down well and stops it just inside the rope, but in doing so injures his leg. Just as the physio reaches him, he gets up and half-trots, half hobbles back to his position. "I think he thought I was going to kiss him!" jokes the physio. "I'd get up and run off too if I thought you were going to kiss me!", replies a spectator on crutches. Kisses or no, the fielder fails in his bid to carry on, and limps off at the end of the over, his fielding duties done for the day. Wickramarachchi strikes again, bowling Hazel with a ball that was quick and kept low, and Essex are 29–2, though Derbyshire will need to keep an eye on the extras that are accumulating.

Freestone, the young Essex batsman, is playing beautifully, with correct technique and elegant strokeplay befitting his county's 2017 Ability Player of the Year. His partner, Martyn Doe, taller and ponytailed, and with a bat seemingly held together only by the tape wrapped copiously around it, cuts the ball strongly through the covers. A few catches go down, to the frustration of the Derbyshire supporters, runs start to come more rapidly, and when drinks are taken, Essex have a solid-looking 86–2 on the board. But, with the score just nudging three figures, the excellent Freestone is well caught low down by Darkins for 33. It's a timely wicket, as he was just starting to cut loose. The new man in, Flowers, is immediately in the thick of it, surviving a loud and prolonged run out appeal. He quickly starts scoring runs, and he and Doe have put on another 29 when Doe is caught, putting a smile as wide as the pitch on the face of the bowler, Martin Taylor. Derbyshire's wicketkeeper, who has two artificial knees and plays for his local able-bodied team as well, leans forward, hands on knees, head down, and blows hard.

More catches are missed – Derbyshire have had five good opportunities now that they may rue later. Their followers know that catches win matches, and offer plenty of words of vocal advice. Wickramarachchi, who looks a very useful cricketer, shows how it's done to end Aust's innings, but Flowers is taking full advantage of Derbyshire's profligacy, pulling a loose ball from Jones to the ropes to reach a fine, if not chanceless, 50. Having achieved his half century, he has to retire, and the Derbyshire players watch him depart with some relief. Wickramarachchi, too, has to be withdrawn from action when Fryett becomes his third victim, the score on 173. With the 30th over approaching, Coles and Gibbons have little time to get going, and the Essex innings closes on 187–7. No fewer than 47 of those are extras, and Derbyshire have effectively given Essex an extra batsman or two. With the dropped catches as well, they've made things hard for themselves if they're to reclaim the title, and their supporters are concerned.

Bill has kindly invited me to share lunch in the pavilion. Armed with a plateful of sandwiches and cake, I am introduced to Paul Roe, who founded Derbyshire's disabled cricket club after his own able-bodied side took on a team of disabled cricketers from across the border in Nottinghamshire and were roundly beaten. That was in 2004, and he's still heavily involved in the club today. For the first two years, the club never won a game, but they set themselves small targets for improvement. In their third year they batted a complete forty overs for the first time, and claimed their first win at the end of that season. Further gradual improvements followed, and by 2015 they were national club champions. Today they have around forty players and play twenty-odd matches a year, more than most of the other county disability sides. But triumphs aren't just measured in terms of wins and trophies. "We are, first and foremost, a cricket team. But, we've had a player who, when he started, couldn't catch a ball from one metre. Now, he can catch from six metres. That's a triumph for him. We've another player who doesn't like talking and struggles to interact with people, but since he's been playing cricket he's had to shout 'yes, no, wait' and has become more vocal and confident". Indeed, confidence building is, Paul tells me, one of the biggest benefits that participation in disability cricket can bring. "For a lot of these players, they were used to being excluded, not being able to take part in sport. Now they are able to be part of a team and enjoy the camaraderie that comes with that. It's a steep learning curve for some, but also offers a massive boost to their self-esteem and confidence." That said, there's real cricketing ability here too. Derbyshire have one disabled cricketer, Jamie

Goodwin, who is not only part of the England squad but plays Premiership-level club cricket too.

If Derbyshire are to win today, though, they will need to muster all of that ability and come out of the blocks fighting. Instead, the Essex opening bowlers send down a succession of tightly bowled overs, and the earlier fears of the Derbyshire followers are justified. Just five runs are conceded from the first three overs, and the start of the fourth sees Darkins back in the pavilion for a duck. Doe, running in from the pavilion end, ponytail streaming behind him, is too quick for the Derbyshire batsmen to handle, though perhaps trying a little too hard for pace and chalking up a few wides. At the other end, Fryett is desperate for a wicket after two, admittedly optimistic, leg-before appeals are turned down. When a third beats the static batsman and gets the same response from the umpire, the bowler slumps to his knees and looks to the heavens as if in supplication. Deflated, his bowling loses a bit of discipline. "We don't bowl well to right-hand, left-hand combos", laments one of his coaches. This triggers a conversation about the importance of partnerships in disability cricket, where having the right support at the other end of the pitch can, it seems, make a huge difference to a batsman's mindset and concentration.

In contrast to Derbyshire, Essex are as nimble in the field as they were running between the wickets. "There seem to be more of them", grumbles a Derbyshire fan, and it's understandable; they have far fewer gaps in their field, and for all their strokes and pushes and nudges, the Derbyshire batsmen, Theobald and Jones, can't get the innings going. Essex change their bowling, and Ben Aust prowls like a young Stuart Broad while repairs are carried out on one of the batsmen, who has scraped his arm diving for the crease. He soon gets his man, too, taking a fine catch off his own bowling to remove Theobald. Jones's stubborn resistance ends next ball and he throws his bat away in disgust. When Arthur falls for a duck, there's a loud sigh from a Derbyshire supporter. "Goodnight Irene", he says, simply, and it's hard to disagree.

Donovan comes on to bowl for Essex. As a wheelchair user, he can deliver the ball from outside the crease, closer to the batsman. His appearance prompts a groan from George. It's the hardest thing to bat against someone in a wheelchair", he says. "He gets to bowl from much closer and if you hit him you get no sympathy – but he's trying to bowl me out!". That's not the only problem Donovan poses for batsmen. His delivery suggests he's a right-hander, but he actually bowls with his left arm. It's his own version of the wrong 'un, and it works. Hopkins, still playing himself in, looks understandably confused and is beaten with successive balls. Whale, meanwhile, picks up two quick wickets, both ducks, and when Ben Aust gets his third the match is all but over. He clean bowls Charlie Harrison with a full toss, though that's not how the batsman sees it as he comes off. "I tell you, a bouncer, then onto the pegs…". Two spectators cast a knowing glance at each other but prudently decide its best not to disagree with a batsman when he's just got out and still has his bat in his hands. Donovan goes around the wicket and still proves hard to hit away. "Just ping one straight back at 'im, that's what I'd do", says George, but his advice goes unheard, or at least unheeded. It's up to James Cole to seal the title for Essex when he bowls Harrison Jones and wheels away with a jubilant, triumphant, yell. Derbyshire, long since resigned to defeat, take it sportingly. "Well", says one of their players phlegmatically, "we just need to improve for next year".

After that, there are presentations, the reins of disability cricket are formally handed over to the ECB, and there are well-deserved thanks for Bill and his team for the work they have done to get disability cricket in the healthy shape it's in today. It's been one of the most enjoyable afternoons of cricket of my season, and an eye opener into a form of cricket that deserves a wider audience. "I know people who've played cricket for 20, 30 years and don't know about disability cricket", says Paul. I confess that, until today, I was one of them. I hope the ECB and Counties continue to drive it forward – perhaps into the Paralympics? – and keep on board the small army of volunteers like Bill and Paul who do so much to enable others to play the game. It's fitting to leave the last word to Bill. "It's cricket", he tells me, "as it is meant to be played".

**Essex Disabled CC**

| | | | | |
|---|---|---|---|---|
| B. Saville | lbw | b Wickramarachchi | | 0 |
| M. Hazel † | | b Wickramarachchi | | 15 |
| J. Freestone | c Darkins | b H. Jones | | 33 |
| M. Doe | c Arthur | b Taylor | | 18 |
| J. Flowers | retired not out | | | 51 |
| B. Aust | c Wickrama'chi | b C. Jones | | 12 |
| B. Fryett | | b Wickramarachchi | | 4 |
| J Coles | not out | | | 1 |
| B. Gibbons | not out | | | 6 |
| Extras | | 8b 2lb 13nb 24w | | 47 |
| **Total** | | 30 overs | 6 – | 187 |

**FoW:** 1–2, 2–29, 3–98, 4–127, 5–169, 6–173
Did not bat: J. Whale, B. Donovan *

| **Bowling** | **O** | **M** | **R** | **W** |
|---|---|---|---|---|
| C. Wickramarachchi | 5.3 | 1 | 10 | 3 |
| A. Gillott | 2 | 0 | 19 | 0 |
| A. Darkins | 6 | 1 | 29 | 0 |
| H. Jones | 6 | 0 | 43 | 1 |
| C. Jones | 6 | 0 | 39 | 1 |
| M. Taylor | 4 | 0 | 37 | 1 |
| C. Harrison | 0.3 | 0 | 0 | 0 |
| Fielding extras | | | 10 | |

**Derbyshire Merlins Disabled CC**

| | | | | |
|---|---|---|---|---|
| C. Theobald | | c&b Aust | | 12 |
| A. Darkins | | b Doe | | 0 |
| C. Jones | c Aust | b Whale | | 23 |
| M. Hopkins | c Doe | b Aust | | 14 |
| K. Owen | c Aust | b Whale | | 0 |
| J. Arthur | lbw | b Whale | | 0 |
| A. Gillott | not out | | | 30 |
| C. Harrison | b Aust | | | 10 |
| H. Jones | b Coles | | | 8 |
| Extras | | 1b 8nb 24w | | 33 |
| **Total** | | 30 overs | 8 – | 135 |

**FoW:** 1–5, 2–29, 3–53, 4–62, 5–87, 6–87, 7–114, 8–125
Did not bat: C. Wickramarachchi, D. Arthur

| Bowling | O | M | R | W |
|---|---|---|---|---|
| B. Fryatt | 5 | 1 | 15 | 0 |
| M. Doe | 5 | 0 | 26 | 0 |
| B. Aust | 5.1 | 0 | 32 | 3 |
| J. Whale | 2.2 | 0 | 13 | 3 |
| B. Gibbons | 0.5 | 0 | 9 | 0 |
| B. Donovan | 3 | 0 | 21 | 0 |
| J. Coles | 1.3 | 0 | 18 | 1 |
| Fielding extras | | | 1 | |

**Toss:** Derbyshire Merlins elected to bowl. **Umpires:** Not known
**Essex Disabled CC win by 52 runs**

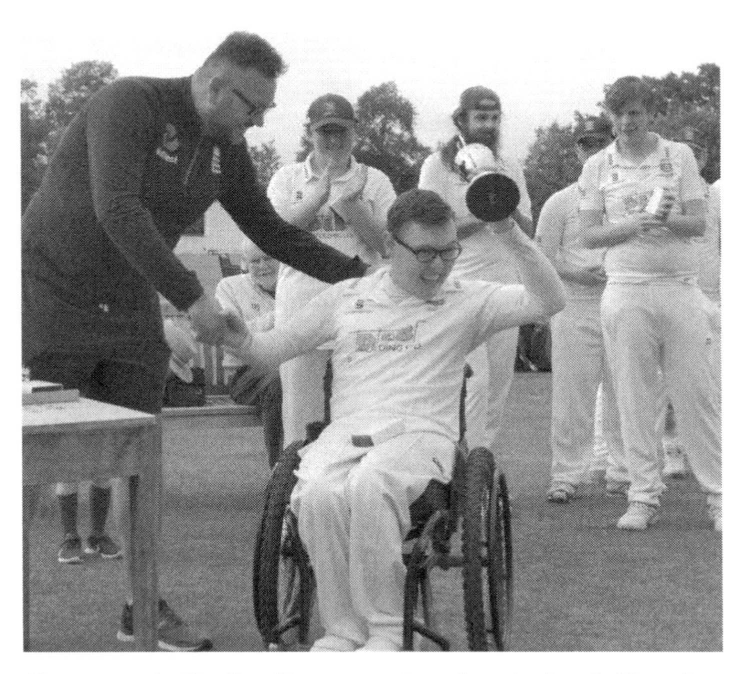

Essex captain Bradley Donovan enjoys the winning feeling after his side's victory over Derbyshire Merlins

# Chapter Fourteen

## The Schools Match

English Schools Cricket Association
v MCC Schools
Lord's, London
Tuesday 4 September

Play begins early today, at 10.45 now we are into September. It is as if we are being hurried to get things done before we must go indoors for the winter. MCC Schools have won the toss and are fielding. Overhead is all cloud, but it's warm too, and the MCC captain, Gay, clearly feels his bowlers can prosper. Das, the ESCA opener, thinks otherwise and plays some elegant strokes before Balmforth, riled by the impertinence, gets one to beat him. His success prompts enthusiastic applause from a man in a striped blazer behind me. Two balls later and Das edges Balmforth to the slips and departs. "YESSSS" cries my neighbour, who I suspect may be Balmforth senior. "It was worth coming now", he says in a broad Yorkshire accent, before asking his companion if she captured a photo of the moment. He immediately phones someone to update them on events, a faux pas that earns him a ticking-off from a vigilant steward. Meanwhile, De Caires, ESCA's captain, pulls a delivery from Brookes beautifully for four. The ball is flying off the hard pitch – the result of more dry weather and Lord's remarkable drainage system – but the bounce is even and De Caires looks hungry for runs. He may have to get a few, as he soon loses a second partner, Smeed's mistimed drive caught well by Fernandez.

It is, not surprisingly, a largely empty Lord's today. One or two boxes are open in the Grandstand, with a few spectators clustered beneath and an assorted sprinkling of parents, players, friends and teachers occupying the pavilion benches. Behind them, the Long Room looks resplendent, the finest MCC silverware sparkling in the sunlight ahead of what will clearly be a splendid lunch for those connected with the teams. Out in the middle, De Caires has a long chat with the umpire before greeting his new partner, Evison, not with a punch to the glove, but to the arm, in a pleasingly old-fashioned gesture. Or perhaps it's ultra-modern, and glove punches are out of fashion on the school playing fields. Either way, Evison is grateful for the support, with the bowlers, buoyed by early success, looking to get on top. Brookes, tall and slim, with a smooth action, is bowling a good line and length and making the batsmen play the ball. It's intelligent bowling. After an expensive start – 20-odd runs from off his first two overs – Balmforth has found his stride too, and beats the batsmen five times in a maiden over. He finds another edge too, Evison prodding tentatively outside off-stump, but the ball drops short of second slip and escapes, and the batsman sneaks two runs.

Despite the rising number of balls that beat the bat, De Caires and Evison keep the scoreboard ticking and the 50 is up in the 17th over. It's steady, rather than spectacular, but having played himself in, Evison starts to combine a very correct defence with some more expansive strokes; De Caires, on the other hand, is less comfortable; his feet have taken root, and he's not getting to the pitch of the ball. After one hour that produces 14 overs – the scourge of slow over rates found even among the nimblest of players – there's a change in the bowling, as Gay comes on from the Nursery End. He pounds in and bowls fast, and very chest-on, but Evison has his measure and despatches successive balls to the boundary. There's another change of bowler for the next over, when Gordon joins the attack. "Oh my God", cries a delighted female voice, its owner spying the scoreboard, "look at the bowlers! I remember trying to learn the Gay Gordon years ago". Her companion suggests a post-match ceilidh in the Long Room, though I suspect the MCC's hospitality, generous as it is, won't stretch that far.

ESCA's skipper, meanwhile, is still struggling for runs but, as all good openers do when they're in that position, stubbornly defends. He may be a little out of nick, but he's not going to give his wicket away cheaply, and his attitude does him great credit. It's a shame he's not a few years older, after Alastair Cook's announcement yesterday that this week's Test against India will be his last. As drinks are brought out, Evison takes fresh guard and De Caires practices a range of expansive strokes somewhat at odds with anything he's played up until now. A rumour spreads that the ESCA coach has sent out a message to the pair that they are not running hard enough. The rumour appears to be confirmed when De Caires promptly strikes his first boundary since the very early overs; his partner, though, fares less well, nicking a ball to King behind the stumps and departing for 36. Three down quickly becomes four as Wijeratne is dismissed cheaply, for the second time at Lord's this season. Having made 5 for Harrow against Eton in June, he manages one fewer today, a victim perhaps of Lord's nerves. One can only sympathise. His departure leaves ESCA on 92–4. Whether any of the ESCA players will eventually make the England side, only time will tell, but four wickets down with under 100 on the board certainly has an authentic England feel. Of course, if any do reach international level, they'll be in good company. Plenty of past and present England players have come through ESCA's ranks, not least of all Jos Buttler, Ben Stokes, Jonny Bairstow and current skipper Joe Root. This schoolboys match may not quite have the social cachet of Eton v Harrow, but it certainly offers a glimpse of what the England team might look like in ten years' time.

For now, though, ESCA have more pressing matters to attend to. De Caires still offers few strokes and even fewer chances, and with those two quick wickets, the virtues of his old-fashioned anchor role are increasingly apparent, even if they are at odds with the "positive" batting mantra we hear so much of. As the 100 comes up, De Caires is on 30 from 23 overs. "Going slowly, isn't he, for one-day cricket", asks one old boy. "I mean, it's ok for Test cricket but a bit slow for this stuff." Perhaps de Caires has exceptional hearing, or possibly it's the introduction of spin into the attack, but he is finally tempted to swing the bat once or twice, using his long reach to good effect. It is, alas, his undoing as he is rapped on the pads and falls, agonisingly, for 49. He cuts a frustrated figure as he walks slowly off, replaying the ball as he goes and wondering what might have been. His innings may not have been scintillating, but it's been a steady anchor role that's held his side together, and the applause for him is appreciative, if mingled with sympathy.

With ESCA on 128–5, MCC Schools might be forgiven for thinking the gates have opened and they can wrap things up early, but any such thoughts are soon banished. De Caires' wicket turns out to be the last success for the MCC bowlers, as the fair-haired Harry Duke and the taller, darker Luke Doneathy wrest control away from them. Doneathy swipes three balls to the boundary in succession as runs start to flow, mostly at the expense of the unfortunate Dilkes, and the scoring rate hits five. Carson, arm uncoiling like a snake, tightens up one end, but ESCA have seized the initiative. Duke brings up the 200 with a paddle shot, while the more conventional Doneathy drives and cuts, bringing up his 50 at barely more than a run a ball. His celebration is understated – there is work still to be done – and he immediately takes fresh guard. With the end of the innings nearing, his batting is explosive, sixes coming freely. He offers half a chance in front of the pavilion, but the fielder has just too much ground to make up, and though he gets his fingers to the ball, he can't quite hold on to it. Apart from that, it's runs galore, and he moves swiftly through the 60s, 70s, 80s. A six into the Grandstand is followed by a streaky boundary, which takes him into the 90s and he calls for a drink. Thirst quenched, he, digs out a yorker from Brookes, and heaves at the next but can manage only a single. Dukes tips the next ball over his head – ESCA's coaching manual clearly not following the MCC's – and takes a single off the next to put Doneathy pack on strike. The tiring Brookes does his best, but Doneathy, with fine timing, sweeps the ball brutally to the Grandstand once more to bring up a Lord's hundred in grand fashion. The standing ovation he gets is no more than he deserves. It's left to Gay to bowl the last over for what may be a slightly demoralised MCC side, with ESCA passing 300 to set a challenging target.

During the interval, I cast my eyes over the scorecard. It's not difficult to spot a common theme among the players from both sides. Of the ESCA team, only three are at a state school; for MCC, just one. It's a telling illustration of the decline of cricket in state schools, and the growing dominance of the private sector. It's reflected in the national team. Of the eleven England players who took the field against India at Lord's last month, seven were partly or exclusively taught at independent schools (another, Keaton

Jennings, was educated in South Africa). Of the English-born batsmen, only Joe Root had any state education experience, and even that ended when he won him a scholarship to Worksop College. The last entirely state-educated regular England batsman was Paul Collingwood, and he retired from international duties seven years ago.

It wasn't always thus; of the twelve players who regained the Ashes in 2005, nine were taught by the state. But, fast forward thirteen years and the game has all-but disappeared from most secondary schools in the country, their playing fields sold off to cover increasingly squeezed budgets. Even if they have somewhere to play the game, many schools struggle to find any teachers with the time or inclination to supervise it, let alone offer proper coaching. Compare that with the infinitely superior facilities and resources available to independent schools and it's not hard to see how the divide has become a chasm. Writing in the *Daily Telegraph* in 2015, Simon Briggs reported that one private school, Millfield, had no fewer than 12 teachers coaching 15 sides[14]. No state school can come remotely close to that; nor can most cricket clubs for that matter, many of which struggle to find 11 players to make up a side at weekends.

It's not just a problem with schools, though. Since the game's authorities took television coverage of cricket from free-too-air channels and handed it to Sky, most

[14]www.telegraph.co.uk/sport/cricket/international/england/11546893/English-crickets-public-school-revolution.html

children have lost exposure to the game. Put simply, it's no longer on their radar. Meanwhile, the rise of the all-powerful Premier League in football has pushed cricket out of the way even further. For all the ECB's worthy schemes, such as All-Stars Cricket, fewer and fewer children are playing, watching or even being aware of cricket. It is a sad loss. As a child, I would play cricket not just at school but, weather permitting, on every day of my summer holidays, along with all the other local youngsters. It's nearly 20 years since I last saw children, other than those from an Asian background or supervised by adults, playing cricket for fun. And even that was in Frinton-on-Sea, a town generally reckoned to be located not so much in Essex as in 1955. Today, it's a very different tale. According to statistics from www.statista.com[15] published just last month, children's participation in cricket is in sharp decline. Among 5–10-year-olds the trend is less marked, thanks, perhaps, to those ECB schemes, dropping from 6.6% in 2010/11 to 5.3% in 2017/18. Among the 11–15-year-olds, it's a sorrier tale – in 2010/11, participation was 17.3%; in 2017/18, just 12.6%. Cricket clubs tell a similar story, of youngsters dropping out of cricket in their teens, probably never to return. All-Stars claims to have reached 55,000 5–8-year-olds this year, 18,000 more than last year. I hope they're right, but I fear more, much more, will be needed if cricket is not to become an increasingly elitist, even marginal sport for young people.

[15] https://www.statista.com/statistics/421078/cricket-sport-involvment-children-england-uk/

There are certainly no state representatives among the MCC openers, as Fernandes (Oundle) and King (Stowe) take guard, though Kalley (Barking Abbey), ESCA's opening bowler, does wave the state school flag. Meanwhile, there is confusion for one spectator, presumably here to lend moral support rather than being an aficionado. "I'm confused", she says, "when it ended the other side were still in and they hadn't got out". The concept of limited-overs cricket explained, attention turns back to the game. MCC come haring out of the blocks, and have 33 after just five overs, prompting the entry into the attack of batting hero Doneathy. Perhaps his captain thinks he is on a roll and can bring his form with the bat to the ball as well (if so, he's on thin ice – a former captain once did just that with me, putting me, a medium-pace trundler, on as opening bowler after I'd knocked the opposition bowling about a bit with late-order abandon. The batsmen took about two overs to more than account for the runs their bowlers had conceded to me, and the experiment was swiftly abandoned, never to be repeated). In Doneathy's case, he certainly slows down the batsmen's charge, especially when he beats Fernandes twice with balls that move away, but it's Sullivan who makes the breakthrough. Bowling somewhere between medium pace and spin, with an action that nods to Derek Underwood, he will prove pretty deadly himself today. He tricks Fernandes into reaching too far, and Das gratefully snaffles the catch. Gay comes in, and another 20 or so are added, but then it all goes suddenly, horribly wrong for the MCC. The run rate is halved, and three wickets fall for four runs.

Reduced to 77–4, MCC need their equivalent of Duke and Doneathy's earlier stand, but after Scott and Dilkes take the score into three figures, both fall in quick succession to the impressive Sullivan, who ends with 4–20. It's a fine return from ten overs and has done as much to destroy MCC School's innings as Doneathy's century did to lift ESCA's. When the trophy table appears on the pavilion steps, it suggests the organisers reckon the end is nigh, and the required run rate has climbed to Twenty20 levels, but Price and Carson offer dogged resistance. There's something of Mike Atherton about Carson's gait and stance, but there's no comparison in the mistimed hoik he plays to De Caires, which Evison grabs at mid-off. MCC still need 145 with just 13 overs left and they are running out of wickets. With nothing to lose, Brookes and Price swing the bat with some abandon, and to great effect. Suddenly, without warning, the bowling looks tame and the batsmen can do no wrong. The pair's scoring rate hits ten an over, and runs come from all directions. The 50 partnership takes just 15 minutes and 31 balls, and ESCA seem to have no answers. Brookes, in particular, strikes one lusty blow after another. He sweeps and cuts his way to his own 50, and now just 68 are needed from six overs. Surely MCC can't pull this off? Doneathy comes back to stem the flow, but he's also deposited into the Grandstand for yet another six. The turnaround prompts chanting, no less, from the spectators, despite their lack of numbers. "I've never heard singing at a cricket match before", says the confused voice from earlier; "it's a new experience for me".

Brooks has reached 57, but his frenetic knock is ended by a sharp catch by Smeed. There's some confusion as to whether or not he's out, but the umpires decide he has to go. "That could be the turning point of the game" utters a sage at the back of the seats, who also repeatedly asks no-one in particular if he's been run out. Price reaches his own half-century, but in the heat of battle seems unaware of it until he hears the applause. The bowlers are feeling the pressure too – they are, after all, still schoolboys and this is Lord's – and wides start appearing, to the sage's dismay. "Come on, you're handing it to them", he grumbles. MCC find the boundary again, and it's followed by another wide, and a collective groan issues from the spectators. It's not enjoyable, seeing your young offspring's side collectively crumble, and here of all places. Doneathy, hero with the bat three hours ago, cannot find his line and his ten-ball over ends with MCC just 33 short of their target, with 18 balls with which to get them. Kalley bowls what would have been another wide but Price improvises a paddle shot from somewhere close to the adjoining pitch. Gordon edges two more fours, one deliberate, the other rather less so, and 23 are needed off two overs. Doneathy begins the penultimate over and Price, with an unlikely victory within reach, has a rush of blood, charging down the pitch with no chance of a run. He is stranded mid-pitch, run out by a distance and

ESCA may just have snatched the match back. "So does that mean they're both out?", asks my still-confused neighbour. MCC Schools are down to their last wicket, but after 45 minutes in which they have seemingly turned around a lost cause, momentum – always a fickle companion in cricket – has abandoned them as swiftly as it previously embraced them, like air escaping from an untied balloon. Doneathy, who cannot keep out of the action, applies the final stroke when he bowls Balmforth for a single. MCC Schools are all out for 285, beaten by 19. For a team that looked dead and buried at 160–7, they've done remarkably well to make such a contest of it, and can take heart from their fightback, even if they did ultimately fall just short.

Around the presentation table in front of the Long Room, MCC President Lord McLaurin reminds everyone of what a privilege it is to play at "the greatest cricket ground in the world". He introduces David English, a man once described by Stephen Fry as "eccentric to the point of sectionable derangement", who through the Bunbury English Schools Cricket Festival has probably done more than anyone in the game's history for school-age cricketers (the festival has, we are told, helped 91 future Test players and a thousand first-class cricketers along their paths).

He gives a characteristically eccentric but endearing speech, and hands over to England all-rounder Jos Buttler. Buttler presents the trophy to Josh De Caires, Nigel Wray, a rugby man from Saracens, gives the man of the match award to Doneathy, who has gloriously upheld the honour of the state sector, and English hands out fluffy bunnies to Buttler, the umpires and anyone else he can persuade to take one.

I gather up my belongings and take a final, reluctant, look around. Lord's does look very lovely. The hanging baskets and planters and flower beds, full today of pink and white petunias, are still dazzling on this late summer evening. The hedges are as neatly trimmed as in the primmest suburban garden, and everywhere looks just, so, well, pretty. And English. It's really rather hard to imagine that I will not be back this year, not for another eight months perhaps. It is with a pang of wistful sorrow that I head through the gates and along the nearby streets, passing a small group of tourists taking photographs of Paul McCartney's London home. The sadness at leaving Lord's is tempered, slightly anyway, by the fact that, unlike the last time I was here, I won't have to queue for ages in pouring rain to get into the tube station. Small compensation, granted, but enough to perk me up as I walk along the Wellington Road for the last time this year.

**ESCA**

| | | | | |
|---|---|---|---|---|
| J.M. De Caires* | lbw | b Dilkes | | 49 |
| R.J. Das | c Dilkes | b Balmforth | | 16 |
| W.C.F. Smeed | c Fernandes | b Brookes | | 1 |
| J.D.M. Evison | c King | b Gay | | 32 |
| R.S. Wijeratne | lbw | b Gordon | | 4 |
| H.G. Duke † | not out | | | 60 |
| L. Doneathy | not out | | | 113 |
| Extras | | 2lb 8nb 15w | | 25 |
| **Total** | | 50 overs | 5 – | 304 |

**FoW:** 1–24, 2–34, 3–83, 4–92, 5–128

Did not bat: F.E.H. Geffen, E.S. Kalley, H.T. Crocombe, H.A. Sullivan

| **Bowling** | **O** | **M** | **R** | **W** |
|---|---|---|---|---|
| Balmforth | 10 | 1 | 40 | 1 |
| Brookes | 10 | 0 | 75 | 1 |
| Gay | 8 | 0 | 44 | 1 |
| Gordon | 6 | 0 | 37 | 1 |
| Carson | 6 | 0 | 22 | 0 |
| Figy John | 2 | 0 | 14 | 0 |
| Dilkes | 3 | 0 | 30 | 1 |
| Price | 5 | 0 | 37 | 0 |

**MCC Schools**

| | | | | |
|---|---|---|---|---|
| S. Fernandes | c Das | b Sullivan | | 27 |
| A. King † | c Evison | b Sullivan | | 26 |
| E.N. Gay * | lbw | b Geffen | | 11 |
| C. Scott | lbw | b Sullivan | | 23 |
| J. Figy John | c Smeed | b Geffen | | 1 |
| I.V.A. Dilkes | | b Sullivan | | 14 |
| O.J. Price | | run out | | 60 |
| J.J. Carson | c Evison | b De Caires | | 19 |
| E.A. Brookes | c Smeed | b Doneathy | | 57 |
| T.D. Gordon | not out | | | 18 |
| B.J. Balmforth | | b Doneathy | | 1 |
| Extras | | 8lb 1nb 19w | | 28 |
| **Total** | | 49 overs | 10 – | 285 |

**FoW:** 1–52, 2–73, 3–75, 4–77, 5–108, 6–119, 7–160, 8–244, 9–282, 10–285

| **Bowling** | **O** | **M** | **R** | **W** |
|---|---|---|---|---|
| Kalley | 9 | 0 | 66 | 0 |
| Crocombe | 5 | 0 | 36 | 0 |
| Doneathy | 9 | 1 | 43 | 2 |
| Sullivan | 10 | 0 | 20 | 4 |
| Geffen | 8 | 0 | 55 | 2 |
| Evison | 3 | 0 | 21 | 0 |
| De Caires | 5 | 0 | 36 | 1 |

**Toss:** MCC Schools elected to bowl. **Umpires:** R. C. Hampshire, B.J. Peverall
**ESCA win by 19 runs**

# Chapter Fifteen

## The Roses Match

Yorkshire v Lancashire
Emerald Headingley Cricket Stadium, Leeds
Monday 10 September

If there are any road signs in Leeds to Headingley, they disguise them well. Not for the first time this season I give an offering of thanks for the invention of SatNav as I eventually escape Leeds city centre and find the pleasant north western suburb of Headingley, with its attractive rows of terraced houses and scores of university students scurrying to lectures and coffee shops. I make my way to the Len Hutton Gates where a sign proudly boasts that this is the home of The Yorkshire County Cricket Club. Not just Yorkshire, but *THE* Yorkshire club, as if to establish its claim to supremacy over any pretenders to the throne that may have the temerity to set up as rivals – which, given the often turbulent history of Yorkshire cricket, is a not entirely inconceivable notion.

As I approach the gates, a woman turns and asks me abruptly if I'd like a free ticket, before thrusting one into my hand. Before I can reply, she is away. I catch up with her and offer my thanks. "They were giving them away at t'local building society branch this morning" she tells me, and once more she is off. It's one of those moments that can catch southerners off guard – that strange, seemingly incongruous mix of kindness, generosity and bluntness. Welcome to Yorkshire. I am touched by the gesture, even if my thanks go unheeded, and gratefully put my wallet back in my pocket. Never mind, Yorkshire – sorry, The Yorkshire – I'll buy a beer or two later to put the money back in your coffers.

Headingley is another ground undergoing much change. It is also, of course, one of the most historic cricket venues in England. It was here in 1930 that Don Bradman made what was then the highest score in Test cricket, 334; here where Geoffrey Boycott became the first batsman to reach his hundredth hundred in a Test Match; here that England overturned odds of 500–1 to beat Australia. But despite its long history, by the end of the 20th century Headingley was in decline, standards falling far short of modern grounds and anti-social behaviour making it all too often an unpleasant place for fans and players alike.

Solutions were hampered by financial wranglings that left Yorkshire in a sorry pickle, and the fact that, until 2005, the ground was owned not by the cricket club but by the Leeds Cricket, Football and Athletic Company. Various redevelopment plans were announced, and in 2014 the club unveiled an ambitious 20-year, £40 million masterplan to turn Headingley into "one of the finest cricket grounds in the world". Even so, as recently as last year those plans – and, again, Headingley's Test status – were once more in serious doubt due to more funding problems. However, with private funding secured late in 2017, it now seems the ground's redevelopment, and the continuation of Test cricket here, are secure.

One of those recent developments is the Carnegie Pavilion, a vast modernist structure built in partnership with one of the local universities. Designed using giant triangular segments that stick out at odd angles, it looks like an enormous lunar lander, or a building that's half-crushed itself under its own weight. On the southern side of the ground, the huge bulk of the new Emerald Stand is taking shape. The stand is two sided, serving the cricket club on one side and the rugby league and union teams on the other. Three clubs, two grounds, one stand. After years of financial turmoil, Yorkshire's famous thrifty common sense is, I'm relieved to find, alive and well after all.

I'm glad the ground has received this new lease of life, for like many of my generation, some of my earliest and finest cricketing memories were forged here. In 1977, Geoffrey Boycott, local hero and recently returned from England exile, scored his hundredth first-class century. No-one had ever done that in a Test, and he did it on his home ground to boot. I nearly missed the moment though, thanks to our television set choosing just the wrong day to break down. Thankfully, a sympathetic engineer took pity and came around speedily to repair it. He managed it just in the nick of time for me to settle down and see Boycott drive

Greg Chappell for four to spark perhaps the biggest pitch invasion in cricket history, and the largest in these parts since Robert the Bruce's army came calling. Four years later Headingley was the setting for perhaps the most famous match of them all. Like Robin Hood and Dunkirk and the Beatles, the 1981 Ashes series is embedded in the English DNA. People with no interest in cricket know of Ian Botham and his exploits, having absorbed the information while still in the womb. Led with psychological mastery by captain Mike Brearley, with his degree in people, first Botham, following his personal *Boy's Own* script, and then an inspired Bob Willis, eyes fixed as if in a hypnotic trance, performed miracles that have become as much a part of English sporting folklore as 1966 and all that. Forced to follow on against Australia, and reduced to a sorry 135–7 second time around, still 92 behind, somehow England turned things around and defeated an unsuspecting, unbelieving Australia, and set the tone for perhaps the most extraordinary series in cricketing history.

The man who co-ordinated England's unlikely comeback in that series was Mike Brearley, re-appointed captain after Botham had pre-empted the sack by resigning. Brearley was a mystical sage, a philosopher who blended the ancient wisdom of an Eastern guru with the magical talents of Merlin. He was one of England's greatest captains, and almost certainly their cleverest. Many years later I met him, at a Twenty20 match at Lord's when we were both guests in one of the private boxes. This being Lord's, everyone was in regulation navy blazer, but it was a sultry midsummer evening and jackets were removed and placed on a large rail at the back of the box. When the time came to leave, there was, needless to say, total confusion as almost all the male guests tried to identify their own blazer out of the rackful of identical garments. All except Brearley, who had come prepared in a cream jacket. Yes, damned clever chap, Mike Brearley. They say you should never meet your heroes, as they will only disappoint you. He didn't.

No blazers are in sight today, though, of any colour. It is a gloomy, almost miserable grey day, a day for jumpers and warm, zipped-up autumn jackets. The short-sleeved Gleeson, newly signed from Northants and fielding in front of the Western Terraces, has overestimated the temperature and calls for a sweater. "Yer nesh bugger", calls out an unsympathetic – and warmly clad – Yorkshire supporter. The threat of rain hangs over us, and the floodlights are trying to break through the murk. Even so, there's a good crowd in, maybe three thousand, the largest I've seen at a Championship match for a while, but then this is no ordinary county match. It was 150 years old last year, this fixture, and rivalries were forged and attitudes cast by a few centuries of neighbourly rivalry before that. There are always more than mere points to be won and lost when these two counties meet, but there's an extra edge today as both sides are in danger of relegation. Only Worcestershire are below them, and the white roses trail their red rivals by a solitary point, though with a game in hand. Both counties must still play

Hampshire, who sit just above Lancashire and are far from safe themselves, and Yorkshire also have to travel to Worcestershire, who will need a spectacular turn of events to avoid playing in division two next year, so this Roses Match has even greater significance than usual. Lancashire, not surprisingly, have decided it's a morning on which to bowl. Bailey opens with three straight maidens, though Onions is despatched with equal regularity to the boundary by Lyth. Lyth has a point to make. One of the umpteen openers tried and dropped by England in recent years, he'll be well aware spots are up for grabs, with Alastair Cook playing his last-ever Test innings 300 miles south this very day. The Yorkshireman, though, has lost much ground after a modest year. He's yet to make a first-class century this season, and his last half-century was back in July, oddly enough against Lancashire. But, fine ends to a season have propelled more than a few players onto winter tours.

Just after 11.00, Onions claims the first wicket as Raval is comprehensively bowled. Born in India, but schooled in New Zealand, for whom he plays Test cricket, Raval made his Championship debut just last week, and is clearly still trying to figure out English conditions. He's not the only one, as Yorkshire wickets tumble under the heavy, grey clouds. Before long, the strapping Bailey has reduced them to 33–4. In nine miserly overs he takes three wickets for seven runs. As one fan wearily informs his companion, "Our batsmen haven't been scoring runs and our bowlers haven't been bowling teams out. That's why we're at the bottom". Lancashire, meanwhile, despite their struggles, possess the division's two leading wicket-takers in their opening pair, and the conditions are favouring them. With Yorkshire's innings in disarray, Tom Kohler-Cadmore and Tattersall are left to pick up the pieces. I've heard much of Kohler-Cadmore this season, all of it impressive. Though born in Kent, he grew up in Yorkshire and learned his cricket in these parts, but then got packed off to Malvern College where he was Wisden Schools Cricketer of the Year and snapped up by Worcestershire. When he scored a century for them against Yorkshire last year, his home county realised they'd let a blossoming talent slip through their fingers and promptly agreed to re-sign him from his adopted club. He's making a name as a big hitter in one-day cricket, but showed last week that he can do it in the longer game too, making a century against Nottinghamshire. His name has cropped up a lot this season, and I'm looking forward to seeing what he can do. It won't be easy for him. The sky is now as grey as the half-built stand behind the bowler's arm, where the only splashes of colour are from the high-viz jackets and dayglo orange trousers of the workmen who wander to and fro, hoisting scaffolding and huge bags of building materials, drilling holes here and inspecting work in progress there. With the stand being built behind them, the two batsmen set about doing rebuilding work of their own. Kohler-Cadmore, crouching low, springs up as he receives the ball, and leans back to play the shot of the morning – admittedly against slim competition – driving

Gleeson beautifully through mid-off. Another fine shot takes Yorkshire past 50 and Kohler-Cadmore is looking as relaxed as his teammates were uncomfortable. Onions is brought back but run making is suddenly, inexplicably, easy. Kohler-Cadmore is playing a different game to anything we've seen this morning, a heady yet controlled mix of powerful drives and wristy flicks. It's one of the curious quirks of cricket, that so many batsmen can find making runs nigh on impossible, and then, with wickets tumbling, another comes in and makes it look the easiest thing in the world. The more restrained Tattersall, meanwhile, blocks everything in sight, and when the lunch interval arrives Yorkshire have scrapped their way back in the contest at 86–4.

Lunch, as ever, means a trip to the shop to sample what's on offer. Amid the usual collection of shirts, tops, bats and assorted equipment, my eyes are drawn to the book stall. Somewhat optimistically, not one but two copies of *Jonathan Agnew's Cricket Yearbook 2009* are still on sale. Even more hopefully, the asking price is still the full £24.99. While I'm browsing, word starts filtering through that Alastair Cook has reached an emotional century at the Oval. A few minutes later it's confirmed on the PA system, and I expect an outbreak of, if not wild cheering, at least warm applause. Instead, there is virtual silence.

Lunch over, the players return, hands buried deep in pockets. The umpires feel the cold too, and are retreating as far into their coats and hats as possible. David Millns is recognisable only by a nose peering between collar and hat, while Rob Bailey looks like Grandma from the Giles cartoons. Kohler-Cadmore picks up where he left off, flashing a shot through the covers to reach his 50, and an imperious cut brings up the 100 partnership. Tattersall looks completely absorbed in his task, and when Kohler-Cadmore wanders down for a chat, he is promptly sent back. When the two do meet, it is with only the most perfunctory of glove punches. A couple of workmen, legs dangling over the edge of the stand, watch proceedings as they eat their sandwiches, but when Tattersall tries to be more forceful, he takes his eye off the ball and falls leg before to Onions for 33. The partnership has re-set the Yorkshire innings after a calamitous start, but its end signals another mini-collapse. Within minutes, two more wickets fall to Onions and the Tykes are back in the mire at 144–7. Patterson, Yorkshire's captain, gets some streaky runs, and when Onions pulls out of a delivery for the second time in a couple of overs, there are catcalls and cries of "Get on wi' it" from the frustrated home supporters. Kohler-Cadmore continues to pull and cut and drive with impunity but he's starting to run out of partners when Patterson is bowled. He has a long, hard chat with new batsman, Jack Brooks, whose bright orange boots stand out on a drab, colourless day, and the new man clips his first ball away for four, but then unwisely keeps the strike and is caught trying to hook Gleeson. Kohler-Cadmore is three short of his hundred and Yorkshire down to their last man, Ben Coad. Coad has been much spoken of as an up-and-coming prospect, but not for his batting. He swishes wildly at his first ball and again at his second, and Kohler-Cadmore, helpless at the other end, goes for a long walk to calm his nerves. Coad blocks the next ball, the one after that races past him for two byes, and he leaves the last to survive the over. Two balls later, Kohler-Cadmore drives Gleeson gloriously for four to a roar from the crowd and a warm embrace from his partner. It would have been a fine innings in any match, but in the context of today it's been nothing short of magnificent, a glorious exhibition of power and strokeplay, and it's kept Yorkshire in the game – and possibly in the division. Coad adds a couple of boundaries., which earn his side their first batting point, to the relief of the crowd, but when he lobs a catch to Bohannon Yorkshire are all out for 209, half of them scored by Kohler-Cadmore. With a win needed, it's well short of what Yorkshire would have hoped for, but we won't know how far short it is until Lancashire have batted.

There's no rest for Coad, who's straight on to attack the Lancashire openers, Davies and Brown – not quite Francis Thompson's ghostly Hornby and Barlow of long ago, but we live, sadly, in a less poetic age. Brown hogs the early strike, and looks like he'll require a bulldozer to evict him from the crease, but Davies, taking risks, bags the runs. Coad changes ends after three overs, and there's much raising of arms and cries of "'Owzat?" from the slips at regular intervals, but none of it makes any difference and the batsmen progress without difficulty. Patterson, aping

Onions, pulls out of a delivery at the last moment but this time there are no jeers or catcalls, until a sole Lancastrian, feeling he should say something, makes a half-hearted call of "Get on with it" and is promptly told to shut up. The crowd is, in fact, quiet all round. Not even the inhabitants of the Western Terraces can muster up any insults to hurl at their trans-Pennine rivals. I should actually say West Stand, for the club renamed the area a few years back, part of an effort to improve the behaviour here. Always a home for the more, ah, vocal supporters, the terrace had become a place where even Australians might fear to tread, with the sort of abuse more usually found at football grounds. Nasser Hussain, a few years ago, said he would not take his family to this part of the ground, due to the "alcohol-inspired environment", and the club admitted they'd lost control of the stand during the 2013 Test against New Zealand. Since then they've taken various measures to, in their words, "move away further from the bad-boy reputation of the Western Terrace that was". Today is not a Test Match or a Twenty20 sell-out, so it's hard to judge how much success they've had, but the crowd is certainly docile. I abhor the hostility and aggression of football crowds, but I must admit, I had hoped for a little more good-natured banter today. Perhaps it's just too cold – and besides, the Yorkshire supporters know their position hardly lends itself to baiting the opposition, even if it is Lancashire.

The afternoon rolls on, the sun briefly emerges, only to swiftly change its mind, and with nothing in the pitch for a rather blunt bowling attack, the batsmen continue to accumulate runs. Davies's come mostly through boundaries, not all of them chanceless; the more circumspect Brown's through an altogether more mysterious process. Like an over-tired child fighting off sleep, the innings starts nodding off until it eventually grinds to a halt. With Yorkshire's bowlers producing a decent line and length, Brown adds nothing to his score for 20 minutes. The Yorkshire slip cordon, when they're not making optimistic appeals, keep themselves amused, and hands warm, by joshing and teasing one another, including a game of 'guess which hand it's in'. Raval comes down to our part of the ground to field and with little happening in the game to require his attention, strikes up a conversation. "I wish the sun had been out this morning", he complains. "How are England getting on?". "India are one for two, Anderson's got both of them", booms a spectator with an earplug in one ear. A couple of minutes later the peace is broken again. "One for three – Kohli out to a golden duck!". Unlike Cook's century earlier in the day, this news does raise a murmur of appreciation from all around. Raval returns from fielding the ball and takes some convincing of the scoreline from the Oval, thinking the locals are having some fun with the new boy. When the score is confirmed, he sucks hard and winces.

Eventually, Davies decides it's time to stop the scoreboard from seizing up and reaches his 50. It's too little, too late, for one man. "I'm off", he pronounces, "I've 'ad enough. It's like watching paint dry". He has a point. Brown has taken two hours for his 35, though his job is to keep Lancashire in the game and Division 1. Dazzling, entertaining batting can wait. Patterson, though, sees things differently, shouting "This is awesome, Coady". Lancashire are simply determined to keep their wickets intact ready for the morning, and even the century partnership is brought up by byes, rather than a scoring shot. In the gathering gloom, Brown, perhaps suffering a rush of blood to the head at the thought of a hot shower and a beer, suddenly finds the boundary, and when the umpires finally pick up the bails, Lancashire are 105–0, halfway to Yorkshire's total and well set for the morrow. They'll sleep the easier tonight.

**Yorkshire first innings**

| | | | |
|---|---|---|---|
| A. Lyth | c Vilas | b Bailey | 16 |
| J.A. Raval | | b Onions | 8 |
| H.C. Brook | c Vilas | b Bailey | 3 |
| G.S. Ballance | lbw | b Bailey | 5 |
| T. Kohler-Cadmore | not out | | 105 |
| J.A. Tattersall † | lbw | b Onions | 33 |
| T.T. Bresnan | c Vilas | b Onions | 0 |
| M.J. Waite | c Vilas | b Onions | 0 |
| S.A. Patterson * | | b Gleeson | 17 |
| J.A. Brooks | c Maharaj | b Gleeson | 6 |
| B.O. Coad | c Bohannon | b Gleeson | 12 |
| Extras | | 2b 2lb | 4 |
| **Total** | | 60.4 overs | 10 – 209 |

**FoW:** 1–20, 2–23, 3–32, 4–33, 5–138, 6–142, 7–144, 8–177, 9–187, 10–209

| **Bowling** | **O** | **M** | **R** | **W** |
|---|---|---|---|---|
| T.E. Bailey | 14 | 4 | 18 | 3 |
| G. Onions | 21 | 6 | 76 | 4 |
| R. J Gleeson | 15.4 | 2 | 74 | 3 |
| D.J. Lamb | 2 | 1 | 5 | 0 |
| K.A. Maharaj | 8 | 1 | 32 | 0 |

**Lancashire first innings**

| | | | |
|---|---|---|---|
| K.R. Brown | c Tattersall | b Coad | 43 |
| A.L. Davies | lbw | b Brooks | 87 |
| S.J. Croft | c Lyth | b Brooks | 11 |
| L.S. Livingstone * | | b Brooks | 7 |
| D.J. Vilas † | lbw | b Brooks | 0 |
| J.J. Bohannon | lbw | b Brooks | 10 |
| D.J. Lamb | c Tattersall | b Bresnan | 9 |
| T.E. Bailey | c Tattersall | b Waite | 16 |
| K.A. Maharaj | c Patterson | b Coad | 38 |
| G. Onions | | b Waite | 3 |
| R.J. Gleeson | not out | | 9 |
| Extras | | 13b 2lb 4nb | 19 |
| **Total** | | 84.2 overs | 10 – 252 |

**FoW:** 1–105, 2–145, 3–153, 4–157, 5–166, 6–175, 7–198, 8–212, 9–221, 10–252

| **Bowling** | **O** | **M** | **R** | **W** |
|---|---|---|---|---|
| B.O. Coad | 17.2 | 5 | 57 | 2 |
| J.A. Brooks | 17 | 4 | 66 | 5 |
| S.A. Patterson | 22 | 6 | 40 | 0 |
| T.T. Bresnan | 17 | 3 | 58 | 1 |
| M.J. Waite | 11 | 5 | 16 | 2 |

**Yorkshire second innings**

| | | | |
|---|---|---|---|
| A. Lyth | c Vilas | b Onions | 7 |
| J.A. Raval | lbw | b Bailey | 10 |
| H.C. Brook | | b Bailey | 5 |
| G.S. Ballance | lbw | b Maharaj | 85 |
| T. Kohler-Cadmore | lbw | b Maharaj | 63 |
| J.A. Tattersall † | c Vilas | b Bailey | 22 |
| T.T. Bresnan | c&b Maharaj | | 20 |
| M.J. Waite | lbw | b Onions | 15 |
| S.A. Patterson * | | b Bailey | 9 |
| J.A. Brooks | c Croft | b Gleeson | 1 |
| B.O. Coad | not out | | 7 |
| Extras | | 4b 20lb 4nb | 28 |
| **Total** | | 101.2 overs | 10 – 272 |

**FoW:** 1–17, 2–19, 3–27, 4–175, 5–192, 6–214, 7–238, 8–250, 9–254, 10–272

| **Bowling** | **O** | **M** | **R** | **W** |
|---|---|---|---|---|
| T.E. Bailey | 29 | 6 | 69 | 4 |
| G. Onions | 24 | 5 | 77 | 2 |
| R. J Gleeson | 10.2 | 3 | 31 | 1 |
| K.A. Maharaj | 32 | 12 | 52 | 3 |
| D.J. Lamb | 2 | 0 | 13 | 0 |
| L.S. Livingstone | 1 | 0 | 3 | 0 |
| J.J. Bohannon | 3 | 1 | 3 | 0 |

**Lancashire second innings**

| | | | |
|---|---|---|---|
| K.R. Brown | lbw | b Bresnan | 10 |
| A.L. Davies | c Tattersall | b Coad | 8 |
| S.J. Croft | c Raval | b Brooks | 13 |
| L.S. Livingstone * | | b Brooks | 28 |
| D.J. Vilas † | | b Coad | 10 |
| J.J. Bohannon | c Bresnan | b Coad | 13 |
| D.J. Lamb | lbw | b Coad | 0 |
| T.E. Bailey | | b Coad | 7 |
| K.A. Maharaj | | b Brooks | 18 |
| G. Onions | | b Brooks | 4 |
| R.J. Gleeson | not out | | 0 |
| Extras | | 2b 19lb 2nb | 23 |
| **Total** | | 48.1 overs | 10 – 134 |

**FoW:** 1–11, 2–31, 3–66, 4–81, 5–87, 6–87, 7–85, 8–122, 9–134, 10–134

| **Bowling** | **O** | **M** | **R** | **W** |
|---|---|---|---|---|
| B.O. Coad | 15.1 | 6 | 24 | 5 |
| J.A. Brooks | 15 | 4 | 47 | 4 |
| T.T. Bresnan | 7 | 0 | 17 | 1 |
| S.A. Patterson | 9 | 3 | 23 | 0 |
| M.J. Waite | 2 | 1 | 2 | 0 |

**Toss:** Lancashire elected to bowl. **Umpires:** R. Bailey, D. Millns
**Yorkshire win by 95 runs**

The Oval's famous gasholder looks down on play against perfect blue skies and autumn sunshine

# Chapter Sixteen

## Stumps

Surrey v Essex
The Oval, London
Thursday 27 September

There is an air of finality about The Oval in September. Over decades of cricket watching, I have come to associate the Oval with endings. It is, traditionally, the venue for the last Test Match of the summer, a place where not just matches but series are won and lost, outstanding matters resolved, loose ends tied, and farewells made. It was here, in 1882, that English cricket itself died, the body being cremated and the ashes taken to Australia. It doesn't get much more final than that. It was here, too, that the greatest Test career of them all, Don Bradman's, came to a sorry end when he was bowled for a duck by Eric Hollies. Later it was said his eyesight was blurred by tears. As a child in 1976, I watched enthralled as that hottest, driest of all summers came to an end at a sun-bleached Oval, Viv Richards climbing 291 steps to take his rightful place at the top of Olympus. And could anyone forget Kevin Pietersen's nonchalantly dismissive batting against Shane Warne and

Glenn McGrath in 2005, or Billy Bowden's theatrical lifting of the stumps to signal the match was drawn and 19 years of hurt had come to an end? So for me, the Oval is where the extended drama that is the cricket season reaches its final act, its denouement. Sometimes it slips away quietly, in other years it goes down fighting gloriously, but it always provides, to borrow from Julian Barnes, the sense of an ending.

So when I sat down in the depths of last winter to work out the itinerary for this book, it was the simplest of decisions to make the Oval my last port of call. Surrey at home, underneath the famous gas holders under grey, chill autumnal skies. What could be more apt to mark the passing of another season, and the end of my own journey around the country? Well, the gas holders are here, unused nowadays but listed and preserved, but it's 22 degrees and rising, and the sun is shining out of one those perfect cloudless skies to which we've become accustomed. Yet on Monday, when this match began, it looked like I would have to make alternative arrangements. Surrey – the newly crowned county champions, unbeaten all season, who would in all probability have come into this game on the back of ten successive wins had Storm Bronagh not blown the covers away and ruined the pitch at Taunton last week – yes, Surrey had been bowled out for 67. Sixty-seven. Undone by Essex at that, the deposed champions keen to leave a parting message. This was meant to be Surrey's triumphant sign-off to a glorious season, a four-day lap of honour in front of their supporters. But by close of play, the party-pooping

Essex boys were already out of sight on their way to 477–8 declared. With the hosts needing a world record comeback to win, the chances of this match making into a third, let alone a fourth, day were already distant. But true champions are made of stern stuff, and Surrey have somehow clawed and clambered and scrambled their way back into this match. After three days, they are, with pleasing symmetry, themselves on 477, five wickets down, 67 runs ahead. Another 100 or so today and Essex will find themselves facing one of those tricky totals – the sort a side should make, but all too often gets bowled out in trying, never quite working out how to make it. And so a match that was to all intents and purposes over after day one now has the makings of a dramatic climax to the season.

Ironically, it is also the only match in this final round of games to have made it this far. One by one, all the other eight games around the country have been decided. Lancashire have been relegated, Nottinghamshire surviving by the skin of their teeth, despite a sound beating by a Somerset team helped by two hat-tricks. Warwickshire will replace the Red Roses, having put Kent in their place with an innings thrashing to take the second division title. Kent's consolation is promotion, though their triumph may be tinged with reminders that their batting order will need strengthening for life in the higher division. Elsewhere, every other match has ended within two or three days. It is as if the cricketers of England, their work done, have collectively been allowed to finish early and bunk off for a few pre-holiday drinks, like office workers on Christmas Eve.

Only here, in an unexpectedly balmy corner of southeast London, does the cricket season live on, for a few more hours at least, like a holidaymaker draining the last few drops of warm Spanish sun before they return to the reality of dark, dreary, drizzly days. To mark the occasion, or perhaps to encourage as many fans as possible to be here for the post-match trophy presentation, Surrey have thrown open the gates for free entry. It's a generous gesture, as the crowd may be close to 1,000, despite it being a working day. That said, most of the spectators gathered here look as if their working days are well behind them. Still, it's good to see a decent turnout when a great many of the non-cricketing public assumed the cricket season finished weeks ago. When I told people where I would be today, they invariably looked at me with wide and questioning eyes, as if I'd told them I was going to a concert by someone they thought had died in about 1995, or Phil Collins. "Cricket, at this time of year?" In fairness to them, it is just three days shy of October. The first frosts of autumn are rumoured to have appeared, and not that far from London either. But on a beautiful day like this, it feels like the season could last forever, and everyone here is willing to suspend belief. The departure of the cricket season is an unwelcome reminder that winter will soon be upon us. As long as play continues, we can defer the inevitable, like young children willing their pre-bedtime TV programme to last just a few minutes more.

As I walk around the ground to my seat, it is impossible to escape the past. The Oval, more than any ground, even Lord's itself, is imbued with history. It hangs heavily all around here. Lord's may be older, but it was here where the first ever Test match in England was played. It was at the Oval where, two years later, the Ashes came into being when the upstart colonials had the temerity to beat the Mother Country. The first FA Cup final was played here, Wanderers beating Royal Engineers 1–0, and the first-ever international football match, England sharing the honours with Scotland. The England rugby union team played their first home match at the Oval, and it even hosted the first Varsity rugger match. But it is cricket that dominates, and everywhere there are reminders of its glorious past – the matches, the players, the feats, the characters. You can enter the ground through the Jack Hobbs Gate or the Alec Stewart Gate and sit in the Mickey Stewart Pavilion if you're a member, or the Peter May stand if you're not. On your way, you might visit the Ken Barrington Cricket Centre.

Wherever you find yourself, you'll walk past banners recalling the great players – of whom there are many – from Surrey's history, ancient and modern. Here is Andrew Sandham, who scored 41,000 runs in his career and was still overshadowed by his partner for most of them, Jack Hobbs. There is Tom Hayward, the first batsman after WG himself to make 100 centuries, and he took 436 wickets to boot. There's the Guv'nor, Bobby Abel, who once made 357no and was the first Englishman to carry his bat in a Test Match; and George Lohmann, taker of 1,221 wickets and dead from tuberculosis at 36. Well over a century after his demise, Lohmann still holds the lowest Test bowling average for anyone save for two players with three Tests between them. We can read of Tom Richardson, who took 252 wickets in a single, glorious summer, and of Douglas Jardine of Bodyline infamy. I wonder if his image stays up when Australia are in town? There are posters of Peter May and Stuart Surridge, John Edrich and Pat Pocock, the Bedser twins, and, still together, Tony Lock and Jim Laker. They once took all 20 Australian wickets between them in an Ashes Test, these two, though Lock took just one. Every Surrey side that's won the Championship is remembered with a plaque. They need plenty of room for the 1950s, when the pennant flew over the Oval for an unprecedented seven consecutive years. They played 28 matches a season in those days. Their 2018 equivalents are playing their 14th and final game today, and there are some who think that's too many.

No, history here is inescapable, as the players of yesteryear gaze down upon us, off drives and off breaks frozen forever in black and white. Cricketers never die here; instead, spirits are absorbed into the Victorian brickwork, from where they watch over matches for eternity as silent judges of their modern counterparts, reminders of what's expected here. Perhaps what finally makes someone a Surrey cricketer is not just pure skill or talent, but how much inspiration they can draw from their surroundings. For some, the weight of expectation may simply be too heavy.

But it's not all gas holders and black and white images and Victorian moustaches. Amid all the history, there is modernity here too. The Vauxhall End is dominated these days by the impressive OCS stand, a vast, sleek, silver beast that curves around nearly half the arena and is as contemporary a piece of architecture as you'll see on an English cricket ground. Behind it is a vast living green-wall, dripping with plants and harbouring an entire ecosystem. There's even a terrace garden in the Peter May Stand, though you'll search in vain for geraniums or petunias – here it's all spiky shrubs in gleaming white planters, the sort of roof-top garden you'd expect to find on top of one of the numerous tower blocks that are starting to dominate the skyline round here. It must make a wonderful vantage point from which to watch a floodlit Twenty:20 game, a glass of something refreshing in hand and room to stretch out.

But, enough. There is work to be done and a match to be won. Surrey's batsmen Will Jacks and Ryan Patel, local lads both, have been sent out with the assurance that this thing can be done. Play steadily, no rash shots and the runs will come. Another 100 runs and Essex will panic and collapse. Do they know it will be a world record if they pull it off? Jacks, just 19, is 52 not out, his maiden half-century. Patel, barely older, is on 19 and, despite the warmth, he is pleasingly attired in a traditional cable sweater rather than the skimpy polyester ones favoured these days. Earlier this summer, Patel took his county some way towards the title when he polished off rivals Somerset with six for five in just eleven balls, but it's his runs they need today. Matt Coles and Matthew Quinn are the bowlers who want to dismiss the home side before the target becomes awkward and Coles soon delivers. With just a single added to his overnight total, Jacks drives at a ball that swings away and he is caught by Harmer. It catches the crowd, still settling into their seats, unawares and they seem uncertain as to how to react, as if not entirely sure if that was a wicket or just a warm-up. They revive quickly, though, to greet the arrival of Rikki Clarke, born in Essex, once of England, Surrey through and through, and the sole survivor of the county's last Championship-winning side, back in 2002.

The powerful Coles, tattooed biceps bursting from his shirt sleeve, comes down to third man to field and gazes into the stand as if looking for old mates, before shouting encouragement to his fellow bowler. Quinn, though, is far away, lost in his own thoughts. He and Coles bowl well, pacey with a good line, and runs are few and far between. There are just 12 in the first half hour, until Clarke breaks the spell and revives the crowd's spirits with successive boundaries. Patel is becalmed, but Clarke, having played himself in, starts scoring fluently, each run accompanied by a peculiar noise, part-sneeze, part bark, from a spectator deep within the stands. In no time at all, Clarke overtakes his partner, who can't buy a run. The crowd are thoroughly absorbed. They are almost all men and noticeably, despite the cosmopolitan nature of the area, almost all white. That said, many are attempting to turn themselves redder as they lie in the sun, shirts off or open to the waist, grey hairs bleaching in the sun. Where Lord's would be awash with panamas, there are none to be seen south of the river. Here the favoured headgear is floppy hats and baseball caps and those pork pie hats so popular with south Londoners and Ska fans. The accents are pure south London, and one spectator near me sounds exactly like Grandad from *Only Fools and Horses*, set just a short bus ride down the road in Peckham. He is one of a group of old friends enjoying their own jolly boys' outing. "Turned aht nice again, ahnit?" he says. "It 'as that", replies one of his companions. "What you got to eat then?" "Just 'am", says Grandad Trotter, who pauses before adding, thoughtfully, "and it's _______ awful".

There's nothing awful about Clarke's batting, which has a liberated, end-of-term ease about it, and when he sweeps the ball through leg side to bring up Surrey's 500 there is loud, prolonged applause. More boundaries follow. and the sneeze-barks get louder, as do the shouts of "Come on lads, keep it tight" from the increasingly concerned Essex captain, Ryan ten Doeschate. He piles the pressure on Patel, who has fielders swarming around him, but unexpectedly it's Clarke, who has made scoring look as easy as Patel has found it difficult, who falls, edging a ball from Coles – who has shrewdly switched to round the wicket – into the welcoming hands of the substitute fielder Pepper. "Oh Rick", says Grandad Trotter wearily, and I half expect him to add "you plonker". Instead he sighs, a resigned lament that seems to take all of Surrey's hopes with it as it fades away.

Surrey, though, are 122 ahead and still have three wickets. The new batsman is Morne Morkel, who's had a fine season with the ball, 50 wickets in the Championship, but he looks distinctly uncomfortable with bat, rather than ball, in hand, and swiftly returns. The game is shifting back towards Essex, though the crowd are sanguine about it, in the ways only champions or the condemned can afford to be. Dernbach comes in, swings and misses at everything and there are theatrical oohs and aahs from the spectators. Surprisingly, though, it's the cautious, watchful Patel who falls, caught behind, though not everyone shares the umpire's conviction that he's made contact. Coles has five wickets and Essex are eager to wrap things up. Virdi plays a nice-looking stroke for two and is as applauded as warmly as if he'd reached 50, but any hopes he has end when Dernbach's middle stump is uprooted. The final equation is revealed: Surrey are 541 all out, setting Essex 132 to win. Their openers negotiate a single, tricky over of spin, and lunch is taken.

~~~~~~~~~~~~~~~~~~~~~

The Oval, like Canterbury, is one of those grounds that lets spectators onto the outfield at lunchtime – in fact, onto the square, without so much as a rope to mark off the pitch, just a solitary steward and an invisible line that everyone somehow sees and respects. Even so, any closer to the pitch and I'll need a bat. It is the closest one can get to seeing a Test ground as Alastair Cook or Joe Root would see it. As I stand gazing at the pitch, I think of the cricketers who have
~~~~~~~~~~~~~~~~~~~~~

stood within whispering distance of where I am now. Jack Hobbs, cut and drove and glanced his way to countless centuries here. Hutton and Laker and Bradman, even WG himself, stood here, sporting knights of the round table weaving tales as legendary as any from Camelot. I half close my eyes and look for ghostly figures, but it's too sunny a day for ghosts. For a ground so imbued with history, I am dragged back to the present.

The crease is showing its age, cratered and crumbling. There are rough patches at both ends, and strips of green still filter down the pitch. There is help here for the bowlers, and this match is far from settled. An old regular says it looks the same as it did yesterday, but has no answer for what happened on Monday. He does, though, tell me he was there on that famous day in 1982, when the same two sides met at Chelmsford and Essex bowled out Surrey for a beyond-embarrassing 14. Surrey managed to draw that one, somehow, so recovering from 67 should hold no fears. As I make my way back to my seat, I pass two staff members, ID badges dangling from lanyards. "Have a good winter if I don't see you", says one. It seems out of place to be talking of winter, but it's another reminder that we are on borrowed time. That sense of finality again. Near me, in the media areas, a young man with a contented air sits behind a laptop, though he is more absorbed with sending messages and occasionally having conversations on his mobile. Is he, I wonder, the person who posts all the updates and tweets on the BBC website's match coverage? If he is, he may have a busy afternoon ahead.

The ever-willing Morne Morkel has been called upon to launch one final effort. He takes up the ball, and runs in toward the crease, each delivery starting with him trotting away from the batsman before turning tightly to face him. He rises once more to the occasion, clattering Vijay's stumps in his second over. He may not be quite as fast as in his heyday, but he's still too hot for Westley, who prods and fumbles and looks at sea. There are strangled appeals and scrambled singles, and nerves get to Browne too, who is caught in the slips. The Surrey boys have the wind in their sails, and there is much gesticulating and shouting of encouragement. Their captain, Rory Burns, born and bred within the county's bounds, calmly marshals his forces, adjusting the field to keep the batsmen guessing and stop them getting settled. The fielders, and the crowd, all do their bit and applaud the bowlers long and hard. Lawrence aims to take the fight to Surrey and strikes Virdi for six, scattering a group of pigeons who fly away, noisily and indignantly. My mind goes back to another unseasonably warm day, at the other end of the season and the far side of town, and discussions on the respective pedigrees of Oval and Lord's pigeons. I'm forced to admit that the ones here do seem a bit, well, scruffier than those from NW8.

Lawrence, though, soon pays for his insolence, edging a ball from Dernbach that keeps low and turning away with resigned dismay. Essex are still 90 behind and three down, and the first chants start up from the Peter May stand. When Ravi Bopara departs minutes later, Virdi wheels away in delight, arms as wide as the wings of an albatross and he leaps almost high enough to say hello to one. The happy Surrey faithful sing "Oh, goodbye Bopara" to the White Stripes' *Seven Nation Army*. Westley, meanwhile, looking nothing like a man who made 134 in the first innings, scrapping his way to 20 before he too is caught by the ever-grateful Clarke, and Essex now have half their men back in the pavilion but for less than half their target. Surrey's confidence is growing as visibly as Essex's is crumbling.

The Essex captain, and possibly their last hope, receives a friendly greeting from the opposition. "Come on Ryan, you can't improve your average this late in the season!". He decides attack is the best defence, and sweeps successive boundaries off Virdi. Wheater, at the other end, is caught like a rabbit in headlights and the resulting appeal is long and loud, but he survives. Every delivery is now met with gasps, the Surrey fielders loudly encouraging each other whenever ten Doeschate lays bat to ball. Virdi and Burns consult long and hard, but to little effect as ten Doeschate strikes three boundaries in the over that follows. The target is down to 42, the pendulum creeping inexorably back once more. The Essex skipper sweeps and cuts and scurries for all he's worth, moving through the 20s and into the 30s. The compact Wheater keeps up his end, and as the partnership reaches 40 there's an inescapable sense that it's now or never for Surrey. Morkel clearly feels it to, and hurls down a delivery that deceives the batsman, who mistimes his stroke and is caught. A thousand people make the noise of ten times as many, and Surrey have renewed hope, but

Essex now need only 35 more. Morkel welcome Harmer with a beauty that cuts away and beats him outside off stump; his next ball is a yorker that the batsman just digs out, but the third is unplayable, Harmer waving his bat ineffectually outside off stump and edging the ball to Foakes. The last three balls he has had to face this season may well have been the most torrid innings he's endured all campaign, and he looks to the heavens as he leaves. The new man, Jamie Porter, has a long discussion with his captain, the crowd roar Morkel on and the ball flies past the outstretched bat of Porter, who has no more idea of its whereabouts than he does of Blackbeard's treasure. It's been a magnificent over from Morkel, and ending a partnership that looked to have taken the match away from Surrey, and dragging them back into the contest.

At the Vauxhall End, Dernbach replaces Virdi, who's taken vital wickets but at greater cost than his side can afford. Essex reach 100 with a bye, and then Morkel concedes four leg byes and the target comes down a little more. At the other end, Porter is beaten repeatedly. He receives advice from his captain, who is promptly left all ends up himself, but survives. "Do the job Morne" cries a voice from the crowd, and with Essex on the dreaded Nelson, 111, he does just that, Porter out lbw to another ball that fails to rise. Twenty-one more runs are needed by Essex, two wickets by Surrey. Coles is beaten by the fired-up Morkel, there's a long silence and then Surrey decide to appeal anyway, but get nothing more than chuckles from the crowd, who've never had so much free entertainment. Coles wags a finger at himself and the tension ramps up another notch. Ten Doeschate clips two balls off his legs for two more boundaries, and just 16 are needed, and when Coles sends a ball to third man the target is down to a dozen. Suddenly there's more of a pleading quality to the shouts of encouragement from the spectators, but their players are still fighting. When ten Doeschate cuts the ball away and looks for two, no fewer than five Surrey fielders converge on the ball from all angles, restricting Essex to a single and crucially getting Coles on strike. He plays a nice stroke through the covers and the batsmen take two more comfortable runs. But pressure does strange things, even to seasoned professionals. It's the only explanation for the confused panic that suddenly attacks the batsmen as they decide to turn for a third, impossible, run. Coles is run out by half the pitch, and he stares in disbelief at the wreckage of his wicket, wondering in despair what on earth he's just done.

Henry Newbolt's Victorian poem, *Vitai Lampada*, may not be read much these days, but suddenly its words drift back across the ages: "There's a breathless hush in the Close tonight / Ten to make and the match to win / A bumping pitch and a blinding light, / An hour to play and the last man in." Well, there are only eight to win, not ten, but in other respects Newbolt's otherwise dated poem suddenly seems surprisingly relevant. Ten Doeschate meets the last man, the New Zealander Quinn, though not quite with "his captain's hand on his shoulder smote", and I doubt his exact words are "Play up! Play up! And play the game". While Ten Doeschate's greeting will probably be less poetic, it's unlikely to be far removed. Quinn, testing the nerves of Essex supporters, looks no batsman, but makes up for technical shortcomings with determination as he blocks, blocks, and blocks again – if not with his bat then with whatever bit of body he can put in the way. He survives the over, and ten Doeschate regains the strike. He steers Dernbach's first ball away and there's no run, then swings and is beaten. The third ball is pitched shorter and races down to third man for two runs. Six to win. There's a loud appeal off the fourth ball, and the fifth, and the tension is like an elastic band wound to breaking point. Burns, remaining calm and focused, instructs his fielders to move in closer. As they edge closer, a wag calls out "Where's your sense of drama?", and even the players laugh with relief. The last ball of the over is clipped away for a single, fielders scurry in all directions, Quinn collides with one of them and amid the chaos his skipper keeps the strike. He has 46, and five more are required.

Morkel is back on, from the Pavilion End. He turns, bowls, ten Doeschate considers a single, mid-wicket twitches, but the batsman thinks better of it and stays put. The crowd cheer on the bowler, but the Essex man clips the second ball to square leg and picks up two more runs; three to win. But when he manages just a single off the next delivery, Quinn is left to face the mighty Morkel. The South African sends down a bouncer that hits the tailender and leaves him requiring attention. Drinks are brought on – doubtless a canny ploy by Burns to break the batsmen's concentration – and the Surrey skipper delays proceedings further still with painstaking changes to the field. It is a full, agonising five minutes before Morkel, having caught his breath, eventually bowls the next ball. Quinn starts his innings afresh and defends, this time with bar rather than body. It's ungainly, and there's no run, but crucially there's no wicket either. Ball in hand, Morkel tears in again and this time thuds the ball into Quinn's hands. The unfortunate New Zealander withdraws his hand in pain, but the ball falls short of the fielder and somehow Quinn has survived a torrid, testing time. And ten Doeschate is back on strike.

The crowd know full well that Dernbach's over will be the last of the match – and of the season. The only thing they don't know is which team will win this extraordinary match. Dernbach sends down the first ball, it hares past the batsman and there's an optimistic shout from behind the stumps, but no-one's fooled. He comes in again, the ball is on ten Doeschate's favoured leg side and, again, he plays it comfortably off his pads. The ball runs away to third man and, despite the frantic chase from the Surry fielders, crosses the boundary. Suddenly, at 3.40 on a still-warm afternoon, it's all over. Essex have won, the world record attempt defeated by the narrowest of margins. From 410 runs behind Surrey have pushed Essex to the very brink. Ten Doeschate raises his bat and helmet aloft in triumph, but it's the Surrey fans who are singing, "Championes, championes" ringing out from the Peter May Stand – though what the urbane May would have thought about that, we can only wonder.

It has been an enthralling, absorbing, captivating final day, and a truly epic game of cricket – one nobody of sound mind could have predicted on Monday evening. Surrey's magnificent fightback has fallen agonisingly short, but it would be wrong to say it was for nought. It has provided the most dramatic of endings to the 2018 season, and sent a reminder, at the very death, that across all the ways in which county cricket is played, nothing can rival championship cricket at its best. Some claim the Championship is living on borrowed time. From what we've seen today, it's very much alive and kicking. And so, we have the unusual spectacle of the losing side, having shaken hands with the departing batsmen, hugging one another and celebrating. After all, a title has been won, and there is the coronation to come. The deposed champions form a guard of honour for their successors and everyone makes their way to the pavilion. Alec Stewart, widely credited, as Surrey's Director of Cricket, with shaping their success this year, is interviewed by his former teammate, Mark Butcher. The electronic scoreboards are turned into screens so we can all see the interview, but someone's turned the sound off. Rikki Clarke is cheered, and, sound restored, tells of his satisfaction at adding a second title to his medal from 16 years ago. Ricky Burns – upgraded to England status for the winter's tours – emerges to the loudest cheers. He has led his side superbly all season, and averages in the high 60s. Will he be the consistent opener England crave? Today, he is proud of all his players and the backroom team and of his side's comeback in this match: "It's the fight we've shown all season – we've won a few from behind. Recovering from 67 all out shows our character". It's all predictable, of course, these things always are, but that matters not a jot to the fans, who are simply happy to share the moment.

The Surrey players raise the trophy high, spray champagne even higher, and no-one thinks of leaving. An hour after the match ended, the pavilion steps are still the scene for a happy party in the sun. Players chat and shake hands with anyone near enough, hundreds of phones take thousands of photos and it all seems likely to go on for a long while yet. I take one last look around. Behind the players, ground staff are busy dusting the pitch, and there's a small army of lawnmowers at work, all underneath the empty frames of the gas holders. Their emptiness seems fitting. Another season is over. Soon it will be time for Burns and others to get kitted out with England blazers and board the plane to Sri Lanka. They'll be playing there in little more than a week. For others, there will be contacts in South Africa or Australia, or the IPL, or coaching roles at schools and colleges. Or, for an unfortunate few, uncertainty.

As I leave the pavilion and out through the Jack Hobbs Gate into the quiet streets beyond, I spare a thought for Ryan ten Doeschate. Amidst the Surrey celebrations, his half-century was largely forgotten. He did improve his average after all.

**Surrey first innings**

| | | | |
|---|---|---|---|
| R.J. Burns * | c Harmer | b Quinn | 19 |
| M.D. Stoneman | c Wheater | b Porter | 2 |
| J.J. Roy | lbw | b Porter | 5 |
| O.J.D. Pope | c Bopara | b Cook | 26 |
| B.T. Foakes ƚ | lbw | b Quinn | 0 |
| W.G. Jacks | | b Cook | 0 |
| R.S. Patel | lbw | b Cook | 5 |
| R. Clarke | lbw | b Porter | 0 |
| M. Morkel | c Wheater | b Porter | 1 |
| J.W. Dernbach | | b Cook | 4 |
| A. Virdi | not out | | 1 |
| Extras | | 4lb | 4 |
| **Total** | | 27.0 overs | 10 – 67 |

**FoW:** 1–13, 2–23, 3–41, 4–41, 5–48, 6–54, 7–55, 8–57, 9–62, 10–67

| **Bowling** | **O** | **M** | **R** | **W** |
|---|---|---|---|---|
| J.A. Porter | 10 | 0 | 26 | 4 |
| S. Cook | 11 | 5 | 27 | 4 |
| M.R. Quinn | 6 | 2 | 10 | 2 |

**Essex first innings**

| | | | |
|---|---|---|---|
| N.L.J. Browne | | b Morkel | 2 |
| M. Vijay | c Foakes | b Dernbach | 80 |
| T. Westley | c Foakes | b Clarke | 134 |
| D.W. Lawrence | lbw | b Clarke | 17 |
| R.S. Bopara | | b Virdi | 8 |
| R.N. ten Doeschate * | c Pope | b Dernbach | 27 |
| A.J.A. Wheater ƚ | | retired hurt | 68 |
| S.R. Harmer | not out | | 102 |
| J.A Porter | lbw | b Dernbach | 1 |
| S. Cook | c Foakes | b Dernbach | 1 |
| M.R. Quinn | not out | | 4 |
| Extras | | 7b 13lb 12nb 1w | 33 |
| **Total** | | 140.2 overs | 8 – 477 d. |

**FoW:** 1–12, 2–158, 3–205, 4–236, 5–276, 6–282, 7–449, 8–456

| **Bowling** | **O** | **M** | **R** | **W** |
|---|---|---|---|---|
| M. Morkel | 30 | 6 | 84 | 1 |
| J. W. Dernbach | 29.2 | 8 | 95 | 4 |
| R. Clarke | 29 | 9 | 65 | 2 |
| R.S. Patel | 25 | 3 | 92 | 0 |
| A. Virdi | 27 | 1 | 121 | 1 |

**Surrey second innings**

| | | | |
|---|---|---|---|
| R.J. Burns * | | c&b Porter | 21 |
| M.D. Stoneman | | b Harmer | 86 |
| J.J. Roy | c sub | b Quinn | 128 |
| O.J.D. Pope | lbw | b Coles | 114 |
| B.T. Foakes ŧ | lbw | b Quinn | 32 |
| W.G. Jacks | c Harmer | b Coles | 53 |
| R. S. Patel | c sub | b Coles | 38 |
| R. Clarke | c sub | b Coles | 39 |
| M. Morkel | c Browne | b Coles | 0 |
| J.W. Dernbach | | b Porter | 2 |
| A. Virdi | | not out | 2 |
| Extras | | 14b 5lb 6nb 1w | 2 |
| **Total** | | 142.2 overs | 10 – 541 |

**FoW:** 1–63, 2–244, 3–249, 4–364, 5–418, 6–479, 7–532, 8–532, 9–539, 10–541

| **Bowling** | **O** | **M** | **R** | **W** |
|---|---|---|---|---|
| J.A. Porter | 26.2 | 3 | 127 | 2 |
| M.R. Quinn | 28 | 3 | 115 | 2 |
| S.R. Harmer | 50 | 10 | 122 | 1 |
| M. Coles | 32 | 5 | 123 | 5 |
| R.S. Bopara | 1 | 0 | 17 | 0 |
| T. Westley | 4 | 0 | 13 | 0 |
| D.W. Lawrence | 1 | 0 | 5 | 0 |

**Essex second innings**

| | | | | |
|---|---|---|---|---|
| M. Vijay | | b Morkel | | 2 |
| N.L.J. Browne | c Clarke | b Virdi | | 12 |
| T. Westley | c Clarke | b Dernbach | | 20 |
| D.W. Lawrence | c Clarke | b Dernbach | | 10 |
| R.S. Bopara | c Jacks | b Virdi | | 0 |
| R.N. ten Doeschate * | not out | | | 53 |
| A.J.A. Wheater ŧ | c Patel | b Morkel | | 11 |
| S.R. Harmer | c Foakes | b Morkel | | 0 |
| J.A. Porter | lbw | b Morkel | | 4 |
| M.T. Coles | | run out | | 5 |
| M.R. Quinn | not out | | | 0 |
| Extras | | 4b 5lb 8nb | | 17 |
| **Total** | | 32.2 overs | 9 – | 134 |

**FoW:** 1–13, 2–26, 3–42, 4–47, 5–55, 6–97, 7–97, 8–111, 9–124

| **Bowling** | **O** | **M** | **R** | **W** |
|---|---|---|---|---|
| A. Virdi | 11 | 0 | 73 | 2 |
| M. Morkel | 12 | 3 | 28 | 4 |
| J.W. Dernbach | 9.2 | 2 | 24 | 2 |

**Toss:** Surrey elected to bat. **Umpires:** M. Saggers, A. Wharf
**Essex win by 1 wicket**

As close as it gets without actually batting.
A wicket-keeper's view of the Oval pitch and a treat for fans

# Conclusion

As I write these words, the 2019 cricket season is taking its first, tentative steps, even though April has not yet arrived. In Dubai, Ollie Pope, overlooked by England for their winter tours, has made 250 for Surrey against the MCC in the champion county match, despite what the BBC describes as “a sandstorm”. Closer to home – much closer in fact, just down the road at Fenner’s – Alastair Cook has notched his 64$^{th}$ first-class century, prompting inevitable calls for him to reconsider his international retirement. Already the nascent season has a familiar feel to it. Yet change is afoot, and no-one can be sure where it will take the game.

Among the alterations this season will be yet more scheduling changes to the Championship, the One-Day Cup and the Vitality Blast, although at least the ECB have the excuse of a World Cup to fit in. Day/Night Championship matches have been dropped for this year, and I suspect few will lament their passing. Of greater concern, weekend Championship cricket is being cut by 44% in 2019, prompting The Cricketer to ask if this “could be the beginning of the end?” And it’s not just scheduling that’s being changed (again). Division 1 is to be expanded to ten teams, which means, this season, one club will be relegated and three promoted. Tinkering, tinkering, endless tinkering.

But the most significant change undoubtedly relates to the biggest talking point by far of the 2018 season, the proposed Hundred tournament, which cast a long, deep shadow over practically every game and every discussion on cricket. The new competition is going ahead, despite the furore surrounding it and the apparently near-total lack of support for the concept outside the marketing offices of the ECB. New city-based franchises will be formed, with millions of pounds distributed to support them when the tournament starts next year. Whether this, and its coverage on free-to-air television, will attract the young, new audience to cricket that the ECB craves remains to be seen, as does its long-term effect on the traditional county structure. But some counties are worried about their futures, and many people have wider concerns about the direction in which the game appears to be headed.

Are they right to be fearful? On my travels around the country last season, there were certainly many disconcerting signs. Crowds at county championship matches were predominantly older, not to mention overwhelmingly male and white. Given the game's popularity in south Asia and, at least historically, in the Caribbean, the lack of diversity in crowds here, especially in areas with large populations originating from those regions, is disappointing to say the least. The lack of children playing the game, and its collapse in the state sector, is also a major cause for long-term concern. Issues around the role of computers and the internet in young people's lives, and the resulting lack of exercise and rise in child obesity, have been well documented elsewhere, but they too are challenges to cricket. If it retrenches further to become a game played almost exclusively by those at private schools, then it will be in deep trouble.

The number of clubs closing down or shrinking is also a serious concern, a point that was made forcibly following the village match I reported on. Buntingford, the losing side that day, survived relegation thanks in part to the team below them, Weston Colville, being unable to fulfil their fixtures. Two months after the season ended, Weston Colville CC's website bore this message:

> "The 2018 season started with high hopes of running two teams in the Cambridgeshire League. Unfortunately, the 2nd XI was withdrawn after one game. Major availability issues continued during the season and the 1st XI conceded a number of games. Relegation for the third year running was a consequence. As a result, the club have entered a team for the 2019 season but have requested a slot in the lower divisions of the junior league. This is intended to encourage younger members to step up from junior cricket to a level that they can compete in and enjoy. Some of the more experienced players wish to continue playing at a higher level and so have left the club. This is perfectly understandable, and the club wishes them well.

> The task over the winter is to increase adult membership to support the team. It is impossible to predict how that search will go but in reality either there will be a team playing in 2019 or Weston Colville will have disappeared from the CCA. Irrespective of the outcome of the above, the junior section of the club will continue. So the club is NOT about to fold. The next few months will determine the direction the club will take, but for now the future of the adult team hangs in the balance."

Sadly, recruitment efforts did not reap rewards, and by spring 2019 the website message had been updated. The club was still running U11, U13 and U15 teams, but "Due to lack of players our weekend team in the Cambridgeshire Cricket Association was withdrawn prior to the start of the 2019 season." It is, sadly, just one of many similar stories occurring across the country in recent years. And then, on a wider basis, there was the constant background refrain lamenting the death, or at least the mortal illness, of Test cricket. Hardly a week went by last season without someone, somewhere proclaiming that Test cricket was doomed unless drastic action was taken. So far, that action appears to amount to a new Test championship finally being set up, the reintroduction of four-day Tests, and players having their names on their shirts in the forthcoming Ashes series (for which, incidentally, most days were sold out long ago).

So with all these concerns, are there any grounds for optimism? Yes, actually, there are. For one thing, attendances at county matches were much higher than I'd expected – tiny, of course, compared with Premier League football, small even against League One games, but far higher than the proverbial two men and a dog. Twenty20 attendances were up for the third year in succession, at 931,000, and average and total attendances for the One Day Cup were up too (at the time of writing, the Championship figures are not available, but recent years have seen increased attendances for four-day matches too). And while the longer games saw mostly older fans, that's to be expected. It is the older generation that has the time to spend watching four-day matches in midweek, when the rest of the population is at school, college or work. Twenty20 matches, in contrast, played at family friendly times, were full of younger fans and families enjoying the occasion together. Besides, go back 50 years or even further and it was still older fans who went to county games, for the same reasons. The writer R.C. Robertson-Glasgow told of the Somerset player Tom Young describing the attendance at a match in Taunton: "I make the crowd 24 – 23 really, because one 'em's died overnight!". That was in the 1920s! The fact that first-class county matches, by and large, do not appeal to younger fans does not mean that cricket itself doesn't, nor does it mean younger fans will not graduate to the longer form of the game as they get older. The ECB's All-Stars scheme certainly seems to be getting lots of young children involved in the game, though clearly much more needs to be done to keep them involved as they get older.

There's hope, too, for Test cricket, despite the comment by ICC chairman Shashank Manohar last month that "Test cricket is actually dying to be honest". Such reports of its death may be exaggerated, at least according to an MCC survey of 13,000 respondents from 100 countries, published this month. In sharp contrast to Manohar's views, the survey found that a massive 86% of fans said Test cricket was their favourite form of the game, up from 68% twelve months ago. The problem is not that people don't want to go to Test cricket – it's more that they can't, because of the cost and the time required.

It was also encouraging in 2018 to see how many people now attend women's matches. One of the happiest sights in English cricket in 2018 was seeing so many girls and young women attending matches, wearing shirts embossed with the names of their favourite – female – players, and talking about playing themselves. It was also pleasing to see how many boys and men were also attending and enjoying those games. Women's cricket still, sadly, has its detractors – mostly men who have never so much as seen a women's match – but the tide is flowing too strongly for them, and women's cricket is finally entering the mainstream, and not before time.

Perhaps, though, the greatest grounds for optimism about cricket's future is in its remarkable ability to adapt. Throughout its long history, cricket has maintained an extraordinary ability to change and develop in keeping with the society around it, adopting fashions and reflecting trends. From the introduction of overarm bowling to batsmen's helmets, limited-overs games to coloured clothing, cricket has persistently and consistently embraced changes that previous generations would have regarded as unthinkable, as marking the very end of the game as we know it, if not of civilisation itself. Time after time, cricket has been written off amid claims of its imminent demise. The writer Simon Raven commented "Indeed it is a commonplace that first-class cricket is already dying." He wrote those words in 1960. Like Mark Twain's obituary, cricket's death notices have always been premature. The game has always survived, and thrived. And I think it will do so again. That is not to say it will survive in its present form. The Hundred may well be the thin end of the wedge, and the enormous changes in society, and the ever-quickening pace of life, may be more than the current structure of the game can overcome. Perhaps in 2058, another chronicler of an English cricket season will write of a game played exclusively in the Twenty20 or Hundred formats, by teams from Leeds and Manchester, London and Birmingham, rather than from Yorkshire and Lancashire and all the other counties. As much as traditionalists will hate the idea, it is not impossible that, one day, all cricket will be played that way. I hope not, for I love the longer, more subtle, more nuanced, more absorbing form of the game, but if it is the price to pay for cricket's survival, it's a price that may have to be paid. And it may not be an entirely bad thing. Eighteen professional teams is an awful lot in a country the size of England. Australia, smaller in population but more successful over the decades, has six state sides. India, it is true, has 37 teams in the Ranji Trophy, but India is a cricket-obsessed land of a billion people, not a country of 66 million in which cricket is very much a minority sport. It might be heresy, but perhaps England would be better with eight, rather than eighteen, teams, if it resulted in greater quality and competitiveness.

But I am getting ahead of myself. The Hundred has not yet begun, and may not even succeed. There is no guarantee that cricket fans will take to franchises in England, a country where allegiances to teams run deep and where there has been little taste so far for franchised teams in any sport. And is the audience for the Hundred really going to be significantly different from those who go to Twenty20 matches, as the ECB thinks? Or will yet another format be one too many, confusing, rather than attracting, casual watchers? Only time will tell.

And so, cricket is at a crossroads, and no-one knows for certain what lies down any of the paths it may take. Just like the country itself, in fact. As I write these words, the UK's future is as clear as mud. Tomorrow should have been the day the UK left the EU, but that's been delayed as the prime minister's deal keeps getting rejected. Last night, MPs considered eight possible alternatives, and rejected them all. The country might still leave the EU next month, or possibly the month after, or possibly much later. Or not at all. And if it does, will it remain united, or will Scotland, and possibly Northern Ireland, go their own way? It is a future fraught with uncertainty, where no-one knows exactly what will happen, or what the future will look like. Which just goes to prove, yet again, that, as Neville Cardus said, cricket really does hold up a mirror to English society.

But is it still, as Geoffrey Moorhouse thought, the best-loved game? On one level, it is hard, in truth, to say it is. Since he wrote his book, football has steamed ahead in all-conquering popularity, a juggernaut that crushes everything in its way. If money talks, football is deafening. And in a land where only one school child in eight plays the game – and then mostly at private schools – and adult participation is below a million, it is hard to argue with the claim that cricket is anything other than a minority sport. And yet… Cricket may have shrunk in popularity, and, for many people, vanished from sight completely, but after centuries of being a part of the very fabric of English life, it still lurks deep in the national psyche. Away from those who openly enjoy cricket, I believe there is still widespread, lingering affection for the game. Ask most people to describe a quintessential village scene, and a cricket match will still feature high in their choices. It may not be the most popular sport in the country, but there remains a deep-rooted affection for the game that makes it impossible to imagine this country without cricket. It is part of our way of life, so much so that I suspect many of those who have no interest in cricket are, nevertheless, glad to know in some way that it's there. And that's why I remain confident that, for all the challenges it faces, and there many, cricket, in one way or another, will survive and thrive.

# Sources

For the most part, the information in this book, at least as it relates to the matches, comes from my own observations. Inevitably, though, a number of books, periodicals and especially websites were needed to confirm background information and to provide supplementary information.

## Books

Booth, Lawrence (ed), *Wisden Cricketers' Almanack*, Wisden 2018

Compton, Denis, and Edrich, Bill, *Cricket and All That*, Pelham Books, 1978

Fay, Stephen, and Kynaston, David, *Arlott, Swanton and the Soul of English Cricket*, Bloomsbury Publishing, 2018

Marshall, Ian (ed), *Playfair Cricket Annual*, Headline, 2018

Moorhouse, Geoffrey, *The Best Loved Game*, Hodder & Stoughton Ltd, 1979

Plumptre, George, *Homes of Cricket*, Queen Anne Press, 1988

Wilde, Simon, *England – the Biography*, Simon & Schuster, 2018

## Newspapers and journals

Chicago Tribune

Daily Telegraph

The Cricketer

The Guardian

The Independent

The Times

Wisden Cricket Monthly

## Websites

www.accringtoncc.com

http://bacd.play-cricket.com

http://barley.play-cricket.com

www.bbc.co.uk

www.bloomberg.com

www.chicagotribune.com

http://cricketarchive.com

www.dailymail.co.uk

http://cricket.derbyshireccc.com

www.ecb.co.uk

www.espncricinfo.com

www.essexcricket.org.uk

www.ft.com

www.icc-cricket.com

www.independent.co.uk

www.lords.org

www.mansworldindia.com

www.mynewsdesk.com

https://news.sky.com
http://nsscpcl.org
www.oxfordstudent.com
https://reaction.life
www.smh.com.au
www.sportengland.org
www.sportingnews.com
www.statista.com
https://talksport.com
www.teamdurham.com
www.telegraph.co.uk
www.thecricketer.com
www.thecricketpaper.com
www.thefulltoss.com
www.theguardian.com
www.totalcricketscorer.com
http://westoncolvillecc.co.uk
www.wisden.com
www.yorkshirepost.co.uk

## Photo credits

Cover photograph: Shutterstock. All other photos ©the author, except for page 219, © Paul Roe.

Printed in Poland
by Amazon Fulfillment
Poland Sp. z o.o., Wrocław